Collector's Guide to

BUYING, SELLING,
and
TRADING
on the
INTERNET

Second Edition

Nancy L. Hix

COLLECTOR BOOKS
A Division of Schroeder Publishing Co., Inc.

Cover design:
Beth Summers

Book design:
Ben Faust

Searching for a Publisher?
We are always looking for knowledgeable people considered to be experts within their fields. If
you feel that there is a real need for a book on
your collectible subject and have a large comprehensive collection, contact Collector Books.

COLLECTOR BOOKS
P.O. Box 3009
Paducah, Kentucky 42002-3009

www.collectorbooks.com

Contents

Dedication

Dedication:
For my mother, Rita Brodsky, who
taught me the value of collecting beauty.

☞Acknowledgments

My deepest heartfelt thanks to my husband, Jeffrey A. Hix, whose technical expertise supported this project. Without his contributions and encouragement, this book wouldn't exist. Your love is everything, Jeff.

Sincere gratitude to Nancy J. Davies for hours of professional editing assistance and for teaching me all I ever wanted to know about action verbs. You are thanked. Or rather, I thank you.

I'm grateful for professional input from James C. Armstrong, Jr., Ila M. Press, Judi N. Fernandez, Bill Younger, and Noel Wiggins.

Thanks especially to Sandy K. Doran — your enthusiasm about things makes you so much fun to know.

Much gratitude to my Internet collecting friends: Laurie Martin, Nancy Guhr, Lynn Berger, Michael Trenteseau, Kristin Sheaffer, Rob Doran, Jay Wanta, Mindy Smith, Janet Cole, Davey and Chris Flanagan, Charlynn Muehle, Angie Jones, Simone Flynn, Ann and George Schmidt, Linda Kowalczyk, Andrius Gerulis, Laura Voss, Karen Rice, Louie Kyler, Ines Morita, Mike Perlman, Karen Gilbert, Sandy Robinson, Velma Weston, Jane Sralla, Sylvia Richards, Sally Simmons, Sharon Radosevich, Suzi Stein, Elaine Dowdin, Claire Boge, and many others.

Special thanks to Randy C. Jones, Patricia Ruocco, Barth Richards, Virginia Meisinger, Betty Jo Akers, and Pat Brown.

My love and thanks for encouragement from my family, scattered about however we are.

Last but not least, my deepest gratitude to my wonderful sons, Jeffrey J. Hix and Chris Colucci, for making your own sandwiches and Hix-Mix for dinner way too many nights in a row. You guys are simply the greatest, and I adore you both. I'm still one lucky person.

Foreword

When the Egyptian king Ptolemy built the famous library of Alexandria in the third century BC, it was the main center of information in the world. With more than 500,000 volumes at his fingertips, an adventuresome person with a lot of time could leaf through the delicate parchment and become acquainted with the known world. Today, the Internet points us to an almost infinite realm of information with over 4,653,382 current Web sites and more than 10,000 added each day.

Clearly, an adventuresome person still needs a lot of time to become acquainted with the known world! Within this electronic latticework lies an abundance of secret rose gardens frequented by clusters of people with similar interests, sharing information, and forging new friendships and frontiers. The Web is a fascinating empowering environment that has, in fundamental ways, made the world a smaller, more intimate place.

When our company tethered onto this budding network in 1995, it was still a small country road. One of the first things we did on our Web site was to add a rudimentary bulletin board. I clearly remember the first collector postings and how, at that moment, the company doors swept open, and we were suddenly working in collaboration with our fans. To produce and market products in an environment where feedback is that instantaneous is both exhilarating and nerve racking. Never before has a manufacturer had the opportunity to have its successes and failures communicated so rapidly.

Beyond its amazing usefulness as a business tool, really the most wonderful thing about the Internet is meeting new people. You start out with a shared hobby, but soon friendships blossom to the point where the hobby becomes a pleasant backdrop to something even more meaningful. Nancy L. Hix's book does a lovely job at introducing this new technology and illustrating how the Internet can enhance our brave new world. After reading her book, Ptolemy would have exclaimed, "AWESOME!"

Noel Wiggins
President, Harmony Ball Company

☞Preface

The second edition of *Collector's Guide to Buying, Selling, and Trading on the Internet* contains updates to keep pace with the evolving World Wide Web. As many chagrined authors can attest, no book with instructions or information about the Internet will ever be completely up-to-date — not now and perhaps not for a long time.

One misconception about this book's first edition was that it's about Ty Beanie Babies®. It certainly is not. While beanbag plush definitely earned its place among classic collectibles, my intent was to recognize the famous Ty product as a catalyst that drew collectors to the Internet. Collector Web sites dedicated to the plush icons sprang up faster than for any other collectible. I have no idea what Ty plans for the future of its product line. But if it launches anything that reaches the popularity that Beanie Babies did, there's little doubt that Internet subcultures will form around those products as well.

For that reason, the Introduction and many parts of this revised text still mention Beanies. Why? Simply because they drew thousands of collectors to the Internet. Once the bottom fell out of the collectible plush toy market, we didn't want to give up our nightly chat-room and bulletin board sessions. Many people decided to collect something else and found an avalanche of wonderful antiques and collectibles through selective Web surfing.

As for the Internet itself, almost everyone's doing it. While prepping me for a root canal, a dentist posed a provocative question.

"So, do you think this Internet will catch on?" he asked. As I took a breath to launch a lecture about how it already has caught on, he laughed and said he was kidding. Then, injecting a fiery stream of Novocain, he asked if I wanted my X-rays in JPEG format. My regular dentist could perhaps view them in Internet Explorer or the Web browser of his choice.

To state globally that "Beanies got us on the Internet" isn't true for every collector. Some folks were on the Web long before I was and remain cyber-footed today, heads and shoulders above where I am. We can't deny, though, that thousands of collectors who got their cyber-feet wet on the Internet did indeed get there because of Beanies. Hundreds of other companies have fabulous Web sites. Surf into any of the collectible-company Web sites listed in Chapter 4 and you'll see what I mean.

Many folks have discovered that the Internet holds an abundance of resources for collectors and dealers of just about anything. As of this writing, I'm waiting for "Weird Al" Yankovic to parody eBay. It might happen.

☛Introduction — Was That Really Me?

I recently came across some e-mail files I had stored from my Beanie-collecting heydays. There were close to 300 of them, all containing in exacting detail a Beanie-trade in the making, and all involving me. Reading a random sample, I have to admit that I was pretty good at it. My Beanie ducks were all in a row.

Then I uncovered the damning photo of three of us in "Show Me The Beanies®" tee shirts. We're standing behind a swap-meet table and proudly waiting for the doors to open and the crowds to descend on our colored velour. We're all smiling proudly, and there is no denying it — that brunette on the right is me. I should have had an inkling that something just wasn't "right" with this picture.

The problem is, I didn't. Somehow being surrounded by a hundred tables piled high with tens of thousands of beanbag toys seemed perfectly normal.

Was that really *me?*

"I Have All of Them"

I first heard about Beanie Babies in 1996, when Chicago's morning news anchor Marianne Murciano talked about them on the Fox Network's *Fox Thing in the Morning.* She mentioned the unique marketing strategy that Ty Inc. engineered by only allowing them to be sold in smaller specialty shops to be sure they weren't mass marketed by the major retail chains.

Months later while catching up with Sandy, a veteran gatherer whose flamingo collection alone hovers around 100, I heard them mentioned again. Sandy built a Beanie Baby collection in her office that often backed up hallway traffic in both directions. She asked me how many I had. Surely, nobody would own fewer Beanie Babies than floppy disks. I told her the grand total of Beanies® I owned: zip.

"Zip!" she exclaimed, incredulously, "only Zip? What about Nip and Flip? And the bunnies, Hippity, Hoppity, and Floppity?"

"No," I begrudgingly admitted, "zip. As in zilch. Zero. Nada. I have none."

Having just offered conclusive proof that I was clueless, I listened to her recite the Web address of the Beanie Babies site, and I dutifully called it up in Netscape. There appeared on my screen a dithered pastel background and three dancing stuffed animals that I later learned to be Bongo, Pinky, and Patti. Clicking on some hypertext, I watched a checklist load. There were over ninety different Babies in this Beanie line. Not wanting to further drop out of her favor, I asked Sandy how many of them she had.

"I have all of them," she said, and proceeded through a litany of how some Beanies in her collection were retired (no longer dancing?) and how proud she was of her rare Humphrey the camel. Through this, I busied myself copying the three dancing Beanies on my hard drive to include in my collection of animated Web icons. At the moment, that summed up my interest in Beanie Babies.

I told my husband Jeff about Sandy's collection, and we shared a moment of tender marital synergy over the antics of one of our friends. So much money spent on toys. Never would we be that improvident!

My First Beanie

The morning before I moved to another department, I found a pink handled gift bag on my desk. Inside was a little unicorn with a note from a coworker:

> *This is unique, and so are you. You will be missed!*   Betty

Attached to the unicorn's ear was a small, red heart-shaped tag that opened, revealing that the little unicorn had a name: Mystic.

I now owned my first Beanie Baby. That was Valentine's Day, 1997. Thinking that if Marianne, Sandy, *and* Betty were wise to these creatures of fuzzy fabric, maybe it was time to get with it. I stopped at a party store on the way home and picked up a Beanie Baby for each of my sons. Just on a lark, I got Jeff a leopard named Freckles and for me, a floppy-eared rabbit named Ears.

"Now this is it, right?" My husband asked, not knowing quite what to do with Freckles. "You're not going to try to compete with Sandy, are you?"

Heavens no. I didn't want all of them. Please! Only the ones I liked.

McBeanies

Jeff and I had lunch at McDonald's the day the first of the Teenie Beanie Babies® appeared with Happy Meals in April of 1997. I wasn't sure what to make of the little purple platypus with gold feet that came with my meal, but I swear it had this aura that made me feel like I needed to have more of them around me. On the way home, we got the little lamb named Chops.

We visited our family in Galesburg that weekend. This historic Knox County town is across Illinois via a route that didn't take us near a McDonald's for many miles. We did manage one stop in

DeKalb but they had just run out of Teenies. Rock Falls came through for us after a long wait in line behind more people than I thought even *lived* in Rock Falls.

When we reached my mother-in-law's apartment, our collection of colorful creatures totaled two each of six different ones, all in sealed packages. Having found out that there were ten different styles in the promotion, I slept very little that night.

I can't remember if I'd ever phoned a McDonald's restaurant. When I ripped through the Galesburg phone book, though, it seemed like the most natural thing in the world to do in order to find out which ones they were giving out. We eventually ended up with two complete sets of the Teenies. Looking back on the weekend's adventure, I couldn't believe the aerobics that Jeff and I went through to acquire them. Such mania! "I will never again go that crazy in search of a Beanie Baby," I vowed, safely at home.

If my nose grew an inch for each time that vow was broken in the months to come, it would reach clear to Cleveland.

The Beanie Famine of 1997

Luckily for our family's moral ground, Jeff wised up and let me peak alone on my Beanie high. "Just remember Sandy," he'd warn, shaking his head as though that would bring everything into perspective. Remember Sandy? How could I not? She had the whole set of current Beanies and most of the retired ones! My collection had only grown to about 20 by then but I was running out of room on both dressers. I considered moving Jeff to the sofa in case I needed his side of the bed for the others.

Out for a drive one day, I stopped at a little shop called "Someplace Else," where they were just unpacking a shipment of Beanies. Later, I had fun explaining the acquisition of 18 more to Jeff.

That was April 18, and would be the last delivery of that size many of us would see for awhile. Limited production by Ty and an untimely UPS strike led to what we came to know as "The Great Beanie Famine" of 1997. When the Beanie well ran dry, I was forced to discover the art of trading. I had no choice but to get back on up the Web in search of those dancing Beanies.

Trading Happens

The Ty Web site's guestbook was teeming with comments about Beanie Babies and offers of sales or trades. I found the sense of trust people had in each other very intriguing. I gingerly posted my own ad requesting a trade and included my e-mail address. I received a reply from Laurie.

Both of us were apprehensive about trading through the mail with someone we knew only from the Internet. We arranged to trade Beanies in person after discovering that it was geographically feasible. Laurie lives in Canton, which is less than an hour's drive from Galesburg, and Jeff and I were heading there to celebrate Mother's Day. The timing was perfect. I needed her Bubbles and Scoop; Laurie needed my Legs and Quackers.

She offered to meet me in the lobby of the Galesburg Ramada Inn on Sunday morning. This also happened to be the day of the famous "1997 Mother's Day Retirement" for Beanie Babies. When we arranged the trade, we agreed to go through with it no matter which ones retired in the meantime. Sunday morning I offered to let her back out of the trade after learning that one Beanie I was to receive from her had been slated for retirement at midnight. She turned down my offer.

"We made an agreement," Laurie insisted, and I added a retired Beanie Baby to my collection that day. I've since based a lot of my trading ethics on that experience with Laurie.

Feeling much more confident about trading with cyber-strangers, I worked out trades with my new e-mail friends and eventually initiated trades with others by answering and entering posts in the Ty guestbook. Within a few weeks, my collection had doubled.

The Beanie Baby trades I made with people I met on the Internet had an amazing success ratio.

Did I stop buying Beanies when my collection was complete? I'm afraid not. Thousands of people bought as many as store limits would allow, and for awhile I was right there with them.

Who Knows Where Goeth Pride?

I'm a technical writer and a wife and mother, and consider myself dignified and successful. Still in all, God help whatever got in my way when someone told me there was a shipment of Beanie Babies being unpacked at the local florist.

One delivery day in particular remains memorable. I was Beanie hunting on my lunch hour when I entered a shop that I knew carried Beanies. There were several customers standing idle, all eyeing me as I entered the store. Instinctively, I *knew*.

"They're on their way, right?" I asked. Heads nodded. "How much longer?"

"Any time now," answered one woman, "the driver is in Downers Grove."

When the UPS driver arrived, they opened the boxes in front of the eager crowd. Instead of being carefully arranged on display shelves, the Beanies® were piled on the floor. People dove. Literally. Only once before had I seen anything like it and that was in fifth grade when our class broke a piñata.

There was a tangle of arms and legs, four of which were my own. By the time I got close enough to pick up any of them, the Beanies® were in smaller scattered piles. I could only find seven different ones. Frighteningly, only about 60 seconds had elapsed since the boxes were first opened.

Three customers, apparently working together, managed to gather up the best of the goods and pile them into a shopping cart. They had many more than their limit of Magic, Lucky, Goldie, Spooky, Teddy, Curly, and Ziggy — the hardest of the hard-to-finds. They were completely oblivious to the cries of protest that arose from other customers. I had to wonder what could cause people to abandon any sense of pride and dignity in a card shop. Despair? Greed? Obsession with beanbag toys?

Beanies-O-Rama

I learned about swap meets that summer. There was one taking place at a local hotel so I eagerly headed for what I thought would be an excited group of collectors carrying similar goods, all with whom I could make trades in an atmosphere of Beanie® camaraderie. I pictured it looking something like a PTA family night, only with Beanies instead of Cub Scouts.

What I found instead were several tables in a smoky lower-level conference room where people had Beanie Babies on display. Standing at the door was a very large, very unkempt-looking dude — a turquoise-studded belt buckle holding up a soiled pair of jeans and a pack of Camels rolled into the sleeve of his tee shirt. He collected two dollars from everyone entering the room and hissed a warning that he'd kick anyone out that he caught selling or trading Beanie Babies without "buying a table." Eyeing his cowboy boots, I took him literally and held my bag of cuddly plush toys tightly closed.

There was a crowd, and the tables I couldn't get near offered the best deals. I meandered around and looked over the retired Beanies that some of the dealers had on display.

Another soiled cowboy walked past me, this one holding his cigarette safely away from something that he lovingly cradled in his other arm. A baby? No. It was the elusive Spot without the spot in a clear display case. One man attempted to lure me into making a costly purchase of a gray Inky the octopus. As he bobbed a cigarette on his lips, he explained the variation created by the way the yarn formed the octopus's mouth. I asked where he learned all of this and he produced a printout from a Web page. "It's all right here," he said, exhaling smoke at me.

After having my feet stepped on, my bag of Beanies bumped, and my tolerance for rude Beanie shoppers tested again, I decided that I really didn't want to be there. I headed homeward, back to the safe, cozy, smoke-free Internet. But not for long.

"You're Gonna Be Mobbed!"

Garage sale days in southwestern Michigan are always fun. My parents have their annual one in August.

When my mother phoned to ask if I wanted to bring anything to sell at theirs, I had an incredible idea. Since she hadn't yet placed the ad, I asked her to include "Beanie Babies — Current and Retired" along with the other stuff she was listing.

Just on a lark, I posted an ad for my "Beanie Baby Yard Sale" in the Ty guestbook and a few Web site bulletin boards. Nancy Lee from Missouri offered to post the ad several more times while I was en route to the sale. I took a few days of vacation from work and headed out on Interstate 94 toward Union Pier, Michigan.

As I neared my parents' home, I had mixed feelings of fear, anxiety, and embarrassment. Would people up there want Beanie Babies? Would I once again vault myself into family legend, enduring eons of kidding from my brothers? Would my father add up all of my Beanie Babies and calculate exactly how much of my hard-earned money I squandered on toys?

As she helped me unpack my garage sale items, my mother mentioned the ad. The desk clerk at the newspaper office had eyed her when she got to the part about the Beanie Babies.

"Lady, you're gonna be mobbed," he told her, jotting down her address and neatly tucking it into his shirt pocket.

Hearing that, my apprehension soared to an entirely different level.

Michigan's Clark Kent was right. We set up my table a distance away from the garage "in case of lines" and my son and I barely got the table carried out when cars started pulling up.

"I saw your ad on the Internet!" some would say, as they piled Beanie Babies into their arms. "I saw the ad in the Ty guestbook!" others said, oblivious to my secondary mark-up. One lady had her daughter from Battle Creek on her cellular phone as she loaded Beanie Babies into a shopping bag that my mother, jaw dropped in amazement, had graciously handed her.

I was right about my father calculating how much I had spent on Beanies, and I had to answer for it the night before. It was forgotten, though, as he sat there in the shade all day watching car after car burn rubber around the corner and my money belt getting thicker and thicker.

"What impresses me the most," he admitted, "is how *knowledgeable* you are about the product!"

I was genuinely flattered. If I could learn this much from web sites and by exchanging e-mail with other collectors, what else could I learn about collectibles from the Internet?

Plenty!

The Internet — It's Ready and Waiting

When the plush toy fad died for me, it died hard. I no longer collect Beanie Babies. Collecting Beanies was fun, partly because of their appeal but mainly because of the great time I had with other collectors on the Internet.

Imagine how thrilled I was to discover that other collectible lines have Web sites with bulletin boards, chat rooms, and links upon links to pages with loads of information about the items! I didn't have to give up my nightly Web surfing sessions. I could just transfer my interest from one collectible line to another!

Now *that's* really me.

Moving from collecting Beanies to other collectible lines introduces us to a whole different atmosphere of fellow collectors. There are some stark differences in the way collectible lines, antique dealers, sports card enthusiasts, and others who share a collecting passion present their items on the Internet. The chapters that follow explain them.

An abundance of information and collectors' networks exist on the Internet. When it comes to building a collection, the Internet has become essential. Getting there is relatively easy.

Chapter 1 — Why Collect?

People collect for many different reasons. Every collector learns his or her own set of strategies for negotiating trades with other collectors, haggling with dealers, when to obtain an extra or two, and how and where to sell their extras.

This knowledge applies to all types of collecting — certainly not just items specifically made as collectibles, but also antiques, coins, stamps, memorabilia, marbles — any collected items. This chapter reviews collecting and how it has evolved into the cyber-hobby of the new millennium.

- An ancient hobby
- What are collectibles?
- How people collect
- The home-office collectible
- How we collected beanbag plush
- Getting past beanbags
- Dealer incentives
- Customer incentives
- Independent collector clubs and networks
- Making the most of it all

While dealing primarily with collectibles manufactured as part of a specific collectible line, the strategies and tactics described on these pages can apply to any collectible or antique, as long as others collect the same type of items. You can find no better place for establishing a collecting network and meeting new "collecting buddies" than on the Internet!

☞An Ancient Hobby

Collecting isn't new. With a natural inclination to surround ourselves with things we like, we're born collectors. Children naturally collect things, although not all of their acquisitions are pleasing to their parents. When my son Chris was barely three years old, I found in his jacket pocket a rather disgusting collection of cigarette butts that he had pulled out of an ashtray at a friend's house.

A trip to any local library, which itself represents a community's literary collection, reveals no limitations to what people collect. Coffee-table books and price guides cover everything from model trains, milk bottle caps, matchbooks, coins, 1950s memorabilia, Depression glass, to old building cornerstones. People have been collecting things for thousands of years as evidenced by artifacts uncovered in ancient tombs. Archeological digs indicate that even

Ugg the Neanderthal may have had a collection of special rocks that held some intrigue or spiritual meaning.

Some collectors revel in the extraordinary. One of my coworkers has a collection of fancy restaurant menus. Another friend collects Masonic Lodge memorabilia and has well over 200 items, ranging from fezzes to Shrine Circus programs.

Collecting Happens

A collection usually starts with one item that holds a particular intrigue; then another is acquired. Other times a person buys an item and later discovers that it's part of a series, and then finds another item in the set. Soon, the hunt is on to complete the set.

As the person grows more and more fond of the items, so does the desire to learn more about them. Books are read. He or she obtains more of the items, all adding to the excitement of seeing how many can be assembled. The owner eventually becomes something of an authority, as his or her collection grows more and more impressive.

By our very nature, we want to surround ourselves with things we enjoy.

☞What Are Collectibles?

Long before companies like Hallmark and Enesco developed and marketed products labeled "collectibles," any piece attracting substantial interest in being collected was considered a collectible. This definition still holds true, but is more commonly used to reference items for which there's a secondary-market value and demand. Their secondary-market value separates collectibles from "giftware."

While the market for manufactured collectibles has taken off with amazing success, the most valuable items in almost any line of collectibles were made before a significant consumer interest rose.

The "first in series" items, those made before a market emerged for their line, usually top the price guides with substantial value. Since the number of items manufactured in a collectible line increases as the line grows in popularity, the debut items usually have the lowest production run. There are fewer of them in existence, so their value rises. Early releases of collectible lines that became popular are prized items, especially if they retained their mint condition. Not many did, since they often weren't bought as collectibles and not cared for as such.

Items that become the cream of the crop in collectibles are those that become collectibles by circumstance.

Bill Younger, president of B.C. Younger & Associates, first developed his line of Harbour Lights lighthouse figures out of his love for the actual lighthouse structures that dot lakeshores and coastlines. He says that Harbour Lights lighthouses were not intended as collectibles, but more in honor of the history each piece represents. He attributes the line's success to two factors: the artistic quality and research that go into making each figure, and the growing interest in the Lighthouse Preservation Society's efforts. That the Harbour Lights lighthouses have become collectibles, he speculates, was pure serendipity.

"The most successful collectibles aren't planned," he told me at a Harbour Lights signing event in Lisle, Illinois. "They just *happen.*"

☛How People Collect

Some collectors focus on a specific series of items, like those that can be grouped by an interest. A collector of world currency might only acquire paper money from countries in Eastern Europe, just as collectors of phone cards might only acquire those issued by a specific type of company.

Antique collectors might buy a certain number of new pieces each year, while bottle-cap collectors may want to pick up new ones whenever they can get their hands on "classics" turning up in antique malls or yard sales. In most cases, the older or rarer the piece, the better. Their strategy for building their collection is whatever strategy they choose, with their collection growing according to their own whims.

If a person decides to collect items that are part of a collectible line, the means of acquiring the items is a lot more defined. There are a certain number of pieces in the collection. Some are special issue, some are limited edition, some are open edition, some are retired, and the collectible company has them all catalogued. Only certain types of shops sell the pieces.

Collectors do hustle for the retired pieces, but there is also a drive to get the newest items in the line.

The collectible company decides how pieces will be issued and which will retire, and the collector can build a collection according to this rhythm. Collecting these items can still be done at one's own pace.

Before the Internet

People who collected worked hard at it. Collections were typically smaller and grew slowly. If a collector couldn't find a particular item in a collectible shop, the options for getting the item included wandering through antique malls, flea markets, rummage sales, paging through catalogs and classified ads, bargaining at resale shops — maybe even bidding at estate auctions.

In those days, a Hummel figurine collector didn't always come home from a collectible hunt with a Hummel figurine, nor did a baseball card collector always find the precise baseball card he was searching for in the first sports card shop he entered.

Some collectors searched for particular items by taking out classified ads in local newspapers, but their audience was limited to a publication's circulation. Finding the exact item often proved impossible, and those who persisted usually built their collections over many, many years.

People collected what was available to them. Over time, and as communication and transportation capabilities grew, so did their collections.

Along Came Computers

Aside from performing mathematical or logical functions, personal computers help us work faster and more efficiently. Instead of spending hours rifling through stacks of loose copy in order to locate a particular word or phrase in a document, we now use a "search" function to get us to the precise word within a few seconds. Instead of countless hours, even days, of searching through books in a campus library, our students can use PC-based encyclopedia software. By entering a string of text in a little box on the screen, they can instantly locate exactly what they need without disrupting their research.

For collectors, the World Wide Web provides a giant search function, but the search isn't restricted to what we have loaded on our PC. Simply stated, the Web allows us to search the entire world — and virtually anyone with a computer can use it.

The Internet

It started out in the late 1960s as an effort to set up a nation-wide communications network that could survive a nuclear war. It was designed in such a way that the destruction of any one computer would not disrupt the network. It was known as ARPAnet (Advanced Research Projects Agency network of the U.S. Department of Defense), and was mainly used by DOD defense contractors and academic institutions. At first it was limited in size and capability.

Once high-speed modems and digital communications were introduced, those interested in high-tech communication began to notice ARPAnet and its potential to reach a limitless audience. Corporations and small businesses alike got connected to the Internet. Before long (around 1996), we started seeing things like http://www.company.com in television and print advertising.

The World Wide Web is actually a subset of the Internet and contains *sites*. The sites are usually accessed using a graphical interface such as a Web browser. Internet users can transfer files in electronic format, send messages via electronic mail (e-mail), conduct research using the vast resources of the Internet, hold real-time "chat" sessions with others connected to the Internet, and so much more.

It took about five years for the Web to catch on in businesses, homes, and schools. Today, almost any fifth-grader can tell you that http://www.hallmark.com is a URL, and that a URL is a Web address. This one can be entered in a special screen on your computer (called a "browser") to reach the Hallmark Company's home page.

Incidentally, a fair amount of these fifth-graders have personal home pages on the Web.

A Collector's Smorgasbord

For many years, my mother has collected fan vases. She has an impressive collection of well over 100 in a brilliant array of colors and styles. Though varied, her collection is somewhat limited to pieces that she found in the Midwest and the occasional find in different parts of the country.

Borrowing my brother's America On Line account one evening, my mother and I sat down together at his computer and called up the eBay auction site. We did a search for "fan vase" and were stunned by the search results that came up in the browser window.

A list of auctions for the most coveted pieces from several continents that would ordinarily represent a lifetime of collecting appeared before us in seconds. All we had to do was place the mouse cursor over some underlined text, click the left mouse button, and beautifully digitized photos of fan vases beyond my mother's wildest dreams appeared on the monitor screen, one right after the other.

We saw auctions for fan vases crafted in Czech deco-art and Depression era glass, Niloak and Hull pottery, antique Fenton and Steuben pieces, and fan vases in styles we'd never before seen or heard of. Fifty-six auctions featuring fan vases ran that evening, over half the total amount of vases that my mother had acquired in 30 years of collecting.

While conducting research on collecting over the Internet, I asked my friend Barth if his collection of Masonic Lodge items has grown much since he got access to the Web.

"Yes," he answered emphatically. "Oh *my* yes." He estimated that in a little over two years, his collection grew by 400%.

A Small Business Boon

And how has the Internet affected the collectible business? Davey Flanagan, president and owner of Heaven and Earth Collectibles in Spring Hill, Florida, estimates that sales to customers who were referred to his collectible shop via the Internet represent ninety percent of his annual business.

"When I advertise on the Internet," Davey explains, "I can reach collectors who are looking for exactly the pieces I have in stock. Many of my customers are right in our neighborhood. They send e-mail to let us know they'll be in to purchase a particular item, so I'll have it ready for them. If I don't have it in stock, I can easily order it online from the manufacturer, with the help of our sales reps. Thanks to the Internet, I also ship many items internationally. I can get the shipping rates in advance right from the USPS Web site."

When away from his shop, Davey stays in touch with his customers using his laptop computer. He predicts his Internet sales increasing every year, as more customers access the Heaven and Earth Collectibles Web site at earthco1000.tripod.com.

Janet Cole, who together with Cyndia Williams runs Old Towne Antiques in San Dimas, California, claims her Internet business or e-commerce, is limited only by the time she chooses to devote to it.

"If I didn't love sailing so much," Janet says, "I would probably become a total workaholic, since the Internet is open 24 hours a day. It affords me the freedom to sail all day and still meet my customers' needs in the evening when the conventional store front would be long closed."

Her specialties include eclectic and varied collectibles, as well as those produced as part of a collectible line. The Internet allows her to develop what she calls a "trust and closeness" through e-mail correspondence with her collectors.

"Repeat sales through e-commerce definitely average higher than at the store level," Janet explains, "but some of our customers who access my Web page don't place orders from there. They look it up to get directions to our shop!" Look for Old Towne Antiques on the Web at www.coleway.com.

Like many other collectible business owners, both Davey and Janet are avid collectors and spend a lot of their free time surfing the Web in search of collectibles — and in the process, attracting repeat customers.

☞The Home-Office Collectible

With the access counter on the Ty, Inc. home page hovering in the billions, significant evidence shows that collectible beanbag plush is still widely traded on the Internet. While collectors of the past spent hours away from home, thousands of Beanie Baby, Barbie doll, and Boyd's Bears collectors build their collections right from their home offices.

On January 1, 1997, Ty made a product announcement about the next set of Beanie Babies to an eagerly waiting public. The announcement included the releases that were about to make their debut on the market. The only medium via which Ty made the information available was the World Wide Web site at www.ty.com. Those who accessed the site found it ran slowly, taking forever to load. But around midnight when most people ordinarily would be ringing in the New Year with family and friends, millions of people instead were watching the long-awaited Beanie Baby news appear on their monitors.

Never before had a collectible been so successfully marketed on the Internet.

The Tao of Ty

A 1962 graduate of Kalamazoo College and former sales representative for the Dakin plush company, H. Ty Warner established Ty, Inc. in 1986 in Oakbrook, Illinois. The first products consisted of plush cats and an Annual Collectible Bears series.

Beanie Babies debuted in 1993 and appeared at a toy exposition. In 1995, Beanies steadily rose in the plush toy market, quickly spreading from the Midwest across the United States.

During this time, Ty developed and launched a Web site. By midsummer 1996, Beanies had carved out their niche in popularity, both as a reasonably priced toy and as a collectible. A rather lucrative secondary market was creeping in. People clamoring for news about new Beanies and retirements absorbed much of their information from the Ty Web site.

What vaulted Beanie Babies into collectible legend was Ty's putting it all up on the Web.

From its inception, the captivating design of the Ty Web site exceeds the level of user-friendliness required by the stuffed-animal industry. It's usable by those who are first dipping their toes into the Internet puddles. With its bold colors, friendly Comic Sans typeface, pretty navigation icons, and sparkling animations, the home page offers a hypnotizing escape into the fluffy, inviting world of plush toys.

With our nurturing instincts tweaked, our curiosity for this new and exciting World Wide Web piqued, and our desire to surround ourselves with things we like so indulged, who could resist?

☞How We Collected Beanbag Plush

Until the arrival of Beanie Babies, many people never considered collecting a specific line made by a single manufacturer. Fan vases, for example, were crafted and distributed by numerous companies with unknown production figures. You cannot likely accomplish "getting the whole set." With collectible lines, you can simply print out the checklist the company provides on their Web site. By checking off each item, you know how many you still need to complete your set.

According to Simone Flynn, who owns and operates Accents Studio in downtown Chicago, almost all of her customers who acquired Beanies strictly for collecting bought at least two of each style, one for their collection and one to trade. Given the frequent shortage of Beanies during their heyday, trading with another collector was sometimes the only way to acquire certain styles. This continues to hold true for other popular, relatively inexpensive collectibles.

This practice probably adds to the supply shortage, but it certainly helps both the United States Postal Service and UPS meet any revenue goals they may have. With the Internet reaching all parts of the world, the packages that people send each other to complete their trades head everywhere.

Most manufacturers of collectibles periodically introduce items and retire other ones. The buying frenzy for current collectible items is the most intense right after the announcements of new releases. Collectors and secondary-market dealers buy multiples of certain styles because they can resell them for much more than the suggested retail price plus sales tax.

The May 1998 Teenie Beanie Babies distributed by McDonald's and the June 1998 regular Beanie Baby announcements brought about another unique concept — the "presale." Prospective sellers entered auctions on the Internet, inviting people to bid on (and subsequently pay for) sets that the seller didn't yet have but was "certain to obtain."

How Beanie Buying Worked

By setting the recommended retail price at $4.99, Ty Warner designed Beanie Babies to be affordable for kids. They sold well and they sold *out* very fast, often before kids could even hope to get their hands on any. Customers were obsessed with them. One store clerk told me that Beanie hunters had "that look." The keen eyes of many experienced cashiers could detect crazed plush seekers across parking lots and through storefront windows before they even entered the shop.

Eager secondary dealers, trying to obtain as many hard-to-find styles as possible, often stood in long lines (accompanied by their cohorts) to defeat shop-imposed limits on Beanies sold to each customer. The boldest ones insisted that their companions, some of whom were infants in strollers, should also get their limit of Beanies Babies.

Many secondary dealers knew this and brought children along (theirs, their friends', and their children's friends) to buffer themselves from the angry stares of other customers as they piled the children's arms high with Beanie Babies. And who was going to protest this, given that these items were, for all practical purposes, *toys?*

Although they politely pretended not to, it was common for secondary dealers waiting in the checkout line to recognize each other from a previous haul. Amateur secondary dealers, not wanting to be caught in the act, invented nieces and nephews who were all eagerly waiting at home for that one noble person who left work at 10 a.m. to buy the Beanies they needed. Of course.

Some secondary dealers made their intentions obvious by shamelessly going through the lines as many times as they could. Many collectors were secondary dealers in denial.

The Beanie Enterprise

And when their collections were complete? Some people either loved them so much or were so compulsive about acquiring them that they couldn't keep from buying at least a few when they'd see them in a store. The result was a cache of extra Beanie Babies and Buddies® at home and the temptation to buy table space at a swap meet to sell Beanies at a profit.

"Some of my Beanie customers would have bought up half my shipment if I'd have let them, and they were in it for big bucks," says Simone. "I used to wonder if they spent more on them than they actually made selling them."

What collectors-turned-dealers found at organized swap meets, though, was competition from seasoned dealers with an abundant stock of both current and retired Beanie Babies and equipment to accept credit card purchases. This was no contest for the amateur Beanie entrepreneur.

Those who couldn't stand up to the competition at swap meets opted for yard sales or something similar. If someone set up a stand in an area experiencing a shortage of Beanie Babies, Salvino Bammers, Furbies, Pokémon collectibles, or any other "hot" item, that person could earn more than a thousand dollars in one day just by asking twice the current retail value — or more.

For awhile it seemed Beanie Babies were sold everywhere — video arcades, gas stations, roadside stands, and especially state and county fairs. Auction sites on the Internet were heavy with people selling the cream of the Beanie Baby crop, and the Ty guestbook was loading up by the minute with entries.

This subculture spawned hundreds of dedicated Web sites and home pages with Beanie Babies as their theme, most offering Beanies for sale. Unless they were purchased at the retail shops with which Ty would accept accounts, customers had to be prepared to pay at least $10 for each Beanie Baby — about twice the retail value. If anyone was determined to collect Beanie Babies, they were available *somewhere*.

For the collector who had the extra time and money, it was relatively easy to assemble a collection of all current Beanie Babies® and at least most of the retired ones in a short time. The Internet made this possible.

However, until new product announcements every six months or so, what was a collector supposed to do in the meantime?

☞Getting Past Beanbags

Armed with knowledge for buying and trading acquired while gathering beanbag plush, many collectors now venture into a different type of product line. Some choose items that are not part of an actual line, like carved birds, ceramic figures, or more traditional collectibles such as Olympics pins or foreign coins. Others find appeal in "getting the whole set" and choose to collect items that are part of a series.

What these folks experience when seeking other collectibles, however, is often dramatically different from what they encountered when they shopped for beanbag plush collectibles when those toys were hot items on the market.

A Dramatic Difference

The lower the retail price, the tighter stronghold the secondary market has on the collectible. This is what ultimately happened with Beanie Babies and Pokémon cards. Other collectible lines rarely sell out completely. Given that most collectibles range from $25 to over $1,000 at retail, it's economically difficult for the average person to buy more than one at a time. Also, the higher the retail price, the more slowly the secondary price creeps up.

Unlike the beanbag plush collectible market, dealers of other collectible lines are usually willing to put a collector's name on a waiting list for the most coveted items and then call the customer when the shipment arrives. Most collectible shops will ship an item with a credit card order. Some will impose one-per-customer limits on limited edition items, but rarely are limits imposed on currently manufactured open edition pieces.

Collectors of lines like Harmony Kingdom, Boyd's Bears, Charming Tails, Cat Hall of Fame, Gene Dolls, and many of the Cavanaugh and Enesco lines usually buy one of each item at a time. Secondary dealer hoarding, even with ample cash on hand, is much less common because the shops don't have hundreds of the items in stock. Beanie Babies came in packages of a dozen and were often shipped by the gross. However, certain limited-edition items in other collectible lines are sometimes limited to as few as two per store, depending on the owner's prior sales of that line.

Collector Camaraderie

Once you get on the Web, you'll eventually meet people who collect the same types of items that you do. You'll notice there's something dramatically different about the way fellow collectors help each other, as opposed to what you may have experienced with so-called "fad collectibles" like Beanie Babies.

During my beanbag collecting, I found that while they were thrilling to hunt for and to collect, they also brought out the inherent greed in people. When I was trying to locate the pink bunny Hoppity for a friend of mine, another friend was lucky enough to have acquired an armload of them at retail.

Since it was needed for a collection, I was certain that she'd gladly sell our friend a Hoppity for the retail price. I was shocked, however, to hear that she wanted the current secondary price for the bunny — eighteen dollars. She appeared distressed that we'd even ask her to surrender it for less than that.

Once I got into collecting another line, I was amazed that people

I had never met face-to-face were willing to purchase an item for me (even a high-demand limited-edition piece) and then let me send them a check to cover the retail cost of the item plus postage. Since the demand for collectibles differs depending on where you live, I've returned this courtesy numerous times.

☞Dealer Incentives

To reward dealers who do a better-than-average job of marketing their products, certain collectible manufacturers offer preferred-dealer incentives. Boyd's Bears has one such program, as does Harmony Ball Company.

Advantages come with being a preferred dealer, but a violation of any of the collectible company's requirements for preferred-dealer status could cost dealers their perks.

Preferred-Dealer Status

Since a better selection of items means more sales for the retailer, many are eager to seek preferred-dealer status. Boyd's Bears dealers can earn Bronze, Silver, or Golden Paw status for ordering a specific amount of the products. A Harmony Kingdom dealer can achieve "Queen Empress" status for ordering a specific amount of Harmony Ball Company products in a year's time. Dealers who have reached Queen Empress status can order more of certain items because their prior record indicates their clientele is steady and future orders are forthcoming.

Queen Empress dealers of the Harmony Kingdom line must meet certain criteria:

- They must have a Web page where they advertise and actively sell Harmony Kingdom products.
- Their business must be in an actual store — not just on the Internet or out of the back of a truck.
- Dealers must agree to host certain Harmony Kingdom special events in their store if asked.
- Harmony Kingdom products must be prominently displayed in the store.
- Product discounting is forbidden.

Auto-Ship

Some companies, such as Harbour Lights, employ a concept known as "auto-ship," where the dealer agrees in advance to buy a certain number of items the company produces.

While dealers risk having overstock if the shipped pieces don't sell right away (Harbour Lights also forbids dealers to discount), shipment of the limited-edition pieces that collectors covet is guaranteed.

No Product Discounting

Most manufacturers of collectible lines want to limit their distribution to a manageable level. When a product overruns the market, collectors might become disinterested, causing lower sales and price discounting. Dealers may turn to the Internet to reach a bigger market in hopes of selling their overstock.

"Some dealers tend to over-spend on a certain collectible thinking they can sell it on the Internet for profit," says Bill Younger, who for that reason will not sell his products to Internet-only companies, "and discounting can kill a collectible."

The only type of "discounting" that dealers can get away with is if they have a shopper's incentive program. Customers get a card punched for a certain number of dollars they spend in the store, and a full card earns a discount on the next purchase of any store merchandise. Some companies allow dealers who are liquidating their business to discount their remaining stock.

☛Customer Incentives

Collectible companies want to produce items that collectors will buy. To keep the customer interested and attract new collectors, they frequently offer incentives or bonus programs for frequent buyers. For years, many of the companies have offered membership incentives to collectors.

Collector Memberships

Memberships in collectors' societies are available through individual dealers or directly from the company. When signing up as a member, the collector pays a nominal fee in return for a membership kit, which contains brochures and one or two special member pieces. Kits that can be purchased right at the dealer's shop are called "instant gratification" kits because the collectors can take them home right away. Other kits must be ordered in advance.

Included in the kit is an application for membership that the dealer fills out and sends to the company. In a few weeks, a membership card and some other perks (like a calendar, item checklist or stationery) is mailed to the new member. Most collectible companies also produce a special quarterly newsletter that's sent directly to members.

In addition to the kit, some memberships include the option to purchase special pieces (separate from the items included in the member kit) called *redemption pieces* that are available to members only. Members receive a coupon for each redemption piece they may order. These pieces are typically top-of-the line in artistic value and quality — the "extra mile" from their creators — and new collectors usually seek them in later years.

You can read more about membership kits in Chapter 3.

Anniversary and Milestone Pieces

Having recently celebrated 20 years of production, Precious Moments released its "Twenty Years and the Vision's Still the Same" commemorative, limited-edition figurine. In 1999, Mattel released the 40th Anniversary Barbie® to honor the milestone for the popular fashion doll.

To welcome the new century, Christopher Radko created *Times Square,* an ornament commemorating New Year's Eve 1999. Numerous other ornament companies created items to honor the year 2000 as we bid farewell to the twentieth century.

Some collectible companies issue an item in memory of a public icon, as evidenced by the many pieces which honor Diana, Princess of Wales, and John Wayne.

Special-Event Pieces

As mentioned before, certain dealers are expected to host special events in their shops to retain their preferred-dealer status. The events revolve around the particular collectible line in the spotlight, and the promise of wine, cheese, chances at drawings, and complimentary items from the company lures customers.

A representative is usually on hand at these special events to answer questions about the line and encourage potential collectors to sign on as members. There is normally a special piece that goes with the collectible line that can only be purchased at these in-store events. On rare occasions, one or more of the artists attend to sign pieces for collectors.

One example is the "Cat's Meow" netsuke piece that Harmony Kingdom's Noel Wiggins made available only in shops that hosted his U.S tour during 1999 and 2000. He brought only 100 Cat's Meows to each shop he visited, and when he left, he took any unsold pieces with him.

Super Special-Event Pieces

Krause Publications sponsors the International Collectible Exposition, or the ICE show. There are two shows each year. The annual spring show takes place alternately in the East and West regions of the United States. The annual summer show takes place in Rosemont, Illinois.

The largest event of its kind, the ICE gives attendees abundant opportunity to see collectibles on the market. Hundreds of booths display collectibles from all types of companies. Some hold drawings for certain pieces. Many manufacturers also use the show to preview products.

The ICE also allows collectors of a common line to meet face-to-face after many months of bulletin board and e-mail exchanges. Some collectible companies take advantage of the event and sponsor social get-togethers for their collectors during the same weekend.

For both yearly ICE shows, select companies produce special pieces to commemorate the event. These special ICE pieces are typically the only collectibles, except for membership kits, that the public can purchase at the event. They only make a certain amount of each ICE piece and sometimes limit purchases. This causes a secondary-market demand for them, especially after the summer show.

If the piece is from a popular line, it sells at secondary prices *before* the ICE closes. One of the event pieces for the 1998 ICE show was Harmony Kingdom's "Sneak Preview," which was limited to 5,000 pieces and sold for $65 at the event. "Sneak Preview" was so popular that purchases were limited to two per individual at the spring show in Edison, New Jersey, and one per person by the time the Rosemont show opened. One eager participant of the Edison show went back to his hotel room and, using his laptop computer, put "Sneak Preview" up for auction on the Internet. The item closed at over $250 three days later.

> ➡ Note: Harmony Kingdom also did the 1999 ⬅
> ICE piece, called "Swap 'n' Sell," and to make things interesting,
> mixed 100 of a special variation in with the 2,500 sold at the Rosemont show. Several lucky collectors brought home a rare variation!

While the public can't buy many products at the ICE events, they can certainly get free stuff, and usually in abundance. Companies dole out buttons, bookmarks, product samples, tee shirts, and other novelties.

Other companies actually produce a small commemorative item that's handed out to their club members attending the ICE events. Many appear at auction on the Internet in later months, coveted by collectors who couldn't attend the ICE or by those who didn't get to a booth in time before all the items were given away.

Since the second year they had a booth at the ICE, Harmony Kingdom has produced a special commemorative pendant that's free for members of their collector society (the Royal Watch) who show their membership card at the Harmony Kingdom booth.

These pendants, and similar items produced by other companies, can later command several hundred dollars on the secondary market. Items like the 1999 Cardew Teapot pin and the Margaret Furlong ornaments available at the ICE shows also sell on the secondary market, especially if signed by the artists.

Super-*Duper* Special-Event Pieces

Since companies generally enjoy getting their collectors together to keep the interest alive, some of them host special events of their own, not associated with the ICE or any other collectible exposition. These special events often yield another item given or sold to attendees.

At the 1997 Harbour Lights Reunion in California, each attendee could purchase two copies of the New Point Loma lighthouse. They were also given one miniature version of New Point Loma. Only 950 full-size New Point Lomas and 480 of the miniature version were produced, making this a highly sought-after collectible. The full-size version sold for $70 to reunion attendees. After the reunion, it sold for over $1,200 on the Internet.

Some companies sponsor collectors' events concurrent with the ICE weekend. During the 1997 and 1998 Rosemont ICE, Harmony Kingdom sponsored a boat ride on Lake Michigan, where collectors were given special pieces designed by artist Peter Calvesbert. Their first collectors' convention happened in April 1999 on a cruise ship that visited Southern California and Ensenada, Mexico. Each passenger received a large commemorative piece and a pseudo-traditional "goodie box," complete with a marble-resin pin, tote bag, and sun visor, all which sold on the secondary market afterwards.

Special Collector-Club Pieces

Some companies create pieces earmarked for independent collector clubs. Since Department 56 doesn't sponsor a membership society for the village pieces (only for their Snowbabies line), a group of collectors started a national club on their own. All local clubs belong to the national club.

Department 56 later created a special item just for the collector-club members. The piece was "generic" in nature and not part of any particular village series. The special piece is similar to what might be in a membership kit. Other collectible lines have since followed the tradition of offering special items to members of independent collector clubs.

New Membership Incentives

If memberships and store events aren't enough to draw collectors to the line, some companies offer existing members an incentive item for signing up new members. If a collector's member number appears on a certain amount of new membership applications, that collector (as the referring member) receives a special piece from the company

In some cases, referring a certain number of new members guarantees your next year's membership free.

☞Independent Collectors' Clubs and Networks

With the right amount of Web surfing and participation in cyber-discussions, you can meet other collectors and maybe become friends outside of cyber-space. It's getting more and more common to see independent collector clubs based around a particular collectible line pop up in different parts of the country.

Most of the clubs elect officers and hold monthly meetings, where collectors can discuss the line and bring in special items from their collections to pass around. Some clubs publish member newsletters with information about the collectible line, and most maintain a Web page associated with the club.

Very often, a collector club will offer to "host" other collectors who are getting together for the ICE or for another event. The club takes care of reserving blocks of hotel rooms, and some of them sponsor hospitality rooms or receptions so the collectors can meet outside of the main event.

☞Making the Most of It All

Often the most exhilarating stage in building a collection is getting the first few pieces and learning about their particular intrigue. With the knowledge of using the Web acquired when you obtained Beanie Babies, Barbie dolls, Furbies, or other items, you're likely to be eager to apply this exciting medium to a new and different line of collectibles.

What you'll find when you venture beyond beanbags is an Internet-based collecting network that operates with a different protocol than the one you encountered in Beanie land.

While exciting, it can be something of a culture shock. Whether you are a seasoned collector who regularly surfs the Web or a novice first plugging in your PC, this book provides the information you need to make the most of your Internet collecting experience.

The chapters that follow will help you learn to use the Internet to your best advantage while building your collection. Be wary, though — your collection will grow *fast*.

Chapter 2 — Accessing and Surfing the Web

The World Wide Web, although still in its infancy, is a place of tremendous possibility and potential for collectors. If your only experience with the Web has been calling up www.hallmark.com or clicking on a few "favorites" provided by America On Line (AOL), take heart. You are not alone!

This chapter covers the basics of Internet use:

- Getting to know the Web
- Accessing the Web
- The Web browser
- Searching for Web sites
- Learning about collectibles on the Internet
- What is Usenet?
- What to do before you start using the Internet for collecting

The information provided here assumes you have or are about to have access to a PC and the services of an Internet service provider (ISP) that offers Web access. If you're using the Web from a library or through your employer's service, consider getting your own connection if you can afford it. It's far more convenient, and your employer will appreciate it!

Since the best testimony to quality service comes from people currently using the Web, ask around before you decide on a service.

☛Getting To Know the Web

Years ago they said that we'd eventually use computers for just about everything. I wonder if anybody thought that would include collecting?

Did you ever dream you'd be able to chat with people all over the world for the cost of a local phone call? Or that you'd be able to tack something up on a bulletin board and thousands of people would read and respond to it right away?

In your wildest dreams, did you ever think that you'd have a computer at home that you could use to bid on items up for auction and have them arrive at your front door only days later?

Those days are here.

"But I'm Computer Illiterate!"

No, you're not. Claiming you're computer illiterate is like saying you can't press the buttons to turn on your computer and monitor, you can't move a mouse around a pad, and you don't understand how the mouse interacts with what appears on the monitor. If you can't handle these simple tasks, then you probably aren't reading this book, either.

Everyone has used computers. They're so prevalent in our most mundane routines that it's safe to say there are no exceptions. Unless you've never used an ATM card, never bought gas with a credit card, never checked out a library book, and never made a phone call, you can be confident that you've used a computer.

Although seasoned technical support persons might argue this, you don't need to format your PC's hard drive, load your operating system, and successfully recover your system from a hard-disk crash to say that you're computer literate. Have you created and saved text files and made changes later? Have you used your computer to update data with new data, like figuring your checking account balance? If you answered yes to either question, then you've made use of the most basic principle from which computers were developed.

If you can call up your Web browser, access a Web site, and click on a hypertext link to get to another screen, then you've used part of the impressive computer network called the Internet.

If you can also send and receive e-mail with attached files, then you certainly aren't computer illiterate. In fact, you've come so far with your computer that in terms of literacy, you're writing poetry.

"What is HTML?"

You'll see this abbreviation whenever you read about creating Web pages. It stands for Hyper-Text Markup Language, which is the coding language used to make pages for the Web.

Chapter 7 contains more information about HTML and its use in dressing up your bulletin board posts and online auction descriptions. Chapter 8 gives you detailed instructions for creating a basic home page for the Web, along with a sample template with HTML coding tags to get you started.

☛Getting on the Web

You can access the Internet any number of ways, depending on what kind of computer you own and how much you want to spend for your connection.

One of the most basic grading factors for Internet connections is how fast the pages load in your browser. Some connections are split-second, while others can be agonizingly slow. Time is money on the Internet, which means the faster the connection, the more you can expect to pay for it.

Making a Trial Run

Another way to access the Web is at a local library that has personal computers set up with Internet access. This is an excellent way to make a trial run and see if you want to use the Internet regularly.

If you can get time (you might have to wait your turn), your Web session will last about an hour. However, right around the time you'll find a plethora of sites that you want to visit, the librarian will be tapping you on the shoulder.

Do you really need a trial run? You're going to love the Web. So, the best advice is to get your own access.

The Fastest Way to the Internet

You can also get on the Internet without using a phone line. The advantage of these alternate methods is that your connection speed will be fast and dependable. Not all of them might be available in your location or with your computer setup, and you can count on them being considerably more costly than a phone-line ISP.

Here are some of the premium ways to the Internet:

- **LAN Connection** – You may be able to obtain a local area network (LAN) connection if you are within a university or large company. A LAN connection means you're connected to the Internet at speeds of up to 100 megabits per second (Mbps) in both directions by way of the organization's internal computer network. Instead of a modem and phone line, you just need a network interface card in your PC. Talk to your organization's system administrator if you need help getting Internet access.
- **Cable TV** – Many cable TV providers also offer access to the Internet. The Internet data is transmitted over the same cable that your TV programs come over. You use your own PC and a cable modem provided by the cable carrier to access the Internet without tying up a phone line in your home. The main advantage of a cable TV connection is that it is *very fast* although it's somewhat more expensive than the service from other providers. It might well be worth the higher price. Your cable TV provider can offer you more information.
- **ISDN** – If you want a faster connection than what's available (or possible) over regular phone lines, consider getting an Integrated Services Digital Network (ISDN) link to your ISP. You might be able to acquire an ISDN connection from your telephone company but it's probably more costly than cable service and not as fast.

- **Satellite Connection** – This runs three times faster than an ISDN connection from your phone company. Hughes Network Systems offers a service called DirecPC which supplies 400 kilobits per second (kbps) download speed and requires a separate modem connection for uploading. The initial cost of around $300 includes an antenna and a special card installed in your PC. Monthly rates run from $20 plus $3.95 per hour to $130 a month plus $3.95 per hour, depending on what time of day you choose to access the Internet.
- **T-1 Connection** – T-1 is a high-speed access method that connects one or more computers to the Internet. A T-1 connection operates at 1.544 Mbps. It can cost anywhere from $150 and $350 per month.
- **ADSL Connection** – Asymmetric Digital Subscriber Line (ADSL) uses standard telephone lines and provides download speeds of up to 7 Mbps and upload speeds of up to 500 kbps. It requires a special ADSL modem on both the customer end and the ISP end. This makes it somewhat expensive. The price may drop as this system catches on throughout the country.

A More Common Way to the Internet

Most people who have Internet access at home use one of the more common ISPs, such as AOL, AT&T Worldnet, or Microsoft Network. The major ISPs will send you an information packet and a start-up diskette if you call and request information about their services. You can also download their software right to your hard drive if you have an active browser with an Internet connection on your computer. For a more complete listing of ISPs, go to thelist.internet.com.

While the faster connections mentioned previously are great, using a common ISP is a lot easier on the pocketbook. They provide unlimited usage at rates from $12 to $30 per month, depending on the plan. You might want to check with people who currently use one of them so you can decide which ISP is best for you.

If you can afford it (or if you have teenagers at home), it's usually a good idea to get a second phone line installed to use when you dial into your ISP. You may not think you'll spend a lot of time online, but once you see the information available on the Web and what it can do for your collecting, you'll use it more than you ever imagined.

Here's what you need to access the Internet over a regular phone line:

- Desktop or laptop computer
- Keyboard
- Modem
- Phone line
- Software required by the ISP for Internet access

Almost every ISP provides you with an e-mail address and the ability to send and receive e-mail — a very important feature if you plan on buying, selling, and trading collectibles with people you meet on the Internet.

Representatives at most computer superstores can give you the information you need for hooking up with an ISP. That's typically part of their job.

A Cheaper Way to the Internet

You may know it as WebTV. This service makes use of a device called a "set-top box" about the size of a standard VCR that sits on top of your TV set with one cable hooked into your set and another connected to a phone line. You must purchase the box and then pay a monthly service fee. The connection is somewhat less expensive than an ISP, but you should know about a few limitations in advance:

- The World Wide Web window is only about eight lines long, so you should plan on doing a lot of scrolling.
- The resolution on the TV screen is nowhere near as good as on a computer monitor, making text difficult to read at times.
- Unless you plug a keyboard into the set-top box, you are limited to read-only, meaning that you can't enter data.

Free Internet Access

If you surf the Internet a little, you'll find several sites that offer free Web access and e-mail. Advertising solely funds these sites. To use one of these services, you first need an active connection to the Internet. You'll most likely use one of these before you end one type of service, because you'll need the connection to download the free site software.

When you surf the Web this way, you'll dial a number provided by the service. Then as you launch your browser, another little advertising window appears on your monitor screen. Throughout your session, you'll see continuous ads from companies that sponsor the site.

At these sites, you'll download a program to your PC so you can dial into their network and surf the Web free.

Uniform Resource Locator	Company Name
www.netzero.net	.NetZero
www.alladvantage.com	.AllAdvantage
www.freewwweb.com	.Freewwweb
www.microav.com	.AltaVista Free Access
www.freei.net	.Freei Net
www.nocharge.com	.NoCharge.com
www.nopay.net	.No Pay Net
www.freepctv.net	.PowerChannel
www.freeppp.com	.FreePPP
www.tritium.net	.Tritium Network

For a comprehensive listing of free Internet access sites outside the United States, check out the Free E-mail Address Directory (www.emailaddresses.com). From the "Free Stuff" directory, click on "Internet Access."

You can find others with an Internet search for "Free Web Access." You'll read more about Internet searches and search engines further along in this chapter.

There are some drawbacks to free Internet access. Response time is much slower and less reliable than what you'll get with a paid ISP, and, of course, the free providers bombard you with ads the entire time you're online. You may also pay by the minute for calls to their technical support.

> ➡ Note: I have not personally used any of these ⬅
> free Internet services. As they say on the Web,
> "YMMV – Your mileage may vary!"

☛The Browser

To access the Internet, you'll need a software package called a *browser*. The browser is the window that you use to access the World Wide Web. Most ISPs include browser software as part of your start-up package.

The two most popular browsers are Netscape Navigator and Microsoft Internet Explorer. Both have the same basic capability in that you can look at Web pages in the viewing area of the window and follow the connections to other Web sites. You might want to experiment with both Netscape and Internet Explorer to determine which one you like better.

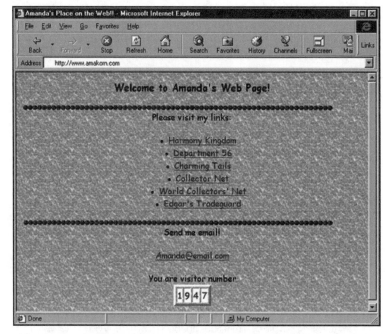

Figure 2-1 shows a sample Web browser with a Web page loaded.

Figure 2-2. The Title, Menu, and Tool Bar on the Browser

Figure 2-2 shows a close-up of the uppermost part of the browser. The top row is the Title Bar, the center row is the Menu Bar, and the bottom row is the Tool Bar. The Address Line is where you type in a Web address, or URL, which you'll read more about later in this chapter.

Title Bar

This area contains the title of the Web page, if the page HTML code contains a title. In the previous example, "Amanda's Place on the Web" is the title that Amanda coded into her page. The title bar might also include the name of the browser, as shown in Figure 2-1.

Note: You'll read more about coding a
title into a Web page in Chapter 8.

Menu Bar

Directly under the title bar is a row of words: File, Edit, View, Go, Favorites, and Help. This is the menu bar. The words may vary depending on what browser you're using, but the functions are similar.

- **File** provides functions for working with your Browser, such as opening Web pages and printing from the Web.
- **Edit** allows you to cut, copy, and paste data, and offers a "select all" and "find" feature.
- **View** lets you alter the way your browser presents the menu and tool bars, and allows some basic browser functions similar to the ones in the tool bar. It also lets you view the source HTML code of a Web page.
- **Go** provides navigation within pages you've visited, or your preset pages, such as your browser's home page.
- **Favorites** allows you to add or delete your bookmarks, which are URLs that you want to keep on file for future visits.
- **Help** contains links to sites on both on the Web and within your browser that offer Internet tutorial assistance.

Tool Bar

The tool bar is right under the menu bar. With the functions provided, you can save files to your hard drive, print pages, return to a page that you visited earlier, and much more.

Each of the tool bar buttons shown in Figure 2-2 performs a unique function to help you navigate the Web. To use them, position your mouse cursor over the button and click the left mouse button.

 Note: This action is known as a "left-click."

I used Internet Explorer in the example here, but Netscape Navigator contains buttons that perform similar functions. The browsers may also differ in future versions.

- **Back** takes you to the last URL location (or Web page) that was loaded in your browser. It only works if you have been to a page before the one that's currently in your browser.
- **Forward** only works if you previously used the "Back" button.

It takes you to the page you were at before you hit the "Back" button.

- **Stop** stops the current page from loading. It's most commonly used if you don't want to wait for the images on the page to load, or if the page is taking a long time to load because the network is running slowly.

- **Refresh** (or **Reload** on Netscape) reloads the current page into your browser. This is most commonly used when the data on the page has changed since the last time it was loaded into your browser. If you post a bulletin board item, for instance, you usually need to refresh the screen to see your posted item included on the main page.

- **Home** takes you to the page that appears when you first bring up your browser. You can set this page to any URL with the "Preferences" option on the top line of your browser. It may be set to a blank page, which allows your browser software to load more quickly.

- **Search** shows you to a Web page where you have access to most of the popular search engines, such as Lycos, Excite, or Alta Vista.

- **Favorites** lists your bookmarks. When you click on this button, you can bookmark your current page.

- **History** shows you the Web page URLs that you have accessed for the period of time set in your preferences, usually one week.

- **Channels** takes you to pre-programmed information sites, like CNN, The Weather Channel, and Entertainment sites.

- **Fullscreen** increases your browser to the full size of your monitor screen. This is usually the default when you start your browser.

- **Mail** brings up your mail screen from which you can send and receive mail. You need to be configured to send mail from Netscape or Internet Explorer.

- **Print** sends the page displayed in your browser to whatever printer you specify as your default printer.

- **Edit** brings you into a program called Front Page Express (or Netscape Composer), where you can edit the Web page if you own it.

You can also access these features by positioning your mouse cursor in the browser window (but not over hypertext or an image) and clicking the right button. This is known as a "right-click" and brings up a menu with most of the navigation functions that appear on the tool bar.

Browsers differ from version to version, so be sure to visit home.netscape.com or www.microsoft.com for more details.

Address Line

The text-entry area under the tool bar is the address line. This is where you'll enter the Web address of a site.

You'll need to know the Web address, or Uniform Resource Locator (URL, please don't try to pronounce it, just say the letters), to visit a site. Type the URL into the address line and hit "Enter." URLs for Web pages start with http:// (which stands for hypertext transfer protocol). This is so common, however, that most browsers don't require it. In fact, most URLs that you see in ads or on package labels no longer include it.

If your browser requires the http:// in the address line, you should probably load a newer version.

> ➡️ Note: For the purpose of brevity, I omitted ⬅️
> http:// from URLs that appear in this book.

➤Searching for Web Sites

If you're using current versions (4.0 or higher) of Netscape or Internet Explorer, there's a "Search" button located on the tool bar near the top frame of the browser. Clicking on the "Search" button takes you to a Web page where you can access most of the popular search engines, such as Lycos, Excite, GoTo, or InfoSeek. From these sites you can type key words and phrases into an on-screen text-input form, called a *search box,* to initiate a Web search.

If you can't find the "Search" button or if the one on your browser limits your search to Web sites within that ISP, you can get to a search engine by typing any of these URLs into the address line:

- www.altavista.com
- www.lycos.com
- www.infoseek.com
- www.excite.com
- www.goto.com
- www.webcrawler.com
- www.yahoo.com

Figure 2-3. Text Entry Area of a Search Engine

You can access many search engines from one Web page called the All-in-One Search Page at www.AllOneSearch.com.

Note: Yahoo works like a search engine, although technically it's not. It's a directory because people make the entries instead of an automated program. You'll see it listed in search engine indexes, though.

Another comprehensive site about search engines is Search Engine Watch at www.searchenginewatch.com.

If search results don't satisfy you, you can always try another search engine. Since the organization maintaining the search engine may not have scouted the Web recently, a different search engine may have more up-to-date information.

How Search Engines Work

To explain it in the most basic of terms, a search engine does the most time-consuming part of your Web-surfing for you.

A search engine uses an index updated on a regular basis. The site has robot-like programs called Web-bots (also called "spiders") that search the Internet and build large indexes of words used on the Web. A search engine differs from a directory in that humans build directories based on information submitted by Web page owners.

After you enter a search string in the search box, all you need to do is click on the "Search" or "Submit" button next to the search box. The search engine will then go into its index files and find as many Web pages as it can that contain all or any part of the string of text that you entered in the search box.

The results appear in your browser, as a list of hypertext links ordered by how likely a page is to meet your search criteria. This likelihood sometimes shows up as a percentage that appears by the item. The best matches list first.

Entering a Search String

When you enter text into the search box, use the most defining words first to make your search as concise as possible. It is not necessary to use plurals; in fact, this could narrow down your search so much that you might miss some wonderful sites.

Suppose you want to search for sites that pertain to collecting on the Internet. A search string you might try is:

collect internet

The search engine hunts for sites containing the word "collect," giving those sites priority because you entered that word first. It's not necessary to enter the entire word because the search function looks for character strings, not words.

Next, the search engine hunts for "internet." Sites that contain both words will list first.

The percent of your search string will be indicated by each result listed. Any results containing the entire search string are labeled "100%" to indicate that all of your search string was found on that page.

After that, sites containing only part of your search string will list and you'll see a percentage less than 100.

Don't get overly excited if your search brings up tens of thousands of sites that matched your search. Most search engines keep grabbing pages down through the lowest particles of your search string. Therefore, the last page of links brought up by this search may be about collective Internet frog jumping.

Most search engines can only display the first 200 listings shown in your search results. If you don't find what you're looking for on those pages, narrow down your search criteria.

Figure 2-4. Typical Results Returned Using a Search Engine

Hints for Effective Searches

To narrow down your search results, these tips work on most search engines (since programs always change, you might have to experiment):

- Don't use punctuation. Some punctuation marks have different meanings from the perspective of the search engine and could alter your results.
- Use lowercase unless you specifically want to search for a capitalized word. If you use uppercase, the results return only uppercase instances of that word. If you use lowercase, it returns items in both lower and uppercase.
- Include a plus sign (+) in front of any word that must appear in the search results. Don't put a space between the + and the word; use a space before it.

- Put a minus sign (–) in front of any word you do *not* want to have appear in your search results. Don't insert a space between the minus sign and the word, but use a space in front of it.
- Add double quotes ("") around any words you want to appear next to each other.
- If the answers are not what you expect, check your spelling!
- Enter a basic and concise search string.
- If you don't find what you want on the first page of results, the rest will be even further off the topic. Use another search string.

To learn more about search engines and how their capabilities match up against one another, simply type "search engine" into the search box of any popular search engine. You'll get a bombardment of links to sites with all the information you need. Plus, it's good practice.

A Word of Caution about Search Engines

For some Internet businesses, hits to their page mean money. This is particularly true of adult-oriented sites. The idea is to get people to the page, show a few "nudie" photos, and then encourage the person to enter a credit card number in return for a special password for the pages that contain the real good stuff.

Getting a search engine to bring up a link to such a site means that Websurfers might go there. Search engine Web-bots look at the source HTML code, and search results list in order of how many times the text appears on a page. To ensure that a site lists in search results, the clever person coding the page tries to include as many instances of "certain words" into the code as possible. All kinds of places give a Web page designer an opportunity to sneak words into the HTML code. These hidden words will be invisible to a Websurfer viewing the page.

This is why page descriptions shown in search results sometimes don't make sense. The words that hide in the HTML code to lure the Web-bots sometimes manage to become the page description. Anyone who's seen a search result listing for an "adult" Web site knows exactly what I mean.

Suffice to say that if your search string contains words like "adult," "pictures," or "free," make sure that before you hit the "Search" button you aren't in a crowded office at work. Be especially certain that your kids aren't looking over your shoulder.

☞Getting Information About Collectibles

You don't need to limit yourself to search engines for finding information about collectibles on the Web. Once you've accustomed yourself to searching for Web pages with a search engine, you're bound to encounter a variety of pages that provide information about the collectible line. Since the very nature of the Internet is to "web" sites together, most Web pages offer links to other pages and opportunities for more surfing.

The Web presents information about collectibles in several ways.

Independent Collectors' Web Pages

Some people become such avid fans of a collectible line that they create dedicated Web pages. These sites are usually separate from and not sponsored by the collectible company.

One of the most well-known independent collectors' Web pages is the Boyd's Collector Forum site at www.boydsforum.com, which is Webmastered by Robin Kralik and Kristin Sheaffer. Micah Kralik does much of the CGI scripting. This site is its own collecting Web community devoted to enthusiasts of Boyd's Bears.

According to Kristin, "The Boyd's Collector Forum is an Internet site where collectors of Boyd's items can gather and share their love of collecting. We've made QVC numbers and item descriptions available, and Boyd's product information as provided by the wonderful Harry and Millie Croft. It's all-around collectible fun!"

For those interested in meeting fellow collectors and friends, The Boyd's Forum arranges a secret pal program, swaps, and cyber-pals listing. The User Comments board is the most popular attraction, where collectors can post exciting details of treasures they found or light-hearted friendly greetings to everyone. Boyd's Forum is a great Internet venue for collectors looking for that hard-to-find piece.

Most of these independent collectors' pages are not sanctioned or sponsored by the collectible company, but the company supports (and sometimes rewards) the efforts of collectors who create pages dedicated to their products.

Collectors' pages provide wonderful sources of information, especially for someone just entering a collectible line. These sites may include any of the following:

- Pictures of early, elusive pieces
- Chat rooms and message boards
- Information about variations, or pieces that were redesigned
- Rumors about new releases and retirements

- Personal collecting stories
- Interviews with the artists who create collectible pieces
- Web-ring links to other collectors' pages
- Links to the Web pages of small businesses that carry the collectible line

The site owners usually include their e-mail address in case a visitor has questions or just wants to make comments about the page. If you have questions about any aspect of that collectible line, you're a lot more likely to get a rapid response from one of these people than from the collectible company itself.

Small-Business Web Sites

The World Wide Web is a growing market for small businesses. Many of the specialty shops that carry collectibles have their own Web pages that allow customers to place orders right from their computers.

Some small-business owners are also collectors, and have a genuine love for the products they market to the public. Because of this, you can find a lot of information about the collectibles from these small-business Web sites. In addition, some provide bulletin boards and chat rooms for collectors. You can meet other collectors this way and small businesses get repeat visits to their Web sites.

An effective small-business Web page includes a catalog of inventory, item prices, the amount of each one in stock, and pictures of the pieces. Sometimes the items in a collectible line are grouped into one picture to save on the time it takes the page to load in your browser. The more images the page contains, the longer it takes to load.

The Web page should also include an e-mail address so you can contact the business to place an order. If the business has a secured Web site, meaning they receive encrypted information, it might also provide an on-line form that you can fill out. You'll see spaces to enter the items you wish to order, your personal information, and your credit card number. A "Submit" button, similar to the one search engines use, transmits your information right to the business.

Whoa, a credit card number? Sure. It's very safe as long as the site uses SSL (Secure Sockets Layer) software when taking your personal information. You'll read more about SSL sites a bit further on.

Some small-business sites offer retired and discontinued collectibles at secondary prices, or they might post their secondary-market estimates for retired pieces. This can be a valuable tool for a collector who wants to determine the value of an item.

One well-known business Web site is the Ruby Lane Antiques, Collectibles, and Fine Art site at www.RubyLane.com. The page contains links to information about all types of antiques and collectibles, fine art, Ruby Lane's Art Courtyard, and Ruby Lane's own online auction site. You'll also find a chat room, message boards, Question & Answer pages, and announcements. You can also read about becoming an affiliate and adding a link to their Web page on your own.

If you're looking to order collectibles at retail from a small business Web site, check out Simone Flynn's Accents Studio at www.accentstudio.com. You'll find Patricia Locke, Just The Right Shoe, Gene Dolls, Harmony Kingdom, and a wide variety of other fine collectibles. You can also check out Ann and George Schmidt's Fin-Alley Pets and Gifts at www.finalley.com for a colorful selection of giftware, collectibles, and interesting pets.

Ordering from a Small-Business Web Site

When you first order collectibles from the Internet, you may want to just go ahead and place a phone call directly to the shop. You'll probably feel more comfortable having a human being take your order than submitting your name, address, and credit-card number to parts unknown. As you use the Web more and more, though, you'll grow comfortable with submitting online orders with a credit card.

Secure Sites

Secure Sockets Layer (SSL) ensures that your browser sends the information you enter in a secure, encrypted form that nobody can read. If the site lets you choose if you want to use SSL, definitely do, even if you aren't submitting a credit card number. It never hurts to protect your privacy.

Your browser may prompt you with a window when you enter or leave a secure SSL site. To double check, look for the little lock image in the very bottom frame of your browser. It's normally unlocked, but if you're on a page with SSL, the lock will be closed or locked.

Here's what the lock icon looks like up close:

Open

Closed

Check for the closed lock at any site that requires you to submit personal information, such as a credit card number. You definitely don't want this information in the wrong hands, and a secure site prevents that from happening.

Other Considerations

If you consider placing an order after finding an SSL site on the Web, be sure that in addition to the e-mail address for the business, the page includes the shop owner's name, street address, and phone number. Use caution with any sites that don't provide this because it might be an Internet-only business. Sometimes, the collectibles available from these sites have secondary-market prices because many collectible manufacturers don't do direct business with Internet-only companies. To acquire merchandise to sell, they typically have to purchase it at retail somewhere and price it higher to turn a profit.

Super-Dedicated Collector Sites

Some Web-site developers go above and beyond the call of collectors seeking information and develop sites that are self-contained collector havens. Small businesses sponsor some of them, while others are the work of individuals with an affinity for both collecting and Web-page design.

Longaberger enthusiasts can check out The Basket Stop — Kelly's Longaberger Land at www.basketstop.com. Collectors can view and place ads and find links to related Longaberger sites.

These types of sites usually cover a collectible line in depth, and often include bulletin boards, chat rooms, secondary price guides, and pictures. Another fine example is Rob & Jay's Harmony Kingdom Page, run by Rob Doran and Jay Wanta at www70.pair.com/robnjays.

Two dedicated Harmony Kingdom enthusiasts, Rob and Jay created a Harmony Kingdom collector's information paradise. Their site includes links to pages with hints and tips for collectors, rumors about Harmony Kingdom pieces and events, classified ads, ICE Show photos, raffles and fund-raisers, and "Stories of Our Addiction" articles written by collectors.

Vivienne Wiltberger manages The Teddies Trader at www.theteddiestrader.com for Cherished Teddies collectors. Fans of the hugely popular Enesco product will find nicely organized links to the News & Info Center, the Contest Corner, the Members Clubhouse, and

Cherished Teddies auctions listed for charity fund-raising, and much more.

You'll find more links to Web sites for collectors in Chapter 4.

Web Rings

Web rings consist of Web sites with a common theme linked by a system of images and hypertext links on each page in the ring. Web site owners can start a Web ring to share their audience with other site owners. A group that manages Web rings can also start them.

To form a Web ring, the page owners determine an order for visitors to view their pages. Each page owner includes a link that guides the viewer to the next site in the ring. The idea is to get visitors to view all pages in the ring before eventually returning to the originally accessed page. Since the Web page owners all need to know when a new page joins the ring, maintaining this type of ring could be confusing.

Several groups on the Web operate and manage Web rings, one of the most common being WebRing, Inc. at www.webring.com. WebRing supports hundreds of rings all over the Web. Like most Web sites that offer users free services, they're funded by advertisements.

If your surfing leads you to a Web ring, ride the ring! You'll be amazed at how much information you can gain from sites you might otherwise have missed. If the sites don't interest you, this will be obvious after you view a few pages and you can use your browser's Back button to retrace your cyber-steps.

Web Rings and Collectors

Many small businesses and independent collectors have their pages linked in rings. If one page in the ring comes up in someone's Web search, that person can surf through as many as a hundred different Web sites from one search result.

When surfing through collectors' Web rings, you'll visit sites run by collectible shops that carry the line you're seeking. They often contain photos and information about each product in stock.

You'll also find Web pages developed by seasoned collectors who want to offer information to others. Some of these folks have collected the line since its introduction and have a wealth of information to share about the items, especially the older ones.

What a wonderful way to gain more knowledge about a collectible line!

LinkExchange

Calling itself The World's Largest Web Site Network, LinkExchange puts free banner advertising on over 250,000 Web sites.

By using their software and your own banner, you display banners for members of the network and they in turn display yours. Some of the banner space is sold to sponsors, but for others, it's free.

Members include the HTML code provided by LinkExchange for displaying banner ads on their Web site, on as many pages as they wish. LinkExchange can verify the placement and correctness of its HTML code on your page to make sure that visitors see it. The member's Web site might display an advertisement from a sponsor, from another member, or from LinkExchange.

When you register your site with one of the exchanges, it comes up at random on other sites that have the link in place. The banners that appear on your page are randomly selected from the pool of other members. When visitors click on the banner, they hyperlink to that site. LinkExchange offers an Antiques/Collectibles exchange, among many others.

LinkExchange lives on the Web at www.LinkExchange.com.

Collectible-Company Web Sites

Web sites operated by the collectible company get right to the important aspects of their products. Professional Web site developers usually manage and maintain a collectible company's main Web site and supply plenty of information and resources for collectors.

If the results from a search engine don't provide you with a link to a collectible company, the independent collector or small business Web pages probably will. Most of the time, the collectible company has its own domain on a Web server. Its URL should be easy to guess, as in the case with www.hallmark.com or www.enesco.com.

Chapter 4 covers collectible company Web sites in more detail.

Online Secondary Market Price Guides

Secondary market price guides are collections of the current market value of collectibles on the resale market. While the most secondary price guides are still in hard copy, more and more are appearing online.

Anyone who used the Internet to collect Beanie Babies should remember the famous Beanie Mom site at www.beaniemom.com. The secondary price guide was periodically updated to reflect the prevailing secondary market values for Beanie Babies.

You'll find one popular secondary market price guide on the Web at www.mapleleaves.net/hk.htm. Michael Trenteseau, an avid Harmony Kingdom and Boyd's Bears collector, publishes a list of current secondary-market prices for retired and limited-edition Harmony Kingdom pieces. He culls closing prices from the eBay online auction site and posts the average selling price for each piece as the current secondary-market value. He updates the list a few times each month to keep it as accurate as possible. When asked why he developed the list to keep track of the values, he replied, "Because nobody else was!"

Other dedicated collectors watch online auction sites and then build price guides based on closing prices. They show them compared against those listed in published monthly price guides. These types of sites are valuable for collectors who need to back-fill their collections with secondary-market pieces.

☛Usenet

Did you ever wonder what computer-junkies did before the Web? We had UNIX. Fifteen years ago, those of us who sent e-mail and participated in UNIX-based Bulletin Board Systems, or BBS's, were called "geeks."

We geeks with UNIX capabilities were in a sub-culture having lots of fun that people with "lives" didn't know about. We met for parties away from our computers, just like collectors who post on bulletin boards do today. We acquired plenty of experience in what the rest of the world still had waiting for them. UNIX-based cyber-land gave us a head start in a very cool medium that we knew we wouldn't be able to keep to ourselves very long.

And we spent hours in Usenet.

What Is Usenet?

When it started in 1979, Usenet was a simple mechanism that allowed people to share thoughts and ideas, and comment on each other's messages. It was the first online bulletin board program that connected multiple computers.

As more topics started and more newsgroups were formed, Usenet's capabilities expanded to include so many that you'd need a very thick user guide to be able to know them all. According to James C. Armstrong, Jr. in *UNIX Secrets* (IDG Books Worldwide, 1999), "Usenet is a complex beast."

It sure is. Usenet is still widely used today and currently has over 25,000 newsgroups split into eight primary categories. Each starts with a name identifier, and extensions to that name further identify (or specialize) the group. The collecting newsgroup is alt.collecting. One of several newsgroups for Barbie doll enthusiasts is alt.collecting.barbie.

I would have to write a separate book to instruct you on using Usenet. I mention it here because it's part of the Internet, and many people who use the Web today got their cyber-feet wet in Usenet.

There are many similarities between the two. In 1988, I saw the same types of information exchanges going on in Usenet as I see now on the Web. While technology has changed, people haven't. When I mention bulletin board etiquette and communicating with people in e-mail, much of my advice comes from my cyber-heritage with Usenet and UNIX-based e-mail correspondence.

I include more about Usenet and its use for collectors in my second book, *Collector's Guide to Online Auctions* (Collector Books, 2000).

Accessing Usenet

Usenet is not limited to Web users. Many people who don't have Internet accounts access Usenet by way of BBS's, AOL, and many other networks. In addition, most ISPs offer Usenet access with their service package.

Presently, you can get Usenet reader software, or access articles on the Web via DejaNews at www.dejanews.com. Numerous other Web sites exist where you can access and read the many Usenet newsgroups. The following table lists a few of them. A search engine can help you find more.

Uniform Resource Locator	Company Name
www.remarq.com	RemarQ
www.dejanews.com	DejaNews
www.randori.com	Randori News, Inc.
www.liquidinformation.com	Liquid Information
www.supernews.com	Supernews

☞Before You Begin

As you travel through cyberspace enlightened by what Internet has to offer collectors, be sure to make frequent stops. There are many, many articles out there written by people who want to share their knowledge with the world, and their knowledge might be about the collectible line of which you've recently grown fond.

Once you see the endless supply of information available on the Internet, you might be tempted to jump in headfirst. Without the right preparation, this can lead to some costly mistakes.

At this point, it's a good idea to review what you need to know about collecting, especially once you get started on the Web.

Chapter 3 — Starting Your Collection

Now that you know the history of the Internet and have experienced first-hand how much a collector can learn from it, you're probably eager to get on with your collecting.

Whether you've just decided on a new collectible line or already have a collection going and want to get more serious about it, this is a good time to review the main concepts associated with collecting.

This chapter will help set you off in the right direction for building a collection. Here we cover the basics about collectibles:

- Getting to know a collectible line
- How to know if a particular line is for you
- Collectible shows
- What to buy
- When to buy
- Variations and oddities
- The secondary market
- Secondary-market price guides

☞Getting to Know a Collectible Line

Although the Internet serves as a vast resource of information, you can learn about collectibles other ways too.

There are brochures distributed by collectible companies, expositions and shows conducted solely for collectibles, professional groups that assist dealers in marketing exclusive pieces, and secondary price guides in print. There are "buzz words" that pop up in ads, on Internet bulletin boards, and in chat rooms. Dealers can teach you a lot about collectibles, especially if they're also collectors, like Davey and Simone.

Knowing which pieces to acquire (and in what order) is an important aspect of collecting. The more information you gain, the more likely you'll find yourself making offers for various pieces. But which ones are the best to get? And what should you buy first?

Aside from the Web, several places allow you to view and sometimes even *touch* certain collectibles to learn more about them.

The Store Display

The best way to see a collectible line is to look at the pieces in the store display. Before you think "well *duh*," remember that a lot of thought and planning goes into the display. This is usually the first exposure to a collectible line that customers get, and the intent is to make them look as lovely and irresistible as possible.

If on first glance the items don't appeal to you, then no method of displaying them will change that. You should probably move on. But if the figurines or other items catch your eye immediately, this could be attributed to the work of a very clever and astute display designer.

Props, risers, wooden or glass shelves, and the type of curio cabinet used to hold the pieces can play a big part in the overall "attitude" of the collection.

Once you decide to start collecting the line, you need to determine how you'll display the items in your home or office. If your collection doesn't seem to have the same synergy in your home as it did in the shop, you may want to return there and study how the display is set up. Remember that *something* about the arrangement of collectibles caught your eye, and with a little bit of study, you'll be able to replicate that same aura at home.

Lighting

Pay special attention to the display's lighting. If you plan to buy a curio cabinet for your pieces, consider one with built-in lighting that you can turn off after you show your collection. Some paints and other materials are sensitive to certain ultraviolet light frequencies. You'll especially need to keep your collectibles out of direct sunlight. Talk with your dealer or with the manufacturer about collectibles that might be light sensitive.

Prolonged exposure to direct sunlight can damage any type of collectible, especially those for which coloration is of particular interest.

The Product Brochure

Most collectible dealers supply product brochures issued periodically by the company that designs the product line. These brochures are free to customers and provide a wonderful source of information for the collector.

A product brochure typically includes a full-color array of all the pieces in the line, including those that are retired. The idea is to make the brochure as appealing as possible so the collectible line works its way into the part of you that says, "I really want to own these."

Many new collectors spend hours poring over product brochures. Suffice it to say the brochure itself can make or break a collectible line, since it is often the second exposure that collectors have to that particular line. Some hard-core collectors also keep each year's product brochure as part of their collection. Debut year brochures from collectible lines that became popular can command a significant secondary-market value.

Introductions

Recently introduced items are likely to rank a prominent place in the brochure, maybe even on the cover. Pieces premiering in the current year signify the pride of the line and usually are featured in the promotional material.

The idea behind this is to spark a thought in you: If these are this year's new pieces, what wonderful things await next year?

Pay special attention to how the current year's items compare with the previous year's. This will give you some idea of the artistic direction of the collectible.

Open Edition Pieces

The currently produced pieces that are not limited edition items are *open editions*. Dealers can order them from the factory on a continuing basis. Some collectible lines are mostly open edition items while others, such as Boyd's Bears, have limited and numbered pieces.

Some brochures present the current open editions in checklist form so you can track the progress of your collecting. Others just want you to get a good look at the pieces and realize you simply can't live without them.

You'll want to know how many pieces the line contains for a few reasons:

- If you're a collector who likes to get every piece available, are there more in that line than you can afford or that you have room to display without displacing family members?
- If you aren't interested in getting all of them, is there a particular series in that line you might want to concentrate on collecting that continues each year?
- How prolific are the artists? How many are there? Can they capture many different themes?
- Is there consistency to the line, or do the items wildly differ from each other?

➤ Note: Some collectors prefer specific artists, ⬅ and collect their works as they move from one collectible line to another. One example is Adam Binder, who created his own line of marble resin fairies before doing work for Harmony Ball Company. Many Harmony Kingdom collectors seek Binder's "pre-HK" items.

Series Pieces

Some collectible lines have subsets of the line with a common theme that often continues from year to year. A few examples include the "Lazy Days of Summer" and "Squashville" series featured in Fitz and Floyd's whimsical Charming Tails line. The adventures of Lord Byron the ladybug in the Harmony Garden series of Harmony Kingdom, and Country Lane by Precious Moments are two others.

Because pieces are often seasonal, a display can change during the year. Department 56 and Dreamsicles represent two lines offering special winter and holiday-timed pieces for seasonal display.

Retired Pieces

Part of what keeps a collectible line alive is the cycle of retiring the older pieces, thus creating classics, and welcoming in the newest ones. As pieces retire, new ones debut. Just as companies take pride in their current and new pieces, they hold the pieces no longer made in deep regard. These usually appear in the product brochures because the company is proud to show off its workmanship with the hope of inspiring collectors.

Many retired pieces stay on store shelves for months, even years, after the retirement announcement and mold breaking. How unlike Beanie Babies, where newly retired ones used to disappear from store shelves within hours!

Naturally, retired pieces are the ones to aim for first because there won't be any more once they sell out. Decide which ones interest you and be on the lookout for them.

Limited Edition Pieces

As their name implies, certain items are made in limited quantities. Each bears an individual and unique consecutive number.

Since limited edition pieces are often intended to "define" the collectible line by implying the piece is so special that only a certain number could be made, they usually consist of stellar quality and artistry. For this reason, collectors pursue limited edition pieces, especially if production falls below 10,000.

Some pieces, such as the "Sanibel Island" lighthouse from Harbour Lights, are in such demand they actually sell out (from dealer requests and allocations) and retire months before the first one ships from the factory.

This is similar to what happened with Mattel's 1994 limited edition "Gold Jubilee Barbie." So many sold from pre-production orders that very few made it to the store shelves.

Depending on the line's success and popularity, the limited editions can quickly disappear, especially when a profitable secondary market arises. If you hear about an upcoming limited edition, you might want to get on a dealer's waiting list.

Product brochures may include photos and information about that line's limited edition pieces, but a better source of information would be dealers, because they usually know about limited edition pieces before the public does.

Also, members of collectible societies often receive advance notice of limited edition releases.

Numbered-Edition Pieces

Lines may number pieces according to the production run. Serial number 234 of batch A would be numbered A234. Usually, the earlier batches with the lowest numbers are the best finds.

With numbered-edition pieces, there is no pre-determined limit of production. When the piece retires, the numbers stop.

Limited-Distribution Pieces

Though not actually an official limited edition piece, an item might be limited in distribution. One example is the "Creature Comforts" Harmony Kingdom piece that was only available through authorized dealers in England.

While considered open edition items in the collectible line, limited-distribution items sometimes run slightly higher than suggested retail because of their controlled availability. They might also only sell as a customer incentive, where the customer can purchase one of them at retail only when buying a certain amount of other items with it. Remember when the legendary Princess Beanie Baby first hit the market?

Closed Editions

Sometimes a collectible company suspends production on a certain piece. The mold and designs remain available and further production may resume in the future. If the company decides to discontinue the piece during the production hiatus, then it's officially retired and the mold (if one was used) or patterns are destroyed.

National Association of Limited Edition Dealers

Chartered in 1976 for collectibles retailers, the National Association of Limited Edition Dealers (NALED) is a not-for-profit retailer organization based in Naperville, Illinois. NALED focuses on education and services for retailers in hopes of enhancing the ethical standards and commercial practices associated with the production, distribution, and sale of limited editions and other collectible items.

Certain collectible lines, like Charming Tails and Gene Dolls, produce special limited edition pieces exclusively distributed to registered NALED dealers through the Park West distribution company (www.parkwestpublications.com). A current list of their dealers is available at www.naled.com. For the more popular collectible lines, NALED pieces sell out quickly and often skyrocket in value on the secondary market.

Consumers can benefit from getting to know a NALED dealer, as it has its own collectible information network and often an "inside track" on certain collectible lines, including:

- New editions and changes to existing lines of collectibles
- Access to special sources for hard-to-find items, new and old
- Information about special artist and club events

If the collectible line you're interested in includes any NALED pieces, you may want to consider getting on a NALED dealer's waiting list for any new editions.

Because of their limited distribution, you may not see NALED pieces listed in a regular product brochure. NALED produces a special holiday catalog that covers all pieces distributed through Park West. Obtain a copy of the catalog once you find a dealer who carries the pieces.

You can contact NALED by calling 800-446-2533 or 630-579-3274.

Gift Creations Concepts

This New Brighton, Minnesota-based organization ensures only one Gift Creations Concepts (GCC) dealer in a certain geographic area. A consortium of collectible dealers similar to NALED, GCC also publishes a special catalog of collectible pieces that dealers can "personalize" with the name of their business.

Each year, collectible companies produce special limited edition pieces that are only available through GCC dealers. Collectors can buy them directly from GCC dealers at in-store events or by advance order. Like NALED pieces, these limited-distribution pieces are highly sought-after by collectors.

Contact GCC at 800-328-9572 or 800-287-6363.

Parade of Gifts

Parade of Gifts is another group of collectible dealers, limited to 500 worldwide. They also produce a brochure that dealers can personalize, and companies produce special pieces in their lines that are only available through Parade of Gifts dealers.

Parade of Gifts exclusives have included Seraphim Classics, Boyd's Bears, Dreamsicles, and Precious Moments.

You can request information about Parade of Gifts at 800-336-8666. They live on the Web at www.paradeofgifts.com.

Membership Kits

Most successful and popular collectible lines offer memberships or some type of subscriber benefits for dedicated collectors. The Fenton Glass Company, Boyd's Bears, Royal Doulton, and Cherished Teddies are just a few of the many lines that provide them.

Memberships offer collectors special pieces not available to non-members. Members usually receive a newsletter containing product information and announcements about retirements or new releases in that line.

The Precious Moments Collectors Club, which has been around since 1981, has around 400,000 members. The club is so large that its local chapters participate in national and community service projects. As a perk for members, Enesco hosts its www.enescoclubs.com Web site, where customers can join various collectors' clubs on-line and ask questions about their membership.

The Precious Moments 1998 collector's kit contained the current year's member figurine and membership in the frequent-buyer program. It also contained the current club newsletter, a club binder, a gift registry binder, invitations to club-sponsored events, and a mini-camera to encourage club members to "capture life's special moments." Members also receive special mailings throughout the year.

If you buy a membership kit for a collectible line, pay close attention to the literature (including the product brochure) enclosed with the kit. This valuable material gives you a complete overview of the collectible line and information that you need to build your collection in the best possible way. From the kit inserts, you may learn:

- The URL, or address, of the company's Web site
- When the line was introduced
- Which pieces are in the current line
- The series groupings, if any

- How many pieces are introduced each year
- Price range of pieces in the line
- Who the artists are
- How the pieces are crafted
- How many members are in the collector's club
- Ordering information for member pieces

Along with a product brochure, most member kits include an exclusive piece that's part of the collector's kit. You might also be able to order special member pieces.

Membership kits offer an excellent value and are a good first purchase in a collectible line. The pieces that are included with the membership kit are well worth the cost of the entire kit, even if you don't plan on buying any more pieces in that line.

Some collectors keep a membership kit from each year as part of their collections.

Member Pieces

Your membership kit will contain information about any special pieces available for members only, along with an order form for them. Your dealer may offer to complete this form for you and submit it to the company. The pieces ship to the dealer, who then notifies you when they arrive.

If you bought the membership kit directly from the company, you can submit the order form and payment yourself, and the kit ships to the address you specify.

Member pieces may be larger and more costly than the regular pieces but since they also represent the best of the line, the detail and artistry are usually outstanding. Also, a secondary-market demand usually arises for them in subsequent years.

Debut Year

If you know when the line was introduced, you can get a good idea how successful it's been and if it will remain in continuous production. When a collectible line discontinues, the pieces rarely retain market value. In 10 to 20 years, the market may come around and grab them up as nostalgia items, but who wants to wait that long?

Knowing the production figures (how many of each piece was made) helps you determine which pieces are likely to be harder to find.

Item Checklist

Some membership kits contain an item checklist so people can keep track of their collections as they shop around for pieces.

Checklists are also created and distributed by independent publishing companies and can be purchased separately from the collector's kit. CheckerBee Publishing distributes many of them. If you have opted to collect a line that contains hundreds of pieces, buying a checklist that you can store in your purse or briefcase can be very helpful and convenient.

Introductions

Since most collectible lines produce membership kits annually, you're bound to see information about that year's new releases in the kit also. Some companies introduce pieces at set times each year, while others debut sporadically throughout the year.

Information included in the kit might offer some clues about releases that collectors don't know about yet.

Prices

Few collectible lines set a fixed retail price that applies to all items. Beanie Babies are one exception. Although some limited distribution pieces, like the Princess and Erin bears, sold for hundreds of dollars in some shops, their suggested retail price was the same as for all Beanie Babies.

Most companies set prices according to the size of the piece and the amount of detail and complexity in the design. Limited edition and special-edition pieces may price slightly higher because they're individually numbered and they usually include some type of certification.

Some product brochures contain prices; others don't.

Artists

Your new kit may contain information about the artists. Reading their biography can often help you get a better feel for the theme behind the collectible line, as is the case with Harmony Kingdom artists Peter Calvesbert and Martin Perry. How these artists got together with Noel Wiggins and Lisa Yashon of Harmony Ball Company might give you some insight into the whimsy and popularity of their "Treasure Jest" line.

Another artist with an interesting biography is Cheryl Spencer Collin, who spent her early years in New England. Her love for the area prompted her to use her artistic talents to create lighthouse figures. Her love of animals is reflected in her pieces as well.

With many of the other collectible lines, you may never know the name of the artist who created the piece. Sometimes the person credited with the work is the artistic supervisor and not the actual crafter. In other companies, the sculpture is the star and the artists remain anonymous.

Collector Clubs

The membership kit may contain information about the collectors' club, such as when it started, how many members joined the first year, and how many signed up each subsequent year. Additionally, you might find information about club-sponsored activities or conventions.

☛ "How Do I Know What I Want?"

One true sign that a collectible is for you is when you just can't stop thinking about the pieces! You've got the product brochure in your purse, pocket or desk drawer and you've looked at it so much that it's frayed. You may have even started putting little X's by pieces that you "might want to get."

Maybe you'll find that you've returned to a shop more than twice to "take one more look" at a series of collectibles. Perhaps you woke up one morning to find you were dreaming about living in a cottage on a street called Lilliput Lane and you moved in with tiny people known as the Wee Forest Folk that speak a language called "Furbish." If this happens, there is no doubt that certain collectible items have caught your eye!

Before you make the final decision to go for it, though, you may need to ask yourself:

- Can I afford the pieces in this line?
- Do I have room to display the pieces?
- Am I likely to be interested in these items for years to come?
- Do these pieces appeal to others in my household?
- Is the line popular enough to have a successful future?
- Does the line have a good secondary market in case I decide to collect something else?

If you answered "no" to any of the questions, it could foretell a roadblock in your quest to collect these pieces.

However, if you like change and switching hobbies and interests from time to time, then go ahead and collect them anyway. Since you've got the Internet to rely on, you're going to build a network of trading friends to whom you can sell or trade your pieces should you decide to collect something else.

You can collect infinitely many things. You don't need to concentrate only on collectibles that are part of a company's line. Check out the various collectors' pages on the Internet — you're bound to find something that appeals to you.

Chapter 4 includes more about Web sites that cater to collectors.

☛Collectible Shows

Back in time, we attended flea markets in hopes of acquiring bargains or items for our collections. While flea markets still thrive and are a lucrative business for knock-off and discounted merchandise, collectible shows have taken over a lot of the interest. They're by character a lot classier than flea markets, and some sell outright only to dealers. They invite the public to look and be intrigued.

The International Collectible Exposition

In Chapter 1, you read about the Super Event collectible pieces available at the ICE show that Krause Publications sponsors. Aside from the event pieces, attending the ICE offers an exceptional opportunity for any collector. The show brings together a huge gathering of limited edition collectibles, imaginative artists, and spectacular exhibits that dealers and the general public can experience first-hand.

The ICE weekend offers plenty for the collector to see and do. Dates and times are set up for collector club meetings, artists' signings, informative seminars, and displays of the latest in new collectibles from more than 200 collectible companies. These include (to name a few) The Alexander Doll Company, Anheuser-Busch, Christopher Radko, Fenton Art Glass, Ashton-Drake, Greenwich Workshop, Hudson Creek, Lenox Collections, Precious Moments Company, Steiff USA, Walt Disney Art Classics, and Little Gem Bears.

If you attend one of these events, plan to be on your feet a lot. Be sure to wear comfortable shoes so you can pay attention to all the displays and company representatives who are on hand to answer your questions. You'll be too busy to have to worry about sore feet!

> ➡ Note: If you attended the 1999 Rosemont ⬅
> ICE, you may have seen the author (me) proudly marching in Harmony Kingdom's "Blessing of the Aisles" Independent Collector Club procession. We were the ones with the loud bagpipes.

Here is some advice for the first-time ICE show attendee:

- Stay at a hotel within walking distance of the show. Some hotels provide shuttle service to exhibition centers. Check on this when you make reservations.
- Try to carpool from your home or hotel room. Parking can run anywhere from $5 to $25 for the day, depending on how full the lots are and where you end up parking.
- Be in line when the ICE opens its doors to the public on Saturday morning.
- Once in the door, head over to where they sell the event pieces and buy them first; then take in the rest of the show. The popular ICE pieces sell out quickly and the secondary price may rise 300% before the show is over.
- On the way in, you'll receive a program teeming with information about the show and artists. As you meet them, have your program open to the place where their biography is and ask for a signature. This makes a wonderful keepsake!
- Instead of a purse, pack what you need for the day in a tote bag. The tote bag should be large enough to hold all brochures and novelties that exhibitors hand you, but small enough that you don't give people contusions when you pass them in the aisles. Be sure you can carry it over your shoulder.
- Pick up a schedule of the seminars to read while you're inevitably standing in line.
- Bring plenty of preprinted address labels so you don't have to write your name and address several hundred times when you enter the many raffles exhibitors hold.
- Bring your checkbook and charge cards. While the collectibles are not sold to the public, exhibitors can and do sell their collector member kits, tee shirts, caps, pins, and other items to promote the collectible line.
- Dress comfortably.
- Expect crowds.
- Get in line for the restrooms *before* the need becomes unbearable.

Be sure to check out the schedule of seminars, too. They usually aren't crowded and are an excellent opportunity to rest your tired feet while you hear an informative presentation about collectibles.

The ICE in Rosemont is presently the world's largest gathering of open and limited edition collectibles under one roof.

Swap-N-Sell

This event runs concurrently with the ICE show, but is located in an area separate from the ICE showroom. Private vendors can pay for space units and set up their tables much like at swap meets.

The Swap-n-Sell is a drawing feature of the ICE show, in that the public can purchase collectible items from secondary dealers, often at fabulous bargains!

Theme Collectible Shows

Independent collectible dealers or publications often sponsor their own collectible shows. Dealers can purchase space to sell their collectible goods, and the public pays a small admission fee.

Some organizations sponsor similar shows as fundraisers. They raise money by charging each vendor for table space and by collecting an admission fee from attendees. Sometimes, each vendor must donate an item or two for raffles.

While most swap meets involve more Pokémon, Hallmark ornaments, beanbag plush vendors, and sports-card dealers than anything else, you're bound to see more of these events include other lines as collectors move on to other interests.

What To Buy

If the line debuted in 1992, pieces from that time and the few years following pose special interest for a collector because they are from the debut year. As you recall from Chapter 1, the most sought-after pieces of any successful collectible lines are ones produced before the product caught on in the market.

Only rarely is a collectible a resounding success in its first year, so fewer of the debut items exist. These are the good finds.

Decide What You Like

Start your collection of current pieces with those you find appealing. You'll have time to back-fill your collection with other pieces if you decide later that you want them in your collection.

If you started collecting with the same zest that most new collectors do, understand and accept that you probably will want all of the pieces eventually.

The Collector's Creed

Most people know that moderation in everything is good. Probably 99% of all persons beginning a collection will declare, either out loud or reassuringly to themselves, something like this:

"I don't want all of the pieces. Just the ones I really like."

This is the famous Collector's Creed, and it is a very healthy, sensible approach to collecting.

Some seasoned collectors, with good reason, prefer to call the phrase "the famous last words."

Don't Overspend

Though it's certainly tempting to buy all the pieces you want for your collection in the first week, you might find yourself spending way too much money or "maxing out" your credit card very quickly.

Remember that open edition pieces will be around for plenty of time. The normal run of an open edition piece is anywhere from one to five years, depending on how well the item sells. Even if one of them retires tomorrow, there are bound to be some left at retail for awhile.

Set aside that rainy-day money or room on your credit card for the limited edition pieces or retired pieces that you know will sell out soon. If you get the open edition pieces a few at a time, you'll build your collection at a slow and steady pace. You can take time between purchases to enjoy each and every piece you add to your collection.

Avoid Overdoing It

Again, it's wise to pace the acquisition of new pieces so you can enjoy each one on its own. If you build your collection too rapidly, you may find that you exhaust your interest in the line way too soon.

It's sad when something you'd have crawled over broken glass for at one time later makes you wonder why you ever found it appealing. Don't let this happen with your collections — take it slow!

☛When To Buy

Just like pacing yourself, timing is important in collecting. Knowing what to buy and when to buy it ensures you won't miss out on the choice pieces in the line.

Try to Buy Early

Buy newly released pieces on the first run for three reasons:

1. If it's a limited edition piece, you have a better chance of getting a low issue number. These pieces are typically valuable.
2. The factory might find that a certain part of the item is either too difficult to produce or may violate some copyright. To alleviate this, the artist will redesign that part of the piece, causing those first runs to be very rare and sought after by collectors. If you acquire the new pieces on the first run, you won't have to hunt for them and pay high secondary prices later.
3. Sometimes, for reasons known only to company insiders, an item is suspended or retired right after its introduction. You'll probably want to have that piece before it disappears forever.

➡ Note: The best place to obtain inside ⬅ information about sudden-death retirements is on the Web!

Remember that while you're picking up new releases and low-numbered limited edition pieces, secondary dealers will be right behind you looking for the same items. This alone is another reason to set aside extra funds for these special occasions.

➥Variations and Oddities

I mentioned earlier that some collectible companies might decide to change an item after releasing it on the market. Once two or more versions of the same piece appear, they become *variations*.

Variations can drive collectors batty. A new collector trying to backfill a collection with retired pieces has to locate not only each item, but also every variation if he or she wants a complete collection.

Variations that are scarce often command top dollar. Oddities and differences in pieces that aren't really variations can also affect the selling price.

Factory Flaws

Many collectors ask if a factory flaw, such as a painted-over chip or an upside-down appliqué, affects the value of the piece. It definitely does.

Visual perfection is always preferred. If the factory flaw affects the appearance of the piece, its value decreases by as much as fifty percent. However, if the flaw makes the piece look slightly different from the non-flawed version, this could drive up the value.

One example would be a die-cast model car with an upside-down decal. A flaw like this could make any that shipped before the error was corrected very valuable.

The Beanie Baby line provides another example of this. Beanies with upside-down flags are worth considerably more than their normal counterparts, whereas a missing sewn-in tag decreases their value, even if the item came from the factory that way.

> ➡ Note: Everyone wants their pieces to be ⬅ perfect, but the definition of "perfect" varies among collectors.

Mistakes

Errors in spelling, printing, factual information, and assembly of the piece can create an anomaly out of an item and drive its value skyward. Remember that legendary stamp with the upside-down Jenny Biplane? The border and airplane are two different colors, so each sheet of stamps ran through the printer twice. One sheet went through incorrectly for the second printing and the airplanes appear upside down. The few stamps from that sheet that still exist are profoundly valuable.

Here are some of the more common types of mistakes found on collectibles manufactured as part of a line:

- **Spelling errors** – Sometimes there's an error on the piece or on something attached to the item. Maybe thousands appear like that before anyone catches the error. Sometimes the corrected version ends up being more valuable by the time the piece retires.
- **Factual errors** – A few years ago, Harbour Lights released its version of Split Rock Light lighthouse. The molded-on flag read "Split Rock, MI." More than two hundred of these shipped before the error was noticed. Split Rock Light is in Minnesota, not Michigan. The European artist, unfamiliar with the two-letter state abbreviations used in the United States, thought "MI" was the correct abbreviation for Minnesota. The incorrect version of Split Rock Light commands as much as two thousand dollars on the secondary market.
- **Assembly errors** – A worker not paying attention puts the roof of a miniature barn on backwards. Quality control doesn't catch it and it's out on the market.

Whether pieces with these types of mistakes grow or decrease in value largely depends on the demand for them on the market. If enough pieces exist with the mistake, the item becomes a variation and most collectors will clamor for one.

If the piece is one of a kind it might be very desirable, but that too is unpredictable. Most collectors want flawless pieces although some will search for mistakes. One-of-a-kind mistakes might not have a market category, though.

> ➡ Note: Before paying big bucks for a piece ⬅ with an error, check the Web for information about the piece.

Intentional Variations

Would a collectible company really do that to us? You bet they would!

In order to keep the spirit alive (and sales growing), some companies redesign an item after the first several thousand ship from the factory. "Completist" collectors — those who desire every piece in the line — must hustle to own both the initial release and the version that follows.

No wonder the curio cabinet business is booming these days.

Signed Pieces

Does a piece signed by the artist make it more valuable? Yes, usually. A signed piece can increase in value as much as fifteen to twenty-five percent, depending on a few things:

- Is the artist elderly and about to retire?
- Is the artist reclusive?
- Is the artist popular?
- Does the artist rarely sign pieces?
- Does the artist frequently show up at collectible shows? If so, collectors might prefer to have pieces signed themselves for an opportunity to meet and chat with the artist.
- Is the artist also an entertainer or celebrity? Marie Osmond's signature on one of her collectible dolls would certainly garner special interest. Fitness guru Richard Simmons also has a line of collectible dolls.

> ━━▶ Note: Remember that an artist's signature ◀━━
> on a piece does not attest to its authenticity. When an artist is
> signing hundreds of pieces for long lines of eager collectors at a
> collectible show, he or she does not have time to inspect each
> item. If there are known fakes on the market, only a qualified
> company representative can authenticate the piece.

Coloration

Variations in the color of material used to fashion the piece can drive up its value. Variations in paint used to color the material can be risky. Most companies cannot authenticate the paint on the items because it's too easy to duplicate.

The best way to obtain variations involving paint is to buy them at retail from a reputable dealer before the variation becomes well known. Then you know they're genuine. However, you still might have trouble re-selling them later because other collectors will be understandably wary.

Missing Box or Packaging

I took a poll in a chat room. The question was, if you found an old elusive piece in an antique mall, would it matter to you if it didn't have the correct box?

Just about everyone there asked me if I were crazy. One woman chided that if she found an elusive piece in a ditch she'd be happy — never mind the box! If it's an old elusive, who cares about the box? Having the correct box usually matters in only a few situations:

- If the piece is a limited edition and the serial number is on the box
- If the box bears the name of the piece
- If the box is also a display container for the piece
- If there is a unique and ornate box for each piece
- If there is specially molded packing that fits a particular piece

Some collectors don't consider the box part of the piece, especially if items in the line ship in the same type of box. Having the correct box matters even less if the piece is an extremely rare elusive.

Unless you consider the box part of the item, the importance of having the correct one is questionable. This is one of many decisions left to the individual collector.

☞The Secondary Market

I make frequent use of the term "secondary market" in this book. I ought to define it.

A retail dealer buys a piece from the manufacturer and sells it at the suggested retail price. This is the *primary market*. If that piece is subsequently sold at either above or below the retail value, this is the *secondary market.*

If you started collecting a particular line any time after the debut year, you'll probably end up buying a few of your pieces from the secondary market. This isn't a bad thing, and presumably, every collector has done that at one time or another. If you have ever bought anything for more than its original retail price, even from a retail dealer, you've made a secondary-market purchase.

Most collectibles you acquire over the Internet are secondary-market buys. Anyone who's ever bought a wildly popular collectible item at a swap meet or from an ad on a Web site has usually paid secondary prices for them.

The secondary-market beanbag plush and trading card dealers made a killing. Any collectible that has a low retail price is a target for such dealers. Since they're sold in large quantities, they can be purchased in large quantities and then resold for as much as three or four times their retail price without putting the buyer into serious debt.

When secondary dealers start buying up hot collectibles in large quantities, this tends to create a retail shortage, thus forcing collectors to turn to the secondary market. This is what happened with beanbag plush. It can also happen with other collectibles, but only certain items in the line.

Target Items for Secondary Market Dealers

For more costly collectibles, there is typically no secondary market for current open edition pieces. In fact, if collectors find they have an extra of a current piece that they aren't saving for any particular reason, it isn't unusual to sell it for less than retail price. Why should a collector pay more for something that's still available at retail in any collectible shop that carries the line?

A booming secondary market exists, however, for some current collectibles:

- Limited editions, because their availability is limited and they sell faster in some parts of the country than in others.
- Member pieces and special collector club items (only members can buy them and only during that particular membership year).

- Special-event pieces (limited quantity and controlled availability).
- NALED, GCC, and Parade of Gifts pieces (limited quantity and availability only through certain dealers).
- Any current open edition piece that was redesigned after the initial issue; thus "retiring" the first issue.
- Super and super-*duper* special-event pieces because of the controlled distribution only at special events, and extremely limited production runs.

How Secondary Dealers Work

Secondary market dealers for collectibles usually deal in more than one line. They study the market, look for the buying patterns of collectors, and purchase what's likely to go up in value right away. The more clever (and successful) secondary market dealers spend a lot of time on the Web reading bulletin boards and lurking in chat rooms, and also reading Usenet news groups that are dedicated for collectors of a certain line.

From this type of research, they learn what collectors want and which pieces they're likely to acquire quickly, even at higher secondary prices. Some collectors who live in remote areas or otherwise don't get out and shop much will go right to the secondary market to save time and to ensure they'll get certain pieces.

Buying on the Secondary Market

Secondary market dealers can and often do serve a beneficial purpose for collectors. They spend a lot of time scouring more obscure shops throughout the world in search of those few remaining retired pieces that they can purchase at or slightly above retail price. They buy them and then make them available to collectors who are still on the hunt.

While it's true that anyone can call shops worldwide looking for choice pieces, secondary dealers can save you a lot of time and effort. If their markup is reasonable, it may be worthwhile to pay a secondary dealer a little extra for the piece in return for the effort they put into tracking it down. If the piece is authenticated, certified, or artist-signed, then all the better.

If you know you have exhausted all your options to acquire a piece either at retail or through a trade, you need to be aware of a few important things before buying collectibles on the secondary market.

For starters, bear in mind that when a collectible commands top dollar, counterfeiters sit up and take notice. The vast majority of counterfeited collectible items sell on the secondary market. Know with whom you're dealing and don't be afraid to ask lots of questions about the piece if you consider buying it.

Buy in Person

If you acquire the piece from a secondary dealer at a swap meet or from someone in your local area, you have an advantage. You can check the piece over for any flaws or other conditions that might render the piece undesirable.

If you're making the purchase at a swap meet, expect to pay cash. Most secondary dealers request that payments through the mail be with a money order or bank check. Some secondary dealers accept credit-card payments.

Ask for References

Unless it's someone you've dealt with before, ask the dealer for names and e-mail addresses of a few of his or her past customers if you're buying an item sight unseen on the Internet. You need to safeguard yourself by checking on the dealer's reliability.

You should contact at least four of these references to ask about their experiences with the dealer. Wait for their response before making the purchase.

> ➡ Note: If you know that the seller participates ⬅
> in an online auction site like eBay, which allows users to enter
> feedback about each other, check the seller's feedback file.
> There's more about that in Chapter 6.

Be sure the responses are favorable and that they don't hint at shady practices. If you have doubts, ask questions. If you can't get answers that make you feel comfortable about the seller, then don't buy from that person.

Study the Market Before You Purchase

Know the approximate secondary price for the item you're buying. If you examine the online secondary market price guides, you can determine a price range for the item. You can also check the Internet bulletin board and Usenet newsgroup posts to check the asking price by other collectors who are selling their extras, or by secondary dealers.

At best, determining a secondary market price is an educated guess. The true value is whatever a collector is willing to pay. Accurate indicators are a range of values and the frequency with which the piece comes up for sale on the secondary market.

One way to determine an up-to-date secondary price range for a collectible is by watching closing bids on Internet auction sites. While prices often go slightly higher because of last-minute bidding frenzies, you can still get a good idea as to what you should pay for the piece.

> ⟹ Note: You can read more about calculating ⟸ secondary market prices from online auction closings in *Collector's Guide to Online Auctions.*

Don't Pay Secondary for Current Open Editions

Only under very unusual circumstances would it ever be necessary to purchase a current open edition collectible item for more than the retail price.

Though hundreds of thousands of dollars were made this way on the collectible toy secondary market, that was an anomaly. Furbies, Pokémon cards, and beanbag plush have a relatively low retail price and most collectors could afford to pay a secondary dealer's asking price to avoid standing in long lines.

The secondary dealers, in turn, were making a steady profit reselling current collectible toys for two, often three (or more) times their retail price.

Consumers can keep this from happening with other collectible lines simply by not paying secondary prices for open edition items. If there is no demand, there's no market. The pieces will be available in stores for retail price and not hoarded by secondary dealers looking to turn a quick profit.

Avoid "Make an Offer" Deals

If you see someone asking for the "best offer," this is a seller to avoid. "Make an offer" is the hallmark of a novice seller who's obviously trying to get as much as possible for the item without taking the time to research the market and determine a fair and competitive price. He or she doesn't want to commit to a price in the hope that someone will offer an absurd amount of money for it.

If you're the one making the highest offer, you'll usually find yourself in a cat-and-mouse game over the price of the item with an inexperienced and uninformed seller. These types of arrangements never come out to the buyer's advantage and often don't even result in a purchase.

By asking you to make an offer, sellers may just be picking your brain to get a price range for the item because they're too lazy to do their own market research. Don't waste your time.

☛Secondary Price Guides

You can find hundreds of secondary price guides in print. Publishers who specialize in collectibles produce them regularly. Among them are:

- Price guides by Collector Books
- *Greenbook Collector Guides*
- CheckerBee Publishing's *Collector's Value Guides*

Each volume is dedicated to a particular collectible line and lists secondary-market pricing information about retired, limited edition, special-issue, and current hard-to-find items.

Secondary-pricing information often includes:

- Original retail price of the item
- Estimated current secondary-market value
- Production figures for retired pieces
- Notation as to whether the item is increasing or decreasing in value.

In addition, the books offer an introduction and a bit of history about the collectible line, information about the company and the artists, and some insight into how the collectible line became successful.

Other Price Guides

Several magazines provide secondary price guides for collectibles, one of the most noted being Krause Publications' *Collector's Mart Magazine*. This monthly publication contains their "Guide to Prices and Trends on the Secondary Market."

Premedia Publications' *Figurines and Collectibles* also includes a secondary-market report compiled by the Collectors' Information Bureau.

Collectors' Information Bureau

This not-for-profit trade association located in Barrington, Illinois, gathers information about collectibles and limited edition collectibles through mail and telephone surveys. CIB publishes newsletters, directories, and secondary-market price guides resulting from its in-house research staff and national panel of more than 300 limited edition and secondary-market collectible dealers.

Information provided by CIB is a general guideline because the secondary market for collectibles is huge and changes all the time. The association offers a complimentary quote on the secondary-market value of a collectible if you call 847-842-2200 or write to CIB, 5065 Shoreline Road, Suite 200, Barrington, Illinois 60010.

The price guide comes out twice a year. In addition, selected updates appear each month in various collectors' magazines.

Secondary-market dealers abound on the Internet. You're certain to encounter a few at Web sites that are specially designed for collectors.

Chapter 4 — Web Sites for Collectors

When businesses started using the World Wide Web several years ago, their sites typically consisted of one page that looked like a flat magazine or newspaper ad. More sophisticated sites had several pages that users could hyperlink through, and the most interactive part of the site was a link to an e-mail address. Really hot sites had animated icons. A good number of Web sites were just plain advertising.

But not any more.

In this chapter, you'll discover places on the Web that cater to collectors and how visits to these sites can help build your collection and trading network:

- Web sites with action
- Collectible company Web sites
- Multi-collectible sites
- Collector exchanges
- Web portals
- Bulletin boards and what they offer you
- Chat rooms

☛Where the Action Is

Two of the finest examples of company Web sites with a function for users are home.microsoft.com and home.netscape.com. Both have become Web portals, offering links to information updates everywhere on the Web. Many users of Internet Explorer or Netscape use one of these as their browser home page. The selected site appears the moment they bring up their Web browser to start a surfing session.

As the browser opens, the user sees the top news stories. Some of these sites have options that allow the user to customize the page, so if he or she wants to see the score of last night's NBA game, that information appears when the page loads.

A Virtual Delight

Part of what makes Websurfing so much fun is all of the interactive stuff that companies have on their sites. The term "virtual" describes any situation where a computer simulates an actual event. Collectors have a rich supply of virtual shopping on the Web.

A Websurfer can "browse" the virtual aisles with a virtual shopping basket and can even go on a virtual tour of the product facility. Some companies will send you free samples (real, not virtual) for completing an online interactive survey.

Web pages aren't just flat advertisements any more. They serve as advertisements in a sense, but many are interactive hotbeds of information — and fun!

☛Collectible Company Web Sites

Collectible companies have joined the act. By spinning a Web site, they discovered the fastest way to get product information to their collectors is by putting information right up on the site. Companies that are more astute include their site URL in their product brochures so newly intrigued collectors can run home and call up the site on their computers.

Such Web sites provide dedicated collectors with the most up-to-date information. Some companies update their site daily. Major collectible companies section their site by collectible line, with appropriate links from the main home page. Most of their Web sites also offer all or many of the following features:

- Product-line photos
- Interactive collector club membership sign-up
- Suggestions for use of the products
- Gift ideas
- Interactive programs for kids
- Jokes and stories sent in by visitors
- Shop locations and dealer listings by state
- Product search engines
- Fun and games
- Special functions, like a program to send an e-mail card
- Bulletin boards
- Classified ads
- Chat rooms
- Links to product-line pages
- Dealer directories
- Press releases
- Dedicated online auction sites, or links to other ones
- Upcoming collector events
- Who to contact to place an order
- How to become a dealer of the products
- Changes in collector club guidelines
- Upcoming public offerings
- Links to private collector and collector club sites

- Employment opportunity information
- Biographical information about product artists and creators

www.collectible.com

The following table lists Web sites of many of the top collectible lines. Some are subsidiary sites of larger companies, and others are the host company's Web site. Many of them provide the features listed above, while some offer other features unique to the growing Web industry.

To ensure regular traffic, the content of the sites often changes from week to week, with new features added and others changed or "put on the back burner," depending on what's in the spotlight.

This list of collectible company Web sites ought to provide hours of surfing.

Uniform Resource Locator	Company Name
www.alexanderdoll.com	Alexander Doll Company, Inc.
www.annalee.com	Annalee Mobilitee Dolls
www.ANRI.com	ANRI
www.the-society.com	Guiseppe Armani Art
www.ashtondrake.com	The Ashton-Drake Galleries
www.autographsofamerica.com	Autographs of America
www.barbie.com	Barbie Collectibles
www.brandywinecollectibles.com	Brandywine Collectibles
www.byerschoice.com	Byers' Choice
www.caithnessglass.co.uk	Caithness Glass Inc.
www.cardewdesign.com	The Cardew Teapottery
www.castart.com	Cast Art Industries
www.cathalloffame.com	Cat Hall of Fame
www.catsmeow.com	Cat's Meow Village
www.charmingtails.com	Charming Tails
www.culbricht.com	Christian Ulbricht
www.radko.com	Christopher Radko
www.coca-cola.com	Coca Cola Collectibles
www.collectibleworld.com	Collectible World Studios Ltd.
www.crystalworld.com	Crystal World
www.dccomics.com	DC Comics
www.department56.com	Department 56
www.disneystore.com	Disney
www.disney.com/DisneyArtClassics	Walt Disney Art Classics

www.enesco.com	Enesco Corporation
www.fenton-glass.com	Fenton Glass Company
www.flambro.com	Flambro Imports
www.furby.com	Furbyland
www.gartlanusa.com	Gartlan USA
www.genedoll.com	Gene Dolls
www.mihummel.com	Goebel
www.greenwichworkshop.com	Greenwich Workshop
www.hagaradolls.com	Jan Hagara Collectables
www.hallmark.com	Hallmark Cards, Inc.
www.hantelminiatures.com	Hantel Miniatures
www.HarbourLights.com	Harbour Lights
www.HarmonyKingdom.com	Harmony Kingdom
www.enchantica.com	Holland Studio Craft
www.joyworldcollectibles.com	Joy To The World Collectibles
www.just-the-right-shoe.co.uk	Just the Right Shoe
www.leemiddleton.com	Lee Middleton Original Dolls
www.lenoxcollections.com	Lenox Collections
www.lladro.com	Lladró Society
www.longaberger.com	Longaberger Baskets
www.lornabailey.com	Lorna Bailey Pottery
www.meanies.com	Meanies
www.moorcroft.co.uk	Moorcroft, Ltd.
www.papelgiftware.com	Papel Giftware
www.pez.com	PEZ Candy
www.piggin.com	Piggin'
www.pipka.com	Pipka Collectibles
www.pipkinandbonnet.com	Pipkin & Bonnet
www.pocket-dragons.com	Pocket Dragons
www.preciousmoments.com	Precious Moments, Inc.
www.roberttonner.com	Robert Tonner Doll Company
www.roman.com	Roman, Inc.
www.royal-doulton.com	The Royal Doulton Company
www.sfmusicbox.com	San Francisco Music Box Company
www.steiff.com	Steiff
www.swarovski.com	Daniel Swarovski Corporation AG
www.shelias.com	Shelia's
www.shenandoahdesigns.com	Shenandoah Designs
www.reugemusic.com	Symphony Classic Collectibles
www.thomaskinkade.com	Thomas Kinkade
www.melodyinmotion.com	WACO Products Corporation

www.wade.co.uk . . . . .Wade Ceramics, Ltd.
www.waterford-usa.com . . . . .Waterford
www.wedgwood.co.uk . . . . . .Josiah Wedgwood & Sons Ltd.

The Economical Web

Collectible companies serve themselves well by maintaining Web sites because they can cut down on advertising costs. Compared with print advertising, putting product information on a Web site is dirt cheap. The company can introduce pieces to thousands of collectors with minimal effort. They can update the text quickly and easily. No need to stop the presses!

Since collectors regularly visit the company's site for information, anything placed on the Web site is a direct hit to their customers.

These same dedicated collectors may put up their own Web pages devoted to their collecting passion and will, of course, include a hypertext link back to the main company site. Thus, more traffic to the company's site. Now add all these collectors' home pages to a thriving Web ring, and it's no wonder that page counters on sites like www.ashtondrake.com and www.swarovski.com grow by the thousands every day. Sometimes even more.

While companies transmit vital information to them, collectors can feel like part of the process.

Cyber-Mingling

Communicating with previously inaccessible people has never been so easy. Since more and more authors include their e-mail addresses in their books, readers can communicate directly by sending an electronic message instead of going through the publisher. I know — I received many friendly e-mail messages after the release of the first edition of this book.

As an avid "Dilbert" fan, I sent e-mail to the cartoon strip's artist and creator Scott Adams one lazy afternoon and he floored me by answering. It was only a few sentences, but it came from Scott Adams! On the other hand, when I was a starry-eyed twelve-year-old, I never once heard back from Davy Jones of the Monkees despite many letters I dropped in the mailbox.

For a Sandra Bullock fan, nothing else on Earth would compare with getting an e-mail message from her. For a dedicated collector, something similar applies to hearing from the president or CEO of a favorite collectible company (although many would love to hear from Sandra too).

E-mail entails typing in your message and clicking on the "send" button. No paper, no envelope, no hunting for a stamp and no trip to the mailbox. And unlike more demanding media (like an incessantly ringing telephone), you can read and answer your e-mail according to your own schedule.

Most people who run collectible companies have personal e-mail accounts, and many enjoy hearing from their consumers. What better way is there to have their eyes and ears on their target market? When they communicate with their collectors, they can find out what the fans expect from the line. Moreover, e-mail is fast, easy, and non-intrusive.

Customers find appeal in being able to communicate directly with the collectible company via e-mail or a Web site. It's like grabbing a mitt and jumping right into the game.

Some companies include links to collectors' personal pages right on their Web page if the personal page is devoted to their line of collectibles. There is no better way to keep a collector a product-endorsing fanatic than to bestow such an honor.

Special Events

Collectible company Web sites also convey details about upcoming momentous events, like the introduction of special anniversary or commemorative pieces, store event schedules, sudden-death retirements, or collector-club events.

News and messages from company officials along with artist profiles are just a few Web site features that encourage visits from collectors. There are many, and each site differs in some way.

Any collectible-product representative can tell you that as the popularity of a line grows, so do the rumors surrounding the company, the collectible, the artists, or any other aspect of the product. Stories of buyouts circulate around the Internet and eventually end up on bulletin boards. A few avid collectors claim their niece's third cousin's nephew's friend works for the company and heard an unquestionable "fact" about the collectible line, such as what's next to retire or any fabled lawsuits in the making.

When a company gets wind of rumors, it can use its home page to squelch or confirm any Internet reports.

☛Multi-Collectible Sites

With the collectible business booming, more and more collectors' Web sites pop up. Some host bulletin boards and chat rooms for collectible companies making use of the host site's sophisticated software, while others put up bulletin boards and information about popular collectors to draw visitors. Since many companies get funding through advertising, they want a steady flow of traffic through the site.

A few well-noted multi-collectible sites on the Web are:

- About.com .www.about.com
- Collector Net . . . . .www.collectornet.com
- World Collectors' Net . . . . . . .www.worldcollectorsnet.com
- Collector Online . . . . .www.collectoronline.com

About.com

This incredibly informational Web collection calls itself "the network of sites led by professional guides."

Each link brings up a complete Web site dedicated to a specific topic. A "guide," or company-affiliated subject specialist, manages the content of each About.com site to provide a comprehensive experience for enthusiasts. To qualify as a guide, candidates must apply and complete a certification program in order to maintain an About.com site.

If you click on the "Hobbies" link from the About.com home page, you'll find links to sites with information about Arts & Crafts, Pastimes, and Collecting. You'll also find discussion forums, chat rooms, newsletters, book reviews, and online shopping.

Collector Net

Self-dubbed "The Collector's Edge," this collector's resource uses a sophisticated and user-friendly software package. You can get news and information about collectibles from the home page, and surf over to bulletin boards or chat rooms dedicated to a particular collectible line.

CollectorNet currently offers many dedicated bulletin boards where collectors can mingle online and adds new ones periodically. Here are a few:

- **The HK Exchange** – The official Harmony Kingdom bulletin board and chat room. There is a separate board for posts offering sales or trades.
- **Beanbag Exchange** – A bulletin board for the discussion of various beanbag toys.
- **Crystal Exchange** – The discussion forum for fans of Swarovski,

Waterford, and other crystal products.

- **Greenwich Exchange** – A place where collectors of Will Bullas figurines and more Greenwich Workshop products can meet online.
- **Ornament Exchange** – Share your favorite ornament storage techniques with other enthusiasts, or discuss your seasonal favorites by Hallmark, Carlton, Radko, and many other lines.
- **Shoe Exchange** – Here's a bulletin board devoted to Just The Right Shoe collectors, or those who happen to enjoy collectible shoes.

Hosted by Collectornet.com and the Harmony Ball Company, the site provides links to news and information about the collectibles industry, and a list of online auction sites where you can sell some of your items on the secondary market. One feature of particular value to collectors is the online directory of collectible manufacturer Web sites.

You'll need to register for a log-in and password in order to participate in the interactive features of the site.

World Collectors Net

This United Kingdom-based site is without a doubt one of the finest and most comprehensive sites of its type on the World Wide Web. You can get just about any information you want about a plethora of different collectible lines worldwide. Each line has its own bulletin board and information page, with links to other related sites. New product lines appear periodically.

Here's where the home page links take you:

- **Shopping Arcade** – You'll find hundreds of links to places on the Web where you can buy your favorite antiques and collectibles.
- **Collectibles Featured** – View a list of the collectibles for which you'll find information at the site.
- **Online Magazine** – An online magazine with articles, reviews, and letters about antiques and collectibles.
- **Message Boards** – Close to a hundred different dedicated bulletin boards for collectors of such lines as Charming Tails, Boyd's Bears, Beanie Babies, and Harmony Kingdom. Check back frequently, because they add new ones all the time.
- **Price Guides & Trends** – Visit some of the sites that offer secondary market values for some of your favorites.

- **Links Directory** – Here you'll find hundreds of links to pages with more information about antiques and collectibles than you can imagine.
- **BookStore** – Check out the reviews and descriptions of books about collecting. Click on a book cover and you'll be right at the Amazon.co.uk ordering page.

You'll also find information about collectibles making their market debut. World Collectors Net has a sophisticated search feature to help navigate your visit.

Collector Online

This collector site differs from the other three. It's more of a swap-and-sell area, where collectible dealers can purchase "cyber booths," or pages linked to and from the main page. Collector Online also has a powerful search feature that allows collectors quick access to items they're seeking.

The site operates on the premise that collectors want to be regulars at only a few sites instead of all over the Web; therefore, access to desired pieces should be quick, easy, and offer variety.

The site also includes fresh content articles about collecting from commissioned authors.

☛Collector Exchanges

People who just want to share their love of a collectible with others operate many of the collector exchanges. Others run the site as an advertising-funded business, and offer free user IDs and passwords for collectors at their request.

Many of these sites contain a message board or bulletin board feature so collectors can communicate with each other. Their subjects revolve around a unique theme or collection of items.

Here's a word of caution about communicating with other collectors: enthusiasm is contagious. Once you talk to other collectors about their favorite pieces, their enthusiasm may rub off on you, even for pieces you've resisted buying.

You may find your collection growing!

Uniform Resource Locator	Site Contents
www.wizardworld.com	Wizard World On-line for comic book collectors
members.aol.com/LL2Starks	Our Button Box

autographcollector.com . . . . .Autograph Collector and Pop Culture
www.abanick.com . . . . .Colorado Casino Chip Exchange
www.antiquetoys.com . . . . .Santa Barbara Antique Toys
marshel.simplenet.com/hh/hhexchange.html . . . .The Holly Hobby
Exchange
web2.airmail.net/bo54 . . .Common Card Exchange (Sports Cards)
www.flash.net/~atw . . . . .PrimitiveArt.com (Tribal Art Worldwide)
www.beckett.com . . . . .Beckett Collectibles Online
www.trainfinder.com/default.asp . . . . .TrainFinder Online
(Interactive Toy Train Exchange)
www.dryden.net/~jablack . . . . .JAB's Canadian Coin Exchange
dizzy.library.arizona.edu/users/mount/postcard.html . . .Postcard
Resources
home.earthlink.net/~wce . . . . .Western Coin Exchange
www.home.ch/~spaw1525 . . . . . . .David's Beer Mat Exchange
www.atchou.com/telescan/artcl01.htm .Guidelines for Buying and
Selling Rare Coins
www.wallofbeer.com . . . . .The Nicholson Wall of Beer
(beer bottle and label collecting)
members.aol.com/steins4you . . . . .Thomas Stein Exchange
www.comiclink.com . . . . .The Internet Comic Book Exchange
www.dollexchange.com . . . . .The Doll Exchange International
home.earthlink.net/~bufe/APX . . . . . .American Pottery Exchange
www.lighthousetrading.com . . . . .The Lighthouse Trading Company
www.hmrs.org.uk . . . . .Historical Model Railway Society
www.piston.com/ipe . . . . .Italian Parts Exchange
www.ewtech.com/gijoe . . . . .The Joe Depot GIJOE
www.mortonscrystal.com . . .Secondary-Market Brokerage Service
for Swarovski Crystal
www.flash.net/~gemoore/arkpotx.htm . . . . .Arkansas Pottery
Exchange
www.tmcx.com . . . . .The Militaria Collector's Exchange
www.money.org . . . . .The American Numismatic Association
(Coin Collecting)
www.vintagelighters.com . . . . .The International Vintage
Lighter Exchange
www.wscoin.com . . . . .Washington Square Coin Exchange
www.dollpage.com . . . . .Doll Page
www.collectibleuniverse.com . . . . .Collectible Universe
www.yulelog.com/cgi-bin/Ultimate.cgi . . . . .Yule Log
(Hallmark and Beanies)
www.classiccarmall.com . . . . .Classic Car Mall

```
www.artcellarex.com . . . . . . . . . . . .Art Cellar Exchange (Fine Art)
www.rio.com/~arne/mb_files/garage.html  .The Matchbox Garage
www.atchou.com/cce.html  . . . . . . . . . .Certified Coin Exchange
```

➡   Note: If some of these sites have moved   ⬅
by the time this book goes to press, use any of the search
engines listed in Chapter 2. A search for "Collector Exchange"
will find many more sites of interest to collectors.

☛Web Portals

A Web portal is a site designed to be the epicenter of your Internet browsing session. Many of the classic search engines have expanded to become Web portals, such as these:

Uniform Resource Locator	Site name
www.yahoo.com	Yahoo!
www.excite.com	Excite
www.planetdirect.com	Planet Direct – Your Personal Web Service
www.lycos.com	Lycos – Your Personal Internet Guide
www.altavista.com	AltaVista Connections
www.enetcenter.com	eNet Center Portal
www.realinks.net	Realinks Internet Portal and Web Advertising Network

Portals for Collectors

Many portals cater to collectors, and some are specifically for collectors who want to use the Internet to manage their collecting. Here are a few:

Uniform Resource Locator	Site name
www.beckett.com	Beckett Collectibles Online
www.magicalupdate.com	Magical Update Collectible Web Portal
collect-online.com	Collectibles, Antiques, and Art Online
www.collectiblesnet.com	The Collectiblesnet.com
www.rubylane.com	Ruby Lane Antiques, Collectibles, and Fine Art
www.collectingchannel.com	CollectingChannel.com

www.collectorsweb.com . . . . .CollectorsWeb.com
www.internetauctionlist.com . . . . . .The Internet Auction List

These sites offer collectors a doorway to finding antiques and collectibles on the Internet. Some have links to other sites of interest to collectors, and some offer message boards and chat. You'll also find that a few of them host their own online auctions.

Note: You'll read more about online auctions in Chapter 6.

More Collector Forums and Portals

From the time the first edition of this book went to press in late 1998, many more multi-collectible forums and collector portals sprang up on the Internet. Here are a few very popular ones:

Uniform Resource Locator	Company Name
www.WebCollecting.com . . . . .WebCollecting
www.treasuresinyourhome.com . . . .Treasures in Your Home
www.collectiblestoday.com . . . . .Collectibles Today
www.collectorbee.com . . . . .CollectorBee
www.collectibles.net . . . . .Collectibles.net
www.collectit.net . . . . .Collect It
www.giftline.com . . . . .Giftware Business

☛Bulletin Boards

Internet bulletin boards appear all over the Web. Almost anyone with a home page can set one up. Many sites right on the Web will host your bulletin board for you.

The advantage of Internet bulletin boards is that people can post messages from wherever they can access the Internet. Like the rest of the Web, you can access the boards 24 hours a day, as long as there are no Internet snags.

Many collector sites sponsor bulletin boards where people can "meet" and share ideas. Some folks use bulletin boards to put out feelers for items they want to purchase or trade for, while others list items for sale. Dealers and shop owners might also list items for sale, although some bulletin boards restrict dealer listings. Some companies provide dealers with their own bulletin board for listing retail and secondary-priced inventories.

When another computer hosts your bulletin board, the data is stored on the host's computer, but you manage the board. You design the page, the layout, how many messages can stay up at one time, and build whatever links to other pages you want included. This can include a link back to your home page. You control how long messages remain on the board, and which ones should be deleted. The hosting service usually requests that you credit them with a link to their home page. They occasionally might insert ads on your bulletin board's main page.

> ➡ Note: "Hosting" means storing an image file ⬅
> or a program to make it accessible via the Web. The host
> stores it for you on a Web-accessible computer, and gives
> your item a URL address.

You can also pay a monthly fee for hosting and not have ads on the page, or you can buy bulletin board software and manage the program yourself.

How They Work

A bulletin board system lives on a server that users access through their Internet browser. Some bulletin boards are secured, requiring users to register with a user ID (also called a log-in) and password. Many secured bulletin boards allow you to log in as "guest," but you'll only be able to read posts already on the bulletin board. You must register in order to post items or follow-ups.

When you register, you provide certain information about yourself. You then receive a unique user name and password to use each time you access the bulletin board. This user name becomes your "handle" and will appear by each post you enter, usually as a hyperlink so participants can send you e-mail. Most programs allow you to choose your own handle.

> ➡ Note: When you register to use an online ⬅
> bulletin board, the information you provide is usually available
> to other participants of the board unless the registration
> page specifically states that it's kept private. Look for the
> closed lock indicating an SSL site if registration requires
> entering personal information.

Other bulletin boards are unsecured, and allow anyone to participate as long as they can type characters into the text-entry area and have a browser that's compatible with that program. There are advantages and disadvantages to each type of bulletin board.

Threaded Bulletin Boards

Threaded bulletin boards allow users to enter topics for discussion, or "post" an item. Once the post appears, other users can add sub-topics under the main topic in outline form. This enables discussions to flow easily without a lot of off-topic "drift." If you want to move on to another topic, you simply find one that suits your needs or post a new item.

Some bulletin boards display in a single browser window. When you click on an item to view it, the post loads in your browser. Your Back button returns you to the main page. Other bulletin boards display in a framed browser window. The subjects appear in one

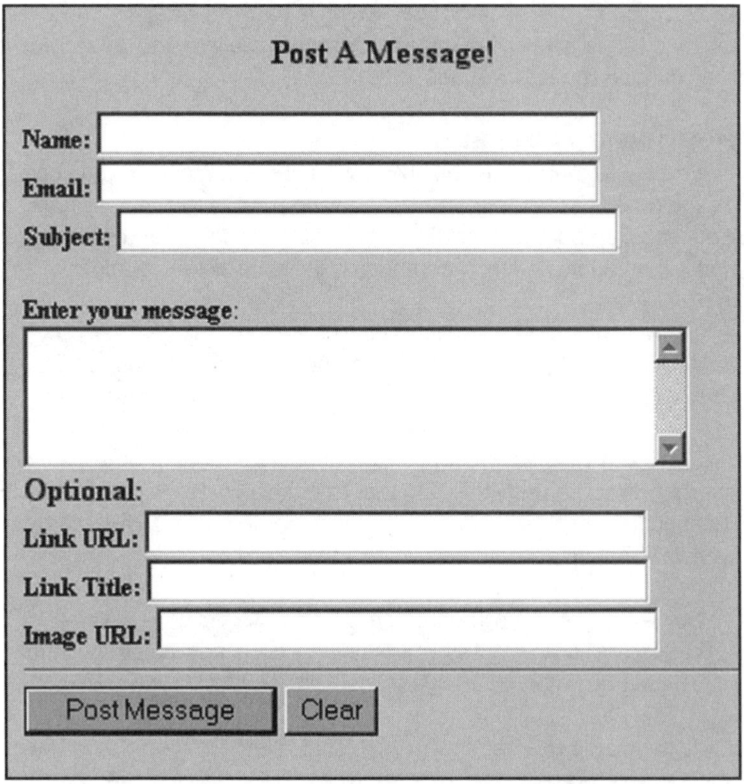

Post A Message!

Name:

Email:

Subject:

Enter your message:

Optional:

Link URL:

Link Title:

Image URL:

Post Message   Clear

Figure 4-1. Typical Bulletin-Board Post Entry Screen

frame, and when you click on one, it loads in another frame. This way you don't need to hit your Back button every time you want to access the main page to view another post.

A user can usually see all the topics on the board. The entry form for new items appears at the bottom of the bulletin board screen or in a different browser frame. You don't need to leave the main screen to enter an item or post a follow-up to an existing one.

The entry screen is a text fill-in form and usually some variation of Figure 4-1.

In each field, you can enter text after you place your mouse cursor there and left-click to position it. Most entry screens accept some HTML tags, which allows you to add images or put in links to other Web sites.

Some of the fields, such as "Subject," accept only a certain number of characters. This design prevents people from putting their whole post in the subject line, which effectively clutters the main page. It takes away the readers' option of clicking on the subject if they choose to read the post.

Posting a Message

Enter your name (or one you want to have appear by your post), your e-mail address, the subject of your post, and the message. If it's a secured bulletin board, you previously logged in and your name and e-mail address are automatically included when you post.

> ═══► Note: Most bulletin boards allow you to use ◄═══
> HTML code in your posts. Remember that you can use any of
> the formatting tags shown in Chapter 7 with your messages.

Enter the URL address and title of your personal home page or another Web page in the Optional URL field. A link to this page is then included with your post. If you include an image's URL, the picture will appear in your post. These fields are optional.

> ═══► Note: If you enter an image URL, be sure ◄═══
> the picture isn't very large. Most folks don't appreciate waiting
> a long time for an image to load unless it's really worth it!

If you decide against sending the post, click on "Reset" and everything you entered on the screen disappears.

When you're satisfied with your post, click on "Post Message." This sends your post to the bulletin board. Some bulletin-board programs allow you to preview and edit your post, but others only give you one shot to get it right. You can't retrieve or delete it once you've sent it.

Your message will appear as a new post, usually first on the bulletin board page. Other users can now read and respond to your post. Their responses will appear indented under your post.

A threaded bulletin board looks something like this:

- Requesting information about a 1997 Barbie – **Mindy in Arizona** Mindy's Cove 11:55:59 04/03/98
  - This tidbit might help you – **Cheryl M.** 12:14:22 04/03/98
  - I have one of those for sale – **Marge McGoo** 14:22:23 04/04/98
    - Marge please read – **Mindy in AZ** 03:24:14 04/04/98
- Has anyone seen the newest Piggin' brochure? It's GREAT!! – **Spinner** 11:43:20 04/03/98
  - Here's what I liked about it – **Cre8vgrl from NC** 12:24:58 04/06/98
  - Gotta have those – **Candy B** 14:23:52 04/06/98

Figure 4-2. Sample of a Threaded Bulletin-Board Discussion

Notice that "Mindy's Cove" appears in underlined text after Mindy's name. This is because she specified the URL to her home page and its title. The program displays the information as a hypertext link. If you click on this text, her page will appear either in a new browser window or in another frame.

This is the most common way bulletin board programs create links. Sometimes the title and the e-mail address are hypertext so readers can send the poster a message. The program interprets the data the poster typed into the screen and formats the post with it.

The subject is also hypertext. When you click on the text, the post loads in your browser window. You'll also see an entry screen in case you want to post a follow-up message.

The follow-up entry screen looks just like the post screen, only the subject of the original message carries over into the "Subject" area of the fill-in form. You can edit the subject if you want.

Non-Threaded Bulletin Boards

Non-threaded bulletin boards list items in the order they came in. Some programs show the newest items first, and others work in reverse. You cannot link your post to another item, only post a new one.

You'll find several collector discussion forums at YuleLog (www.yulelog.com) that use non-threaded bulletin boards. In addition, the Online Traders Web Alliance (OTWA) at www.otwa.com uses Ultimate Bulletin Board, a variation of the non-threaded format. This site is an excellent place for cyber-discussions about online auctions.

The post-entry screen is similar to the one for threaded bulletin boards, but usually allows fewer characters. A non-threaded bulletin board looks something like this:

I have many Hallmark ornaments for sale. Please visit my home page for a list of exactly what I have. Just click on my name to go there! **Elliot** *user1@email.net* 12/14/98 13:24

Just surfed by to say hello! **Amanda** *kornegay@email.net* 12/14/98 12:35

Does anyone know which weekend the Rosemont ICE is supposed to be? I need information on hotels in the area too. Thanks! **Raven** *user3@email.net* 12/12/98 23:56

Figure 4-3. Sample of a Non-threaded Bulletin Board Discussion

Elliot's name appears underlined because he specified the URL to his home page on the entry screen. Amanda and Raven didn't specify a URL so their names are not hypertext and thus not underlined.

One advantage of non-threaded bulletin boards is that you can see all entries at a glance. You don't have to click on subject hypertext and wait for the post to load.

Most Internet guestbooks are non-threaded because guest entries are sporadic and usually don't follow a common topic. Users link to another page to post entries and usually see the current entries only after adding an item. These rank lower in popularity because it's difficult to carry on a "discussion." If you want to respond to a specific message, you must refer to it in detail. This tends to make entries cumbersome and topics rather hard to follow. For this reason, guestbooks are not that widely used as bulletin boards unless there's a specific reason.

Ultimate Bulletin Board

One very popular type of secured bulletin board program is Ultimate Bulletin Board, or UBB. Many companies use UBB software for their discussion forums because it's powerful and easy to customize. Here are a few of the features that registered users of UBB forums can enjoy:

- User registration with logins and passwords
- E-mail notification of replies to topics
- Private forums

- UBBFriend Feature: e-mail a topic to someone
- Forum moderators who can edit/delete any post in a forum they moderate
- User profiles that can be updated by users
- Ability to edit/delete/prune messages

Users can use HTML code to add images and hyperlinks to posts. However, the site administrator may opt to enable UBB codes. Then participants will use a special abbreviated code, similar to HTML but easier to use, to add links, images, and special text features to their posts.

Learn more about the UBB software at www.ultimatebb.com.

Before You Jump Right In

When you first access a bulletin board, remember one point of protocol:

Read; then post.

Some bulletin-board communities have a link to a "FAQ" page. The FAQ is a list of information presented as answers to questions new users often ask; thus, "frequently asked questions." Before you even consider entering a comment on the bulletin board, read this file. The site administrator usually puts together FAQ lists based on input from frequent users. Sometimes a regular participant oversees the FAQ, or it can be a rotating job among the group.

⟹ Note: You'll see FAQs used a lot in Usenet. ⟸
Newcomers who ask basic questions find numerous
follow-up posts saying "Read the FAQ!"

As with any organized gathering of human beings, someone is bound to break the rules or behave obnoxiously from time to time. If enough users complain, the site administrator can decide if a new policy should be developed and added to the FAQ.

Along with reading the FAQ, get to know the attitude of users on the bulletin board. Some are more temperamental and defensive than others and don't like contradictory follow-ups to their posts. Others are friendly and helpful. Everyone has "on" and "off" days. Get a feel for the personalities before you jump in and possibly start a "flame war."

Caution About Bulletin Boards

As easy as it is to access the Internet, it's also easy to post information there. With the right knowledge, anyone can establish an identity, set up an e-mail address, and participate in a bulletin board discussion. Some site administrators hesitate to issue user IDs to those who have accounts at free e-mail sites like Hotmail and Usa.Net, although many decent people use those services. Someone with ill intent pretty much has to strike before he or she can be flushed out.

Therefore, be cautious when talking with people you know only from contact on the Internet. Don't be too free to give out information about yourself. Until you've met the person face-to-face, you can never really be sure with whom you're communicating.

With unsecured bulletin boards, there is no simple way for users to know exactly who posts a message or its origin. You can't trace e-mail addresses through bulletin board posts. The person's Internet provider address shows up with posts on some bulletin boards, narrowing the originator only to a specific Internet service provider. But what if the post came from a library or cyber-café? Or from a friend's computer?

Whatever the person enters is what appears on the bulletin board. There's no audit to check that the data applies to the person hitting the keys. Even a secured bulletin board doesn't guarantee truthful data on the registration screen.

Just as there's no way to verify the data, no easy way exists to prevent a particular person from posting on a bulletin board. Even when identified, Internet troublemakers are next to impossible to stop. Maybe this will change as technology advances.

Free E-mail Addresses

You'll find sites offering free e-mail accounts all over the Web. Here are just a few of them:

Uniform Resource Locator	Company Name
www.juno.com	Juno
www.hotmail.com	Hotmail
www.usa.net	Usa.Net

In addition, most Web portals and free Web page hosting sites offer you a free e-mail account if you use their services.

As I mentioned before, many good, honest people use these services. Sometimes you can't avoid using a free e-mail account, such as when you're away from your ISP and your main e-mail server and you only have access to a Web connection.

Be aware that people may be suspicious of you when your user profile includes a free e-mail address. Once you become a regular participant at a collector forum using one of these e-mail accounts, folks will get to know your cyber-personality a little better, and their apprehension will probably subside.

> ➡️   Note: Many bulletin boards and online ⬅️
> auction sites won't let you register with a free e-mail address.

Bulletin Board Stalkers

Unfortunately, a few lost souls make a sport out of causing trouble on unsecured bulletin boards. They usually read without posting for a while, or *lurk*, to get a feel for the relationships among the participants, and then start trouble. They might post using another person's name, enter something inappropriate, reveal personal information about another participant that they've dredged up on the Internet somewhere, or just generally be obnoxious.

Ignore them if you can, although sometimes that's difficult. Some of them are quite good at what they do and often manage to drag other collectors into the foray. An otherwise informative discussion can easily and quickly turn into something resembling a schoolyard brawl.

Here is an example of a bulletin board stalker in action, impersonating other posters and getting the collectors angry at each other. Notice all the offensive comments were posted around the same time of day:

- Requesting information about a 1997 Barbie – **Mindy in Arizona** Mindy's Cove *11:55:59 04/03/98*
   - I gave you that information last week, can't you read?! – **Cheryl M.** *03:44:22 04/05/98*
      - Cheryl I resent that – **Mindy in AZ** *06:24:14 04/04/98*
         - Mindy I did NOT post that!! – **Cheryl M** *08:03:30 04/04/98*
   - I have one of those for sale – **Marge McGoo** *14:22:23 04/04/98*
      - This isn't Swap and Sell, stupid – **idiot identifier** *03:24:54 04/05/98*
- Has anyone seen the newest Piggin' brochure? It's GREAT!! – **Spinner** *11:43:20 04/03/98*
   - It BITES!!!! – **Real Collector** *04:03:58 04/05/98*
      - YOU bite !!! – **Who cares what you think?** *04:23:52 04/05/98*

Figure 4-4. Sample of a Bulletin Board Stalker in Action

Beware of the malevolent stalkers and resist responding to their posts. Stay on the host topic and leave unrelated discussions to e-mail or the telephone. And whatever you do, don't keep too high of a profile until you know your way around the board.

Flaming

Not everybody agrees with everyone else, especially when art forms such as collectibles are discussed. One person's favorite piece may be the one another collector passes by. We're all unique.

Sometimes people forget that on the Internet, only words appear and the associated emotions are not clear. These words are often misinterpreted. One person posts a response to a comment he or she perceived as malicious, and then another person posts in kind. Before you know it, the board is full of insults and has completely drifted from the host topic. This is a *flame war*, and it's best to avoid getting into the middle of one.

A *flame* is a hostile remark directed at another person, like a sarcastic response to something a person posted. Since written words are easily misunderstood, innocent comments can be interpreted as flames.

Before assuming you know what another person meant, it's best to double check by posting a polite request for more information, or by sending a private e-mail request for clarification. Don't invite hostility anywhere on the Internet, especially on an unsecured bulletin board.

Emoticons

To show emotion on the Internet, we use something called emoticons at the end of sentences if we want our meaning clearly understood. For example, the writer of the following sentence is just kidding around with JD, and JD knows it because of the smiling emoticon:

Hey JD, this isn't a sales pitch, is it? :-)

Here are some emoticons and their meanings:

:-)	Happy, or just kidding
:-D	Very happy, or pulling your leg
;-)	Winking, get the joke?
:-(	Sad
;-(	Crying
:-O	Shocked!
:-x	Lips are sealed
:*)	Being a bozo
:-)8	Wearing bow-tie
8:-)	Bow in hair
:-C	Angry
:-@	Very angry
:-P	Sticking out tongue

: o)	Joking
{ : o)	Joking with hair
: 8)	Acting like a pig
8 -)	Wearing glasses
: -\	Indifferent
} : -)	Being devil's advocate
: o }	Feeling silly today

Your favorite Internet handbook probably contains more, since long lists of emoticons are floating around cyberspace. In case you haven't figured them out yet, tilt your head to the left and you'll see the little faces formed by the characters.

We Learn From Our Mistakes

We sure do. Right after I "promoted" myself out of collecting Beanie Babies, I was thrilled to find the line I had just started collecting had a Web site with a bulletin board. I took a quick glance at the posts, read a few, immediately felt at home (isn't collecting the same everywhere?) and decided to jump right into the mainstream.

Post-O-Rama! I posted advice, reminded people not to post in all uppercase, tried to be funny, and was free with my opinions. I posted the same way I had on a previous bulletin board. At this new site, however, I apparently managed to offend someone in the process. One person obviously didn't appreciate a "newbie" having a high profile.

Nasty posts started appearing under mine, and soon someone was following up every one of my posts with an insult or something obscene. A few collectors posted messages in my defense, but stopped after they were flamed themselves. I felt that the ugly posts would stop if I ignored them. It didn't work. If this wasn't enough, my nemesis went one step further.

The person started posting as me. Since user IDs and passwords weren't in effect on this board, the person could put my name and e-mail address in the entry screen and effectively impersonate me. And the posts, appearing to come from me, were quite often nasty and offensive to other collectors. My impersonator literally built me a whole different identity. Since most people on the bulletin board didn't know me well, they were left to decide for themselves whether I was a troublemaker or an enthusiastic collector being cyber-stalked.

I phoned the collectible company and complained. They were very apologetic and had their site administrator remove the offensive posts. However, the person just came back with more bad posts every time the company cleaned up the board. Since participants didn't need a user ID and password to post, the site administrator had no way to block the person's posts without completely disabling the bulletin board.

This situation made it difficult to participate in the collector discussions. Meanwhile, many of the regular participants were afraid to post on the board. I switched my ISP service to one compatible with the site's chat room and talked to other collectors that way. My impersonator tried to mimic me there too, but was quickly found out. It's much more difficult to imitate a personality during an ongoing discussion than it is to create a few short bulletin board posts.

Gradually, as the rest of the collectors got to know me better, the impersonator's posts stood out as the product of a malicious soul. Others soon realized I wasn't the person posing as my other identity, and once the collectible company changed to a secured board that required IDs and passwords, the impersonating stopped.

This person may have been a fellow collector with an ax to grind, or may have been one of the many bulletin board stalkers who run rampant over the Internet. Perhaps both.

The lesson I learned from the experience is to start slow, mind your cyber-manners, and follow along rather than try to take charge. While the Internet contains a wealth of information, you can cause yourself a lot of trouble if you aren't careful.

Bulletin Board Etiquette

Sometimes people who are unfamiliar with communicating on the Internet commit blunders that really annoy other users and get the person started off on the wrong foot. Such mistakes are easily avoidable if the person learns the basic bulletin board etiquette before he or she starts posting:

- **Show respect for others.** State your opinion rather than admonishing someone else's.
- **State yourself clearly.** Not everyone is the world's best speller or writer. The object is to share ideas, not win a Pulitzer Prize for the most well-written post. How you write is how you represent yourself, though, so your post should be easy to understand.

- **Don't post in all uppercase.** It's difficult to read and looks like shouting. Posting messages in all uppercase letters is extremely poor form on the Internet. If you need to use all caps for emphasis, do so sparingly.
- **Don't post in all lowercase.** Our eyes are trained to read standard upper and lower case sentences. Make it easy for your readers!
- **Don't post "this is a test" messages.** Have something to say, even if it's just to introduce yourself and tell everyone you're new to the group.
- **Don't post e-mail messages.** Unless you have the originator's permission, it's always bad form to post the content of an e-mail message you received privately. If someone sends you a rude message, handle it in e-mail. Posting it will only cost you the respect of others on the board.
- **Don't put your whole message on the subject line.** Since the subject is the only part of the message people see before they click on it to read your post, it might be tempting to put your message there to ensure that others read it. Long titles can clutter the bulletin board. Enter a short subject line and let people decide for themselves if they want to read your post.
- **Don't post large images.** Either reduce the picture so it doesn't take that long to load, or refer your readers to the URL of the image so they can view it later.

☞What Bulletin Boards Offer You

Collectors can benefit from becoming a regular on an Internet bulletin board. You can stay knowledgeable about the pieces you can't get enough of, and you can meet other collectors with a similar addiction. Misery loves company!

Actually, meeting other collectors provides a good way to build your collection. You can buy and trade with people you know and trust.

I've met the nicest people while collecting on the Internet. I'm sure you will too!

Leads for Items at Retail

Some folks are so devoted to their hobby that finding pieces for their own collection isn't enough. They also want to help other collectors in their treasure hunts.

Perhaps a newly retired item you're hoping to purchase at retail is still available in stores, but you haven't been able to find one in your area. Your bulletin board friends can help. Asking if any of them has seen the piece at retail might get you a lead to a shop that will ship you the piece with a credit card order. Many shops will hold the piece pending a check or money order payment.

What goes around comes around. As you browse through shops in your area, take notes if you see retired pieces that you aren't going to buy for yourself. You can bestow yourself a nice warm fuzzy by helping other collectors acquire pieces they've been seeking.

If you're in the mood to receive lots of e-mail, list the retail items you've spotted and post them on a bulletin board. Offer the shop name and number to anyone who sends you e-mail asking for it. Be wary, though, that some of this e-mail might be from secondary market dealers who want to buy the pieces at retail and resell them for a profit. Whether you want to give them the information or save it for collectors is totally up to you.

News About the Collectible Company

Collectors might pick up tidbits about a company before an official announcement is made and pass them along in the form of rumors. You might hear about:

- New company officers
- Changes in dealer and customer incentives
- Changes in collector club guidelines
- Upcoming public offerings
- Buyouts and takeovers
- Gossip — the *good* stuff

While some collectors and dealers do communicate with company representatives and occasionally get the "scoop," it's a good idea to wait for the company to make an official announcement before acting on the news. In the meantime, other collectors can keep you informed of what's going on — or at least what they *think* is going on.

News About the Collectible Line

The same goes for the product line. Some collectors might have an "in" with the powers-that-be, while others pass along their predictions.

Companies occasionally take collectors up on suggestions and use their ideas in new pieces. Usually these collectors are the first to know about pieces created because of their suggestion and eagerly share the information with everyone else.

Questions and Answers

While you might occasionally encounter knowledgeable collectors who like to keep all product knowledge to themselves, these people are (thank goodness) rather scarce.

Remember that many collectors also create Web pages devoted to the product and provide valuable information you may not get anywhere else. These same people often read and post on a bulletin board. This is a great opportunity to rub elbows with the experts.

Don't forget about passing your own knowledge along to others. As you learn more about the line, new collectors will seek answers from you, too.

Advice from Experienced Collectors

Seasoned collectors can give advice as well as information based on their own experience. Suppose you have a dilemma over which item to offer in trade, or how much to ask for a retired piece. Someone who knows the market can help you determine what type of deal would be the best for both parties. Another collector, who may have been in a similar situation, can advise you as well.

Remember that people who've participated on the bulletin board the longest aren't always the most savvy. Newcomers to one collectible line can and do bring knowledge with them about their previous collecting experiences. Take no prisoners!

Offers of Sales or Trades

Trading with other collectors can help you build your collection, and bulletin boards are a great place to arrange transactions. You can usually get references for a person with whom you want to trade. In turn, your trading partner can obtain references from collectors who have dealt with you.

The most common way to arrange a trade is to include in your post exactly which piece or pieces you're seeking. Then, list what you have to offer in trade. This is one instance when it's fine to ask others to make an offer because you've provided them with a list of choices; you aren't asking them to do your homework.

"Who Are My Fellow Collectors?"

In cyber-land, get to know a person before you accept a trade offer or make a purchase from him or her. An e-mail exchange can lead to a phone call or two and before long, you've made a new friend that you can't wait to meet at the next collector club meeting or ICE show.

Cyber-Nicknames

Not everyone wants to use his or her real name in cyber-land. Some people use a cyber-nickname, or *handle*. Be prepared to encounter new and unusual names as you meet people on the Web. You might even want to establish one for yourself, but make sure it isn't one that will draw a lot of negative attention.

Good Choices:	Not-so-good Choices:
Boydslover	Bunghole
~*Issy*~	Easylady
Mapleleaves	Gangbanger
Sunflower	Barfman

One cyber-nickname has a rather interesting story behind it. Charlynn's family calls their cat "Boo." Once when her kids were fighting over who'd play with Boo, Charlynn's husband told one of them, "Don't be such a Boo hog!"

Humored, Charlynn picked up the moniker and became "BooHog" to her cyber-friends.

Shared Knowledge

Just because you're a new collector of a line doesn't mean you're new to collecting. The experience you gained buying, selling, and trading Barbie® dolls or Gene dolls will pay off when it comes to getting into another collectible line. Remember that you may not be dealing with the same types of people in every corner of cyberspace, so know your company!

Collector Whimsy

It was a slow afternoon right before the Christmas holidays and I was in a musical mood. Taking a rare opportunity to wax poetic, I composed a version of the Macarena that included the names of many of my favorite collectible pieces. I then posted this "masterpiece" on our bulletin board along with an animated image of a piece of dancing macaroni. It produced a few laughs.

On slow afternoons, you'll see surveys. One collector will throw out a question and ask others for their opinions. It is not entirely certain what's ever done with this data, but surveys can help get things moving on days when the bulletin board doesn't seem awake.

Conducting a survey is like asking for opinions. Any time you ask collectors for their opinions, you'll get them in abundance.

☞Chat Rooms

What an excellent place to *really* get to know your fellow collectors! While bulletin boards supply a wonderful place to impart ideas and knowledge, chat rooms allow you to converse in real time with other collectors who are right there online and can respond in rapid-fire discussion.

Chat rooms are easy to use. You simply type your comment on a text line and hit "Return," or click an "Enter" button with your mouse. Your comment will show up in queue along with the rest.

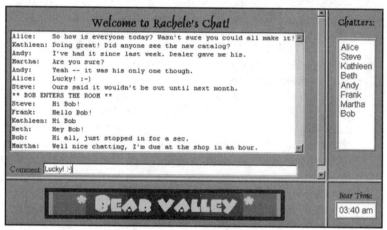

Figure 4-5. Sample Chat Room Screen

With all the special features offered in chat rooms — emotions, color text programs, icons, and sound — you can share the trials and tribulations of collecting in an atmosphere of camaraderie. You may also be given first crack at an item another collector is selling, especially if you were asked for advice on the sale.

Collectors tend to gravitate toward their own kind. If you decide to become a regular participant in a collectible chat room, you're likely to find yourself with many new cyber-friends.

Chat Room Etiquette

The general rule is stick to the topic. If the chat room dedicates itself to Mary's Moo Moos, then keep the discussion as close to that product as possible as long as any others in the group wish to discuss the line.

It's perfectly all right if the discussion drifts off the topic, as long as the host product or collected item takes precedence.

Many participants in collectible chat rooms are friends who meet there regularly. If you find yourself in a discussion that doesn't revolve around the collectible, either join the fun or return the discussion to the host product by asking a question or suggesting a topic.

It's not a good idea to interrupt a friendly off-topic chat just to show people the error of their ways, though. If you have nothing to contribute to the discussion, follow along until something that interests you arises, or exit and visit the chat room another time.

Keep in mind these basic Internet chat room rules of etiquette:

- **Follow the rules.** Be familiar with any rules of order in effect. Read the FAQ if one is available.
- **Use emoticons.** Be sure others know what you mean.
- **Make newcomers feel welcome.** Greet newcomers unless the chat room contains more than fifteen people. A long string of "Hi, BooHog!" can disrupt a discussion in progress, especially if BooHog wants to join in right away. For busier chats, elect a chat-room monitor and let that person do the greeting. In smaller chat sessions, go ahead and greet BooHog. It will make her feel special!
- **Stay on the topic.** If you need to ask another user a question or make a private comment, there is usually a "Whisper" or "Under-the-table" feature that allows you to send your comment privately.
- **Avoid cross talk.** Collectible company chat rooms are not for long-lost friends to meet and exchange family news while others in the room are talking about the latest limited-edition pieces. Unless you're the only two people there, find a private chat room for your catching-up.
- **Don't use all uppercase letters.** The same rule for bulletin-board posts applies to chat, since text in all uppercase (or all lowercase) is hard to read. Posting messages in such style is extremely poor form on the Internet.
- **Don't monopolize the discussion.** Wait for others to respond to your question or comment before entering another one.
- **Be courteous.** If you're using fancy chat-room features such as color text, sound, or special characters, remember that these might have unpredictable results on other people's monitors. If anyone in the chat room asks you not to use them, don't.
- **Avoid topics that might be offensive.** Some places on the

Web welcome discussions about politics, theology, pornography, computer techno-babble, or social controversy. Collectible company chat rooms usually don't.

- **Know your company.** Avoid using the chat room to air your personal vendettas. Someone may have entered the chat room when you weren't looking. A list of participants usually appears adjacent to the main screen.
- **Use the "ignore" feature if needed.** Many chat rooms let you "ignore" another user so you don't see their comments. This comes in handy when "chat spammers" enter and don't respond to subtle requests to take their business elsewhere.
- **Don't be vulgar or obnoxious.** You may lose access to the site and all benefits that go with it.

If you are unfamiliar with the features and/or protocol of a particular chat room, ask the participants. Someone will be glad to show you around the site.

Be Nice!

Web site administrators can and do revoke site IDs if many people complain about a person. When the site is unsecured, the administrator can let the person know his or her participation is no longer welcomed.

Ejection from a bulletin board or chat room on a collectible-company Web site is no laughing matter. This can seriously affect your credibility within your collecting circle. Since you probably don't want this to happen, follow the rules.

Remember to treat someone you meet on the Internet the way you would any stranger. Caution and manners are both important here.

Chapter 5 — Talking to Strangers

As you conduct sales or trades over the Internet, you're going to deal with people you don't know. Just as shop owners don't personally know every customer who walks in the door, you won't know everyone you deal with on the Internet.

It's a good idea to get to know the person you're making a trade with before you actually send an item on its way. Since you probably won't be able to meet for lunch with a person who lives three thousand zip codes away, you'll have to get to know your traders as well as you can by e-mail or over the phone.

Once you become familiar with a person and buy, sell, or trade items with each other, you can develop your own way of transacting — whatever works best for both of you. However, when dealing with someone you just met through cyber-space, you need to take precautions to protect yourself and the investment you've made in your collectibles.

This chapter will help you through that process:

- Knowing when it's time to trade or sell
- Getting the word out
- Collectible frenzy debriefing
- Arranging trades
- The anatomy of an Internet trade
- Trading brokerage and verification services
- Internet good-trader and bad-trader lists
- Selling items
- Packing and shipping

Some of the information provided here might seem as though I'm trying to scare you away from buying and trading collectibles on the Internet. That's certainly not the case. If it were, this book would be titled *Whatever You Do, Don't Buy, Sell, or Trade Collectibles on the Internet.* Quite the opposite.

My intent is to show how to transact with people you don't know without unnecessary risks. Taking as little risk as possible is tantamount to success when you trade and sell pieces. No transaction is risk-free, but you can safeguard yourself as much as possible.

Before you go further on this page, look around and see if anyone is reading over your shoulder. If so, hide the book. What you are about to read is important but somewhat selfish, so keep it to yourself. Here goes:

The object of being successful at trading and selling collectibles is *for you to assume the least amount of risk.* I'm not suggesting that you put the person in jeopardy; be considerate and follow good trading practices. However, if you're an honest person — and you no doubt are — you should understand the logic behind this reasoning.

It's a lot like approaching a stranger on the street. You know that you're OK, but you don't know if the other person is. You need to use caution when dealing with people you don't know. Let the people with whom you deal decide for themselves how much caution to use.

With this in mind, you can be successful in adding to your collection by trading pieces with collectors you meet on the Internet. Hundreds, maybe thousands of collectors trade with each other through the mail every day.

I was very lucky the first time I made a trade with someone I knew only from the Internet because Laurie and I lived close enough to make the trade in person. While this was an ideal situation, I eventually had to trade through the mail with someone I didn't know at all.

☞When It's Time To Trade or Sell

Before you post on the Internet, determine which items you want to sell or trade. This might be a tough decision. If you have duplicates, the decision is easy unless you really enjoy having more than one of something in your collection.

Simply speaking, it's time to sell or trade away a collectible when its current value outweighs the enjoyment you get from owning it.

Compare knowing when to sell a collectible with the headlight rule. When you're driving at dusk and start wondering if it's dark enough to turn on your headlights, this usually means you should. As the outdoor light fades, your intuition tells you that you need your headlights.

When you start thinking about whether you should sell one of your collectibles, this is a lot like the fading daylight. Your intuition is telling you that you might not be as excited about the item any longer, and it's time to let go.

☞Getting the Word Out

Once you make the decision to part with a collectible, contact your circle of traders and see if anyone wants to make the trade with you. If you can't find anyone interested in trading, then it's time to hit the bulletin board or Usenet newsgroup. You have some options, depending on whether you want to sell or trade:

- Post an item proposing a trade — your piece for another one that's comparable in value. Clearly describe the condition of your item and of the piece you're seeking.

- Post a "for sale" item, giving its name and condition (be specific), and the price you're asking for the piece.

Indicate whether you want any "takers" to contact you via e-mail or by posting a follow-up item to yours. E-mail is usually more productive in this situation so that you can proceed with the transaction privately, or off-line.

How Large Is Your Audience?

Collectors of "frenzy items," which are collectible items people hoard, usually address their posts to the thousands of people likely to read them. When dealing in wildly popular collectibles, there's a larger audience and posted messages usually receive a bombardment of e-mail responses after you broadcast a sale or trade offer.

When I posted trade offers in the Ty guestbook, I inevitably received e-mail asking if I was interested in selling something I wanted to trade. I'd get the same offers to trade for pieces that I had posted for sale. Many, many offers, sometimes 50 or more e-mail messages, would arrive all at once offering the opposite of what I wanted.

I'm sure this happened to other folks, because "no trade offers please" or "not interested in selling" started appearing at the ends of people's posts. I began adding this to my posts too, but then I got e-mail asking me if I was *sure* I didn't want to trade instead of sell, or vice versa.

Others experienced this too, and it's probably what led to this type of post occasionally showing up:

Spooky for sale, $25. NO trades. NONE! Don't even ASK! THIS MEANS YOU! For sale ONLY!! I mean it, send me e-mail ONLY if you are interested in BUYING ...

This might make the point to the audience, but it doesn't come across as an inviting offer to purchase a toy. Even a collectible toy.

Collectible Frenzy Debriefing

If Beanie Babies, Furbies, Pokémon, or any wildly popular collectible was your first online collecting experience, you definitely acquired a good education in buying, trading, and selling on the Internet during a frenzy. The basic ideas that you learned are universal to all types of collecting, and parts of this chapter will be a review. It will help you keep your skills honed.

You'll find, though, that the more you get into collecting fine art, figurines, or antiques, the more you'll realize the stark differences in the way collectors of other lines interact with each other.

For instance, my ads offering beanbag plush trades sometimes got this type of response:

Subject: ur post

what do u want 4 ur garcia? lmk asap!!!!!!!!

I usually didn't answer these. Isn't our language at least worth using correctly? Here is the same message, translated into something more English teacher-friendly:

Subject: Your Garcia trade offer

What would you accept in trade for your Garcia? Please let me know as soon as possible!

-Amy

That would have more likely gotten an answer. Just like bulletin board posts, nobody is expected to be a Pulitzer Prize contender when communicating on the Internet. Remember that how we write is how we represent ourselves, though. If people can't take the time to communicate in full sentences, they also might not take the time to carefully pack up and ship out an item to complete a trade.

This is one case where our perceptions of each other will determine how successful we are at our collecting hobby. When you first contact someone in e-mail, that message is the only medium you have to convey any kind of perception about yourself. Make it a good one.

You'll acquire valuable trading skills as you collect various items on the Internet. You'll no doubt develop additional skills the more you use the Internet for collecting. It's important to remember that some ads posted on the Internet reached a much larger audience than others, especially with a hugely popular item. A person making some kind of cyber-faux pas could just fade away and start over at another bulletin board dedicated to the same collectible.

With specialized collectible lines or items like coins, antiques, or stamps, your circles of fellow collectors probably will be much smaller. They'll want to get to know you and share ideas about your collective passion. Cyber-social blunders, even early ones, are often harder to live down in a smaller crowd.

☞Arranging Trades

Further on we'll explore the anatomy of a trade involving two collectors swapping pieces in the mail. This section covers the initial communication that you make with another collector to begin the process.

The best place to start is at the bulletin board. If you prefer Usenet, post your messages in the newsgroup dedicated to your favorite collectible line.

What To Post

When you post a message on the Internet requesting to trade certain collectible pieces, your message should contain everything a prospective trader needs to know about you and your item:

- What you have to trade
- What condition it's in
- What you're seeking in return
- The condition of the item you're seeking
- Your qualifications as a trader
- Assurance that you have the item in-hand
- What you expect from the other person
- How to contact you

> ➡️ Note: Never offer to trade or sell an item ⬅️
> that you don't actually have in your possession.
> You'll read more about that a little further on.

Here's an example of a bulletin board post that gets right to the point and leaves few unanswered questions:

I have a limited edition XYZ that's in mint condition in its original box. I only took it out to inspect it and then carefully stored it. I would like to trade it for a limited edition ABC in the same condition. I have references and will ask that you provide them as well. Please send me e-mail at sally@aloha.com if you are interested in trading. Thanks! – Sally

This post tells the reader what item Sally has, what condition it's in, what piece she's looking for, what condition she expects the piece to be in, and how anyone interested in trading can contact her.

It also clearly conveys that she's an experienced trader with e-mail addresses of people who can vouch for her honesty and that she expects to be able to check references before she'll agree to make the trade.

Caution is a good sign!

In keeping with advisable Internet practice, Sally does not include her last name. That information isn't necessary at this point. "Sally" might even be her Internet nickname! She'll exchange her personal information, such as her full name, address, and phone number, privately (in e-mail or over the phone) when the trade is finalized.

Responding To a Post

If something about a particular post strikes you as odd, unusual, or in any way objectionable, don't respond to it no matter what the offer is. If someone's post puts you off, there is usually a reason. Rely on your instincts before you respond to a "cold call" in e-mail.

On the other hand, if the post is clear and concise and makes you feel at ease about contacting the person, then go for it.

Posting Your Response

If you post a response to a trade offer, it might not be very effective. The person making the offer might not see it if he or she uses the bulletin board only occasionally.

However, the person making the original trade offer may specifically request you to post any responses to the offer. While this isn't the best way to arrange a trade, there could be a reason for this request:

- His or her service provider charges for every e-mail message received, so receiving many messages is costly.
- The trader/seller is in the process of changing e-mail service and doesn't want to miss your message.

If you post your response, you don't need to include a lot of detail. You can exchange that information privately later on. Your post can be very simple:

Sally, I'm interested in making this trade with you. Please send me e-mail and we can work out the particulars! – Charlynn (charlynn@email.com)

You can handle the rest of the correspondence by e-mail.

Sending an E-mail Response

This is the preferred way to respond to a trade offer. If you have the item the person is seeking and are interested in the one offered in exchange, then tune up the e-mail engine and get a message on its way.

When responding to a post in e-mail, refer to what the person offered. Avoid being too brief, as in this example:

Subject: Your post

Hey, I can trade with you! When can you ship?

The person receiving this e-mail might not know which offer you're referring to if he or she has several of them posted at the same time.

Here's an example of an e-mail message sent in response to Sally's post that will make her feel comfortable about considering the trade offer:

Subject: Your XYZ – ABC Trade Offer

Hi, Sally!

I noticed on the Bulletin Board that you have a limited edition XYZ that's in mint condition in its original box and you're interested in trading for a limited edition ABC. I was just about to post the same trade offer, only I'm looking for the XYZ! My ABC is in mint condition in its original box and I can ship it out as soon as we check each other's references.

If you haven't already made a trade agreement with someone, please let me know. I'd be happy to make this trade with you!

Charlynn

Notice that Charlynn reiterates the condition she wants the items in and assures Sally she has traded with other people who can give her a good reference. She also makes it clear that she intends to check Sally's references. Cautious traders are usually good traders.

Follow Up Your Post

Unless the bulletin board moves fast and your post falls far down on the list, you should post a follow-up. Let your readers know you have arranged a trade and the offer is no longer open.

Are You Sure?

If you want to buy an item posted as a trade, there's nothing wrong with asking the person if he or she would be interested in selling if no trade occurs. Request this a day or so after the person posts the trade. By then, he or she may be ready to make a deal.

Use Care When Revealing Your Inventory

You just bought a great, retired piece in mint condition at 75% off the original retail price. The shop was going out of business and the owners didn't know about the piece's value. You're so excited that the first thing you do when you get home is access the bulletin board to tell all your collecting comrades about your good luck.

But should you tell them?

If people know you acquired a great piece for a bargain, they may expect you to pass along your good luck. You may get some resistance from other collectors if you try to sell or trade your bargain-basement piece for its full current secondary-market value.

If your great find will become a treasured part of your collection, share the great news. But if you intend to trade using the secondary value as leverage, it's best to be discreet about how much, or especially how little, you paid for the piece.

Play Your Cards Close

Believe it or not, some collectors on the Internet keep track of your inventory. They might even share the information with another collector to "help out." I was quite taken aback the first time someone sent me e-mail offering to trade for one of my collectibles. She knew I had it because I had posted about buying wonderful retired pieces at retail in an Arizona gift shop. An exciting find for me became a tally on someone's inventory sheet. On the other hand, if I didn't want the information known by others, I shouldn't have mentioned it on the Internet.

Since knowledge is power, the knowledge you keep to yourself about your trading inventory allows you more of an advantage when making deals with other collectors.

During the Beanie famine of 1997, I was lucky enough to trade some of my extra current Beanies for a retired Radar the bat. At the time, Radar had a secondary value of three times what the current Beanies® had cost. What a bargain for me!

I mentioned my luck to another collector from whom I was about to purchase a Canadian Maple the bear. I was in for a surprise when Maple arrived. Instead of money, he now wanted my extra Radar in trade. Since I needed Maple for my collection, he had me over a barrel. Had I never told him about my extra Radar, I could have paid cash for Maple and held onto Radar as the secondary-market value continued to climb.

Be Specific About What You're Offering

If you reveal too much about what you have available for trade, someone might ask you to surrender a prized extra piece. Don't let anyone talk you into making a trade that isn't what you originally wanted.

Let's say you and another collector have pieces that you'd like to trade with each other. His one piece is worth three of yours, so you offer the following in trade for his piece:

Item A, Item B, plus a choice of either Item C or Item D

You don't mind giving up Item A and Item B, but you don't want to give up both Item C and Item D. To keep Item C or D for yourself, you offer him a choice of either one.

In the process, though, you've revealed that you have both Items C and D available. If he needs both, you're likely to get this counteroffer:

Item A, Item C, and Item D

You must now make the choice of carrying out a trade that isn't in your best interest, or of not agreeing to the trade and not getting the piece you hoped for in return.

A better strategy is to find out what the other person seeks. Then, decide if you should include Item C or Item D in the trade offer without revealing you have both. Be as specific as possible about your offer when trading multiples of pieces, or you may end up kicking yourself later.

> ➡ Note: Be wary of prospective traders ⬅ who insist you list your whole available inventory before they'll commit to a deal. They're probably taking notes.

Build a Dependable Circle of Traders

If you've made a successful transaction with someone, there's no need to recheck the person's references if you trade again. Checking references is an important step in the process, but it certainly speeds things up if you don't have to do this.

Some collectible companies distribute their items sporadically in different areas, so it pays to have a "trading relationship" with collectors in other regions. They can get pieces for you that aren't available in your area, and trade for pieces you find that they can't acquire.

If the collectible line contains special pieces available only in certain countries (like the Harmony Kingdom "Gobblefest" event piece variations for the US, Canada, and England), mutual trading with a collector in another country will benefit both of you.

Establishing a circle of trading friends you can trust takes much of the worry out of trading collectibles through the mail. The newly acquired pieces may then have a special meaning for you, since your Internet friends helped you add them to your collection.

☞The Anatomy of a Collectible Cyber-Trade

If you're making an Internet trade with someone you don't know, there is a right way to do so. The wrong way would be to leave out any of the steps. If you take shortcuts, you may leave yourself open to being the victim of a bad trader.

When you follow the steps, you do everything you can to protect your investment and build your collection.

Let's assume you just saw a bulletin-board post by someone named Randy, with whom you have never dealt before. You're interested in his offer. Here's how to carry out the transaction, step-by-step:

1. Send Randy e-mail telling him you're interested in his trade offer. Include details about the piece or pieces that you have to trade. Ask if he's interested in trading with you and if so, ask him to include the e-mail addresses of at least four people with whom he has recently traded. Confirm that he's an adult.

2. Randy returns your e-mail, saying he's willing to trade with you. He includes four e-mail addresses of people who can provide a reference for him, assures you that he's over 18, and agrees not to accept another trade offer for his item until you

have had time to check his references. Randy asks for the e-mail addresses of four people he can contact to get a reference for you.

3. You send Randy the names and e-mail addresses of your four references.

4. E-mail all four of his references, telling them that you're about to trade with Randy Jones at randyj@email.com and would like to know about their past transactions with him.

5. You receive e-mail from all four of Randy's references telling you they had no problems with him whatsoever and to go ahead and trade with confidence.

6. Confirm the trade with Randy in e-mail, and include your shipping address and phone number. Ask what day would be the best for both of you to ship your items.

7. Randy confirms he's heard from your references and agrees to make the trade with you. He includes his shipping address and phone number and tells you he can ship your item on Thursday.

8. You ship your items to each other on Thursday.

9. E-mail Randy and let him know you shipped his item.

10. You receive e-mail from Randy telling you he shipped your item.

11. E-mail Randy to let him know the item he sent arrived in satisfactory condition, and you are pleased with your trade. Offer to be a reference for him in the future.

12. Randy lets you know he received the item you sent, and he's satisfied that the trade went well and offers to be a reference for you in the future.

Sound Good?

This trade went smoothly. It would be great if they all went that way. On Cyber-Planet Web, however, unforeseen things sometimes happen and you need to know how to deal with such problems if they arise. For instance...

No References

Perhaps Randy hasn't traded through the mail before, and therefore has no references to provide you. In this case, you can do one of three things:

1. Tell him you'd prefer not to make the trade.
2. Ask him for the names and e-mail addresses of four people

> who can vouch that he's an honest person who will honor the trade.
>
> 3. Send a few more messages back and forth and try to get to know him well enough to decide whether you want to proceed on good faith with the trade anyway. Randy deserves a chance.

How you want to proceed here depends on how well you trust your instincts to guide you. Here are some things to consider:

- Is the tone of Randy's e-mail personable? Does he write like an adult? If you find out he's less than 18 years old, pay special attention to the next section.
- Does Randy understand that you're cautious, and appear cooperative?
- Does he seem equally apprehensive about *you?* Remember that this is a good sign.

Suppose you don't have any references. If that's the case, you can offer the same information you'd expect from a person who couldn't provide references either. Whether the prospective trader agrees to carry out the trade largely depends on how you come across in your communication.

> ➡️ Note: If you're a regular at an online ⬅️ auction site, you can refer a prospective trader to your user feedback file in addition to providing references. You'll read more about online auction site feedback files in Chapter 6.

He's Under-age

Many children are into collecting and make successful trades by contacting people in e-mail and sending items through the mail. There is absolutely nothing wrong with trading with kids as long as both parties send items in the agreed-upon condition.

However, before you trade, sell to, or buy a collectible item from a minor, confirm the transaction with his or her parents, a guardian, or an adult sibling. It's never a good idea to conduct a trade before getting the approval from an adult supervising the child's end of the transaction. Make this contact on the telephone so you can verify an adult is involved and secure permission to trade with the youngster.

Normally, the adult supervising the child's trade will want to check you out, too. Be sure to cooperate.

No Response from a Reference

Suppose you get three favorable responses about Randy, but the fourth person never answers your e-mail. Then what?

People get busy, go on vacation, change their e-mail addresses, or sometimes just don't feel like turning on their computers for awhile. In cases where one out of four references does not respond to your request, you can either ask the trader for another reference or go by the adage that "two out of three ain't bad."

He Doesn't Have the Item Yet

If you find out Randy doesn't yet possess the item he's offering to send you (perhaps he's waiting to receive it from another trade), cancel the trade and ask him to contact you when he actually has the item. You can renegotiate the trade then.

You definitely don't want the headache of learning that the item he was supposed to send you is hung up in the postal service somewhere, while other trading opportunities whiz past you.

Likewise, never negotiate a deal that involves an item you don't yet have. If the item doesn't arrive when you expect it to, you'll endure endless hassles.

You Can't Ship the Item On Time

If you're unable to get to the post office on the scheduled shipping day, contact Randy immediately and let him know about the delay. If he hasn't mailed his item yet, he can hold off until you're ready to ship. If he already shipped his item, offer to send your item via express or overnight service. He might tell you not to worry about it but at this point, it's his call.

Wimps Need Not Apply!

Notice that I don't suggest you ask the other person to send his item first to avoid the risk of not having your trade returned. In every trade involving two people mailing collectibles, both parties should send their items on the *same day*.

It might be tempting to wait and see if the other person honors the trade, but it's not fair to do this to someone. If something about the person causes you uncertainty, don't agree to the trade.

If a person makes such a request of you, say no. Why should you bear most of the risk associated with the trade? Since your references came through with good reports, you are no less worthy of trust than anyone else.

The practice of delaying shipment until you receive your end of the trade is called *wimp-trading*. This is extremely poor Internet practice. If someone doesn't ship an item to you until receiving yours, never trade with that person again and be sure to explain why.

Wimp-trading can set you up for a scam. The bad trader buys extra time by telling you this is her first trade and she's scared. She asks you to send your item first, and then makes an excuse for not shipping the item the day yours arrives. You allow a little more time to pass before you start to get suspicious. When you finally realize you're a victim, she canceled the e-mail account, abandoned her mailbox-hosting service, and disappeared.

Since collectible trading on the Internet happens in an atmosphere of mutual respect and trust, collectible communities quickly blackball wimp-traders. Offenders find it very difficult to do much trading with other collectors once word gets out.

Keep Good Records

Maintain a record of what you sent, the date you shipped it, what you're supposed to get in return, and the date you received it. This will keep track of your trades if you have several in progress. It will also help you remember a specific transaction if you need to provide a reference for the person in the future.

Here's an example of how you can keep track of trades:

Name, Address & e-mail:	Their Item:	My Item:	Date I Sent Mine:	Date I Got Theirs:	Trade Again?
Laurie Martin Canton, IL laurie@email.com	Reginald's Gourd Costume	Binkey's Acorn Costume	May 1	May 3	Yes
Nancy Guhr Raytown, MO nancy@email.com	1996 Precious Moments Member Kit	1996 Boyd's Member Kit	May 5	May 8	Yes
Carrie Whiner Portland, VA proveit@email.com	MWT Cubbie	MWT Teddy	May 9	May 22	No!! Postmark May 20
Lynn Berger Brooklyn, MN lynn@email.com	One-Mouse Open Sleigh	1998 CT NALED piece	May 10	May 14	Yes

Figure 5-1. Personal Record of Trades

Since Laurie, Nancy, and Lynn sent their trades on time, you noted in your record that you'd trade with them again. There's no need to recheck their references next time, and you can provide good references for them.

Notice, however, that Carrie's trade took 12 days to arrive at your house. Carriers can and do delay packages, so go by the post-mark date to determine if the item shipped on time. Carrie's package was postmarked May 20, so you can rule out any postal delay — she wimp-traded you!

As your record indicates, you won't trade with her again.

> ➡ Note: Save your trading records indefinitely. ⬅
> You may need to refer to them. If you plan on making a lot of trades, it's difficult to remember details like the dates and the exact items traded without good records.

General Trading Guidelines

When trading collectibles through the mail with people you don't know, here's a reminder list:

- Never ask the person to send his or her item first, nor agree to send yours first. Mutually decide on a date to ship.
- Ensure that you both have the items in your possession and can ship them out right away.
- Exchange daytime and evening phone numbers.
- Always check references if you never traded with the person before. Asking for references beforehand is a lot easier than trying to track down a trade later.
- When people respond to your request for references, compare the writing style. Is it similar enough to be the same person? Remember that free e-mail is available all over the Web. Some service providers even let you have several different e-mail names on one account. If a person gives you references that are all @aol.com or @hotmail.com, you might want to ask for different ones.
- Save all e-mail associated with the trade in case any questions arise.
- Keep a photograph or detailed description of the item you sent the person.
- Stay in communication with the person until the trade is complete and answer e-mail promptly.
- Don't get annoyed if the person seems overly cautious of you. This is the best sign you have that the person is honest and plans to make good on the trade.
- Be wary of any suspicious-sounding requests, such as a request that you label the package "gift" or actually gift-wrap

it to avoid taxation. This might be used against you if you need to file a claim.

- You can call off the trade up until the day you both agreed to ship the items.
- Insure the items if you mutually agreed to do so.
- Save all shipping and insurance receipts.
- If the item you were to have sent the other person was damaged or lost before you could cancel the trade, phone or send e-mail explaining the situation as soon as possible. Return the package you receive from your trader unopened. Pay any return postage fee.
- Remember that you are responsible for the item until it reaches its destination. Pack it securely.
- Keep a record of your trades.

Once you get going with your cyber-trading and develop a system for shipping and receiving trades, things get a lot easier because you gain instincts about people that may help you avoid bad situations.

Over time and with experience, you can tell a lot about people just by what they say and how they say it in e-mail.

Identifying a Potential Good Trader

You might wonder why I'm putting this information into a book for anyone to read. After all, if the bad traders know what we'll be looking for, they can act as if they're good traders so they can scam us, right?

I don't think it's that easy. If a person has ill intent, it will usually peek through in some way if you know the signs. The more you communicate with people who are putting up a front, the more likely you are to catch them in the act unless, of course, the bad trader is brilliantly sinister.

Unfortunately, some people do manage to scam others out of valuable collectibles and money. Luckily, they're few and far between. After making more than 300 successful collectible trades with people I've known only from the Internet, I never encountered any of them.

Remember that far more trades work out than don't. If you know in advance what types of people to avoid, the odds favor successful trades.

An honest trader will:

- Appear cautious of you.
- Ask for and check your references.

- Make a point of getting your address right.
- Want to speak to you on the phone before agreeing to trade.
- Mention a preferred method of shipping.
- Be willing to negotiate.
- Show flexibility with the shipping date.
- Have a sense of humor.
- Add a personal touch, like mentioning she can't ship until Thursday because of her kid's recital on Wednesday.
- Mention work, family, or something else indicating that he or she is a nice normal person with a life and not some sociopath.

The idea is to look for signs that your prospective trader is an honest person who will make good on the trade. The more you communicate, the more comfortable you'll feel as the trade progresses.

Of course, there's the other side of the coin. As with any situation where you venture into the unknown, watch for red flags.

Bad Trader Warning Signs

I ran an Internet bad trader list for six months. Since I investigated every situation before posting a name on the list, I asked everyone who sent me the name of a bad trader to include a detailed account of the situation.

As I read their stories, I noticed that in almost every case, some sign could have been recognized as a red flag of warning. Sometimes people don't realize they reveal their intentions through their behavior.

If you know what to look for, you can avoid dealing with bad traders. Here are some of their warning signs:

- They give you their address right away but don't seem as concerned about getting yours.
- They provide you with a pager number instead of an actual telephone number.
- They become hostile if you ask too many questions.
- They don't want to talk to you on the phone, or the phone conversation leaves you feeling uncomfortable about trading with them.
- They want to stay anonymous and ask that you address the package to Mrs. Doe (or something similarly generic) claiming that "it will get there just fine."
- They ask you to write the word "gift" on the outside of the

package or send the item wrapped up like a birthday present.
- They avoid saying anything about themselves.
- They don't offer any references and don't check yours.
- If they do provide references, the responses seem written by the same person.
- They don't "sign" their e-mail messages by ending them with their name.
- Their address is obviously not a residence. Be wary of mailbox-hosting locations.
- They avoid answering questions about the condition of the item they're sending you.
- They seem to care more about how soon you can ship than what might be going on in your life to necessitate a later ship date.
- They don't care about the quality of your mutual communication. Their messages are short and sometimes downright rude, like:

> Subject: [none]
>
> well do we have a deal or not when can u send it i need it now

- They ask you to send your item first and promise to send theirs after they get yours.
- They don't inquire about a glaring error in your address, like only four numbers in your zip code or a missing state or province.
- Their offer is too good to be true.
- They insist they're adults but their writing gives them away as children.
- They just don't seem very nice.

Now for the disclaimer: not all of these are necessarily warning signs. There are, of course, a few exceptions and points to ponder:

- Certainly not all people who use mailbox-hosting services are bad traders. Nonetheless, be wary of those services. Mailbox-hosting services provide people with a street address, and an apartment or suite number represents the box number.
- Not everyone is a fast and accurate typist who can send detailed e-mail messages. The person should at least "sign" his or her e-mail.

- The person might genuinely fear giving out too much informa- tion to a stranger. You can try to ease the tension by exhibiting the good trader signs we talked about unless you don't feel comfortable about the situation. In that case, cancel the trade.
- The person might not be fluent in your language or may have a learning challenge that impairs spelling and grammar.

As I'm sure you can tell, it's important to communicate when you consider trading with someone. You have the right to protect your investments and you're under no obligation to trade with a person if you don't want to.

Remember that you probably can't stop a bad trader, but you can avoid dealing with one. If three or more warning signs are present, or if you feel even the least bit apprehensive about the situation, you should simply tell the person that you'd rather not conduct the trade and don't correspond any further.

What About Post Office Boxes?

Though some individuals are wary of sending something to a PO box, this can be the safest method. People with PO boxes are less likely to cheat because the U.S. Postal Service will get involved in cases of suspected mail fraud, especially where one of their boxes is concerned.

When I started doing a lot of trading through the mail, I rent- ed a post office box so my packages didn't sit outside until I got home. There's less chance of weather damage or of the packages walking off.

When Things Go Wrong

This is by far my least favorite section of this chapter to write. After going on for page after page about how you can pro- tect yourself by identifying and not dealing with bad traders, I have to warn you about things that can happen if you're not careful.

Of course, this could help reinforce the need to keep your guard up and take as little risk as possible. Here is what may happen oth- erwise, along with some counteractive measures:

- **Person does not return the trade** – Since you kept in con- tact with the person after you sent out your item (right?), you need to *stay* in contact. Don't let a day pass without telling the person either in e-mail or by a phone call that the item still hasn't arrived. If this is just a lazy or disorganized person, your daily contact will convey in no uncertain terms that you want your item *now*. Whatever you do, don't lose contact with the person. The longer you're out of touch, the more likely it is that you'll never receive your trade.

- **Person claims the item you sent was damaged, and then sends you a different one back** – This occasionally happens with items that can chip or bend, causing a decrease in value. One way to ensure the person returns your item is to mark it in some way that will not void the mint status of the piece. With plush toys, sew in a thin colored thread that you can see only if you part a seam. On figurines, make a small dot in an inconspicuous place that you can detect only under a black light. Many people discreetly mark and photograph their pieces to safeguard against this kind of scam.

- **Person claims he or she never received your trade** – Contact the post office or carrier and request that they initiate a trace on the item. You may want to use registered or return receipt mail, where the recipient has to sign for the package. If someone else signs for the package once it reaches its destination, that isn't your concern.

- **Person doesn't send the correct item** – Contact the person immediately and explain that the item you received isn't the one stated in your agreement. Ask him or her to send the correct one in the next day's mail, and once you receive it send back the first item. Since the other person made the error, the burden of risk isn't yours.

- **Person sends a non-mint item after describing it as mint** – Contact the person immediately to reverse the trade because the item you received is not in the agreed-upon condition. If the person refuses, then you have to decide if the condition of the item is bad enough to warrant filing a mail fraud claim with the postal service.

Steps You Can Take

Too much time has passed since you were to have received an item from someone. You tried sending e-mail but the reply indicates the e-mail account is no longer active, or you never receive a reply at all. Nor can you reach the person by phone.

What can you do? Several things:

- If you're a regular user of a bad trader list, send the person's name and a description of the incident to the individual who maintains the list. Sometimes this person can send the offender an e-mail message or make a phone call that guarantees a response.
- If you can trace the address to a mailbox-hosting service (like Mailboxes USA), notify them that someone has committed fraud using the service. Mailbox-hosting services can immediately stop delivery to that particular box and return all incoming mail.
- If the address was for a U.S. post office box, call that city's post office and report the person who committed mail fraud using one of its boxes. The USPS takes these claims very seriously. According to Joan, my favorite Warrenville postal worker, "USPS inspectors can be more intense than the IRS if you commit mail fraud."
- Contact the police department in the offender's city and ask to file a report. If the police won't make a report, they might be able to tell you what other action you can take.

Your Legal Rights

The best resource for information is Internet Fraud Watch at www.fraud.org/ifw.htm. This is a good place to learn how to protect yourself from fraud resulting from an Internet transaction.

The Internet Fraud Watch was launched in March 1996, enabling the National Fraud Information Center (NFIC) to expand its services to include situations occurring on the Internet. Its goal is to help people recognize the difference between legitimate and fraudulent Internet promotions, and to report suspected fraud to the appropriate law-enforcement agencies.

NFIS's Web site contains information about the organization, an online incident report form, and valuable Internet-based trading information, such as:

- Basic Internet tips
- Credit card safety online
- Pyramid schemes and illegitimate multilevel marketing
- Scholarship scams

Consumers can contact Internet Fraud Watch by calling the NFIC hot line at 800-876-7060.

☛Trading Brokerages

When you conduct sales and trades with people you meet online, certain resources exist on the Internet to offer you peace of mind if the antiques or collectibles you're dealing with are of considerable value.

All three of these services are types of trading brokerages, also known as *escrow* or *verification services,* that act as a third party during transactions that involve two people sending items to each other for a trade. Alternately, if you're buying an item from someone you know only from the Internet, these services are useful if you've never dealt with the seller before and you have no way to verify his or her previous transactions with others.

> ➡ Note: Escrow services usually aren't necessary ⬅ if you transact through online auction sites. You can read more about these services in *Collector's Guide to Online Auctions.*

Verification and Authentication

A verification and authentication service specializes in examining a collectible item or antique using special criteria before the piece changes hands during a transaction.

The seller sends the item to the service, where it's unpacked and examined by a specialist. When you hear word from the service that the item is valid, you can send payment to the seller. The service forwards the item to you after the seller receives your payment.

Someone who is a well known and trusted expert in a certain collectible line or type of antique might offer this service, for a fee. When a rare item or variation is involved, particularly one that's often misidentified or counterfeited, third-party verification can be an invaluable service.

An expert can let you know if the seller described the item accurately. You can have a few different services performed.

Grading

This determines the physical condition of an item. Given the frequent misuse of the term "mint," a verification service can distinguish mint from "poor quality" and the categories in between. The actual grading system depends on the item. For example, trading cards grade from A1 to F1; coins grade from Poor to Perfect Uncirculated.

Collectibles have grading systems too, including mint, mint in package, collector quality, near mint, slightly imperfect, damaged, or fake. An expert can verify the quality and/or authenticity of the item before forwarding it to the buyer.

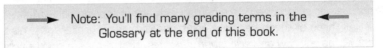

Note: You'll find many grading terms in the Glossary at the end of this book.

Authentication

Authentication relies on the expertise of whoever performs the service. Someone with the right training can easily detect counterfeits from subtle details. If you need an item authenticated before you agree to purchase it, rely on someone you know or an expert with references.

Sometimes a specialist can authenticate a collectible item that's part of a line, especially if there are known fakes on the market, but not always. Marking or signing an item as authentic may require the services of company representative.

Appraisals

An appraiser estimates an item's value using a variety of methods, including examining the item with a trained eye, or estimating the value based on recent sales for the same or similar pieces. An appraised value is usually accurate only at the time of appraisal and for a short time afterwards.

Variation Authentication

In Chapter 3, we discussed item variations. Only someone very familiar with the line, like a seasoned collector who owns the oddity, can authenticate a genuine variation. This is an important service if there are unofficially altered versions turning up on the market.

Clearinghouse Services

Some collectors perform clearinghouse services by listing antiques or collectibles for sale on a Web site. The buyer sends the money to the clearinghouse, who then tells the item's owner to ship it to the buyer. When the buyer receives it in satisfactory condition, the clearinghouse sends payment to the owner of the piece, minus a service fee.

This differs from escrow in that the buyer is actually viewing a classified ad on a Web page.

"Where Do I Find a Verification Service?"

Collector's Universe offers links to their grading services. You can reach the main site at www.collectors.com.

You can also search for "Verification Service" or "Authentication and Grading" with any Internet search engine.

Here are a few verification sites where you can learn more about their services:

Uniform Resource Locator	Company Name
www.isa-appraisers.org	International Society of Appraisers
www.beckettgrading.com	Beckett Grading Services
www.sgccard.com	Sportscard Guaranty Card Grading
certifiedsports.com	Certified Sports Authentication, Inc.
www.psacard.com	Professional Sports Authenticator
www.pcgs.com	Professional Coin Grading Service
www.realbeans.com	Real Beans

⟹ Note: I have not personally used any of ⟸ these sites. By listing them here, I'm shortening your search time – not endorsing the services. Research any online verification and authentication service you consider using.

Before you use any private verification or authentication service, ask for the e-mail addresses people who used the site before. Ask these experienced users what they thought of the service.

Internet Trader Lists

If you do an Internet search for "good trader list," the search engine will probably return 50 links. Some Web sites contain lists of good traders for all different collectible lines. Some claim to cover the whole Internet. People who maintain these lists invite others to submit names of those with whom they've made successful property trades via the Internet. You can do a search for "bad trader list" and get a slightly smaller return.

You're probably thinking, "Gee, she goes through all this and then tells us we can find the names of good and bad traders right on the Web."

Yes, you can find lists containing the names of good and bad traders on the Web for some of the more popular collectible lines. It's not true, however, that the information they contain is completely accurate.

Good trading should be expected. It's nice to see Web sites centered around a warm, positive theme, but very little is done to verify good trader lists. After all, who needs to verify good reports?

I've seen good trader lists abused too many times to consider recommending them as a dependable resource. Some of them attempt control by requiring that three different e-mail addresses must submit a name before it's added to the good-trader list. This doesn't mean three people, just three different e-mail addresses.

Since free e-mail accounts can be established in minutes, what's to keep someone from setting up three e-mail accounts and sending in his or her own recommendation for the good trader list? Absolutely nothing.

If that isn't enough, one good trader site actually *tells* people they can submit their own names that way. Like, just tell me three different times that you're honest, and you can have the combination to my safe and access to all my valuables.

I don't think so.

If a bad trader wants to establish an aura of credibility, an Internet good-trader list provides a quick and easy way to do it. For securing information about a potential trader, good-trader lists are useless.

> ➡️ Note: Some of the so-called "good trader" ⬅️
> and "bad trader" lists that still appear on the Internet are now "cobweb" sites — badly out of date and long overdue for being deleted. Be sure to check when the page was last updated.

Regularly updated lists of bad traders, however, do serve some purpose.

Bad Trader Lists

> ➡️ Note: There are fewer bad trader lists on the ⬅️
> Internet because they require more work to maintain than good trader lists.

My former bad trader list started as a list of problematic traders that one person put together with the help of her own circle of collecting buddies. She originally sent the list to her trading friends via e-mail. Once word got out about the list, she got many requests for it.

I received a Beanie Baby with a missing swing tag from someone and much too hastily sent her name to the keeper of the bad trader list. The same day the trader's name was added to the list, she contacted me apologizing profusely about the missing tag and assuring me that another Beanie in mint condition was on its way. Keep the one without the tag, she said.

I immediately contacted the list's keeper and requested that she remove the woman's name as soon as possible. She did, but unfortunately had e-mailed the list to about 40 people.

Since the list was just a plain-text file with no master copy, hundreds of copies flew through cyber-space with no way to tell which one was the most current version. Imagine how I felt when I saw this woman's name on the bad trader list weeks later.

What's more, imagine how *she* felt.

It was still necessary to warn other people about bad traders. Around the time this was happening, the famous "Christa" bad trader ring had a growing list of cyber-victims.

Christa and her numerous aliases arranged trades for retired Beanie Babies, making off with several thousand dollars worth of items and never returning one single trade. People needed warning.

Spinning a Web

The keeper of the list grew tired of receiving hate mail on her family's e-mail account. I can't say I blame her, but I still felt there should be some way to warn people about Christa and other bad traders.

I decided to maintain the list on the Web so there would only be one copy. This way, people would have one place to access the most updated information.

I found a Web site that offered free home-page space and transferred the text file to the Web directory I created. Next, I established an address with a free e-mail service to provide one point of contact for the list. I put the e-mail address right on the Web page, and included detailed instructions for how to submit a bad trader report.

In order for people whose names were on the list to tell their side of the story, I found a Web site that hosted guestbooks and added one to the bad trader page as a feedback board. Just for kicks, I added a counter to the page. I completed all of this in one evening and none of it cost me a single cent.

Late that night, when I knew Internet traffic in at least the United States would be low, I posted a message about the new bad trader list in the Ty guestbook and included the URL to the page.

Within one hour, the page counter jumped from zero to 400.

My Other Job

As the page counter continued to climb by at least 500 hits every 24 hours, I received a minimum of 20 messages daily from people reporting bad traders. Some had valid complaints, but others obviously wanted names put on the list to seek revenge for a personal vendetta. It was up to me to weed those out.

Before adding any names to the list, I investigated every situation. I dated each entry so I could remove names if I didn't receive more complaints within a certain time.

I also removed anyone's name who sent me e-mail asking me to do so. Because I was only going on he-said-she-said information, there was no other way to be fair. This also helped remove names added because of minor incidents or misunderstandings.

The list warned people about scams like the Christa ring. Since the big-time scammers didn't do much Websurfing except where their potential victims posted trade offers, they were completely unaware the list existed. I never once heard from any of them and the authorities eventually managed to apprehend a few.

As I read and answered e-mail, I was saddened by what was happening in cyber-trading land. Far too many people who were reporting bad traders had obviously allowed themselves to be set up. I had the difficult task of tactfully letting them know so it wouldn't happen again.

I spent as much as five hours every evening answering e-mail seeking my advice about trading collectibles. Though I didn't always have the answers they were looking for, I asked them to let me know how the situation worked out. Before long, I was able to compare situations and give practical advice about conducting safe trades.

I was happy when my intervention helped resolve an issue, even if the resolution involved both parties ultimately blaming *me*. As long as people completed their trades and names stayed off the list, I felt I'd served some purpose. On the other hand, did I really want to carve out my niche on the Internet as someone famous for screwing up?

That's when I had the idea to put all of the information I had gathered about good trading practices into one resource and make it available to as many Internet traders as possible.

Are the Lists Valid?

While good-trader lists are grossly unreliable, bad trader lists do serve some good in warning unsuspecting people about serious bad traders. Since quite often names are submitted to the bad trader list when an item is only one or two days overdue, the person maintaining the list must verify each situation and show what day the list was last updated. A well-maintained list can be very beneficial.

Checking a bad trader list before trading with someone you don't know is not a bad idea, as long as you don't rely on it completely. If you don't see the person's name on the list, this is not a sign to proceed with the trade, throwing caution to the wind. Refer to the advice in this chapter and always check the person's references.

If you see a serious-looking report, it's a good idea to tell the person you aren't interested in trading. If his or her references all report favorably, you might want to give the person a chance to explain what happened, especially if you have no way of knowing when the bad trader list was last updated.

After six months of managing the bad trader list, I finally handed it off to someone who was eager to help others resolve bad trader issues.

Meanwhile, I had a book to write.

☞Selling an Item

This type of transaction definitely poses less risk than trading. You have the goods; they send the money. You can initiate the sale offer the same way you would a trade, by posting on a bulletin board or in a Usenet newsgroup.

Your post should contain the following information:

- The item's name
- A description of its condition
- The condition of any packaging, tags, or included documents
- Your asking price for the piece
- Shipping and insurance costs if not included in the price
- How you expect payment, such as a money order, bank check, or cleared personal check
- How any interested buyers can contact you

Selling and trading both involve an element of risk, and you must know how to safeguard yourself against potential fraud. Keep in mind two rules when selling a collectible on the Internet:

1. *Always* wait until you receive the person's payment before you ship the item.
2. *Always* wait at least 10 business days for personal checks to clear the bank before you ship the item.

If you didn't know the buyer before you posted your item for sale, *never* ship until you've received the payment and any personal checks have cleared the bank. The statement "cleared personal check" in your post indicates you won't consider the payment valid until the check clears.

I've heard a few arguments that sending a payment for an item is just like trading, but this isn't true. When you trade item-for-item with someone, both of you are sending property and the risk is evenly proportioned.

When you sell, however, you have the property and the buyer must pay for it before taking ownership. Isn't this the way businesses operate? Why shouldn't you?

Some people are understandably afraid to send a payment through the mail to someone they don't know. This is a very valid concern, but if you are the seller, you already know that you're honest and that you'll send the item once it's paid for. It's the *buyer's* responsibility to determine if he or she can trust you, based on his or her perception of you during your e-mail or phone contact. Don't let anyone play on your sympathies when it comes to dollars, cents, and valuable collectibles.

Above all, *never* allow anyone to talk you into shipping an item so he or she can examine it before paying. As a last resort, offer a 3-day inspection period with a refund if the buyer isn't satisfied. Be sure both the item and the payment are not out of hand at the same time.

If someone tries to convince you to ship the item the same day he or she sends the payment, say no. You are not trading, you're selling, they're buying, and cash talks. Show me the money!

Types of Payment

The seller should let you know in advance of closing the deal which type of payment he or she prefers. Here are a few options:

- **Cash** – Discourage people from sending cash through the mail. There is no way to trace it if it's lost. If you receive cash through the mail as payment, include a receipt with the shipment. Retain a copy.
- **Personal check** – Accepting personal checks makes the transaction easier for the buyer and the seller usually receives the payment faster. As the seller, be sure to wait until the check clears the bank before shipping the item. This takes a minimum of 10 business days.
- **Bank check** – Most financial institutions will draw a bank

check for you in the amount you specify. There's usually a nominal fee. You pay for the bank check with cash or automatic account withdrawal.

- **Postal money order** – For a small fee, these are available at U.S. post offices and must be paid for with cash. You can cash them at any post office if you produce the required identification.
- **Other money orders** – Most work just like a bank check. You specify the check's amount and pay in cash along with a small fee. You can purchase money orders many places: currency exchanges, grocery stores, department stores, and even convenience shops.
- **Credit cards** – If the seller has a merchant account that accepts charge purchases, this is an excellent way to pay for the item since it protects both the buyer and the seller.

☞Packing and Shipping

This is just as important as any other step in arranging a sale or trade. If an item arrives damaged, everything else was a waste of time.

Use a box that's large enough to allow adequate packing material to cushion the item on all sides.

Remember that you're responsible for getting the item to the receiving location in the expected condition. When you pack it for shipping, make sure it's secure enough to withstand jostling.

It is far better to over-pack and possibly pay a little more for postage than to ship an item without adequate protection.

Preparing the Item

Getting an item ready for shipping is an important part of the buying, selling, and trading process. If the item has accessories, keep a written or photographic record of everything you send to the buyer or person receiving your trade. Here's an example of what you might include in the list:

- Original packaging
- Product documentation or certificates
- All necessary hardware, if the item must be re-assembled
- Assembly instructions
- Anything that came packaged with a collectible item, such as doll clothes and shoes (if it was part of the agreement)

- A book's dust jacket
- Any protective covering or casing you sold with the item

Keeping a record of what you send can also help safeguard you against fraud.

Marking Your Pieces

Be mindful of the *bait and switch* routine. An occasional unscrupulous buyer or trader might use your trade or sale offer to unload a flawed or damaged item. The person will buy an imperfect item at a discount and later buy an identical version in mint condition from you. When yours arrives in the mail, he or she will request to reverse the transaction, claiming the item you sent is damaged or flawed. He or she then "returns" the imperfect piece, keeping your nice one.

One way to protect yourself is to mark your item in some way that will not void the mint status of the piece. With plush toys, sew in a thin colored thread that you can see only if you part a seam. On figurines, pottery, or earthenware, make a small dot in an inconspicuous place that you can detect only under a black light. Scan the front and back of sports cards. Many people discreetly mark and photograph their pieces.

The bait and switch scam isn't that common, but it's still a good idea to protect yourself and keep your photos on file. This documents what you sent.

Packing Material

If it's breakable, wrap it securely in bubble wrap and secure it with packing tape. If the item has several parts, such as a lid and a base, wrap each one separately. They might take a long time to unwrap, but the buyer will be far more upset if the item is broken.

Nest the item in shock-resistant material. Line the bottom of the shipping carton with packing puffies, place the item on them, and cover it with puffies.

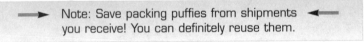
Note: Save packing puffies from shipments you receive! You can definitely reuse them.

If the item is bendable, be sure to secure it in some way so that it will not bend during shipment. If it's a figurine without a box, wrap it securely in bubble wrap, secure the wrap with tape, and nest it in plenty of puffies.

Most collectors who buy and trade through the mail have enough packing material around to last three lifetimes.

Adequate Cushioning

Get a shipping container big enough for the item, the product packaging, and plenty of packing puffies. Be sure the carton is large enough for the item to "float" in the center of all the packing.

Some folks will double-box extremely fragile items. Pack the item securely in one box, then float that box in a slightly larger box by surrounding it with more packing puffies.

Make sure the item can't jostle inside the container once it's sealed. The carrier won't stamp it "fragile" if something bounces around inside when the package is shaken.

Do I Mind If You Smoke?

It's your business if you smoke, but I'd rather not be able to tell when your package arrives. Cigarette, pipe, and cigar smoke has a way of permeating porous items, like fabric and packing material.

If you smoke, try to keep such items in a well-ventilated area so they don't set off the smoke detector when your buyer or the person you're trading with receives the package. I'm not trying to be politically correct about smoking; I just speak from unpleasant experience.

Don't Forget the Enclosures!

Here's a chance to promote good karma, and maybe make a new collecting friend, by enclosing a few other items with the shipment.

When you ship the item for a sale or trade, include a note with the following information:

- What item is enclosed
- What it's in exchange for, if it's a trade
- A note of thanks for making the trade or purchasing the item
- How the receiver can reach you if there are any problems (so the person doesn't have to rummage around for your phone number if he or she has to contact you right away)

Tape the box securely and address it clearly. If you insure the package, do so for the full current secondary-market value of the item. If necessary, mark it "fragile." The post office or carrier can mark the package for you.

Business Card or Brochure

Do you run a collectible business? If so, including a business card or brochure with your shipment is a great way to generate more sales. Your customer will see it when he or she is the most possibly satisfied with you — when the item arrives!

Nice Touches

One seller I buy from writes her shipping letters on homemade note cards. I save all of them. Another collectible dealer includes advertising novelties, such as a key chain or a pen bearing his business logo, with his shipments.

Just for kicks, I included a few unopened packs of Pez candy with some old Pez dispensers I shipped out. Something like that can be touching for some folks, especially those still leery of buying and trading things on the Internet.

Why not use this opportunity to put a little sunshine in someone's day?

A Word of Caution About Sending COD

It's not foolproof. As the seller, COD (cash on delivery) demands a lot more work from you than conventional shipping and puts most of the risk right back in your lap. Not only that, but it takes much longer for you to receive your payment and is a costlier way to ship.

United Parcel Service (UPS) doesn't accept cash for CODs. They will only take payment in the form of money orders, bank checks, or cashier's checks. The USPS accepts cash or personal checks for CODs.

Sending an item COD involves some serious disadvantages. For example, an unethical buyer can make the transaction difficult and costly for you:

- **Refuses to pay** – Lazy buyers sometimes request items sent COD so they have more time to decide about the purchase. If your buyer refuses to pay for the item, then you have to pay return postage.
- **Pays with a check** – If the carrier accepts a personal check for a COD and the check doesn't clear the bank, the buyer may disappear and any settlement claims with the carrier may take months.

All things considered, avoid sending items COD. Again, you know that you're an honest seller and if the buyer is worried that you won't send the item, then he or she should deal elsewhere. Look out for your own interests first.

Once you get used to effectively dealing with strangers on the Internet, it's time to try a more sophisticated method of buying and selling collectibles in cyberspace.

Chapter 6 — Going Once, Going Twice...

I always considered auctions scary. Whenever I think about what happens at one, I picture Rob Petrie bidding without realizing it and taking home something that he and Laura didn't want. That old *Dick Van Dyke Show* episode must have made an impression on me. Not until I accessed the Internet did I ever once bid on anything up for auction.

The Internet provides many user-friendly auction sites that allow collectors to bid on items from the privacy of their homes or offices without worrying that swatting a mosquito will lead to the untimely purchase of an old kitchen table.

In *Collector's Guide to Online Auctions*, I cover online auction sites and their use in managing your collections online. This chapter provides an introduction and overview of how the sites work and what to expect when you explore them for the first time.

After reading this chapter, you may decide to become a regular user at an auction site that caters to collectors. If so, I recommend that you read *Collector's Guide to Online Auctions*. Meanwhile, this book tells you plenty about some of the major auction sites that collectors will find interesting, plus the basics of buying and selling collectible items at online auction sites.

Internet auctions run like any other auction only without the fast talker up front haggling bids out of people. Someone puts something up for sale, and the person who offers to pay the most gets to buy it. The seller sends his or her address in e-mail to the high bidder, who mails in the payment. The seller then ships the merchandise to the buyer.

Collectibles and antiques are among the most popular items listed on Internet auction sites. This chapter covers online auction sites and how they operate.

- Popular auction sites
- How auction sites work
- Types of auctions
- How to bid on an item
- How to put an item up for auction
- User feedback

If you want to visit an online auction site, there are hundreds. The BidFind Web site at www.bidfind.com provides a comprehensive list of online auction sites where you can sell just about anything. This chapter includes a table listing the major online auction sites used for buying and selling antiques and collectibles.

☛Popular Auction Sites

Some companies run Internet auction sites to sell overstocked merchandise at discounted prices. Others let anyone participate and include huge item lists resembling online classified ads. To participate, you need to register with a site ID (some auction sites call it a handle, user name, or user ID) and a valid e-mail address. Also, be willing to provide some personal information. This typically includes your home (or shipping) address and a phone number.

Most online auction sites require you to be an adult who can form legally binding contracts in order to use the auction services. Others ask for a credit card number. Many sites assess a nominal listing fee and sales commission that's charged to your card; some sites use your credit card only to secure your bid.

You may want to verify that the site includes a statement assuring that it doesn't disclose your personal information to any outside party.

The major auction sites, such as eBay and Auctions.com, have strict rules about giving out personal user information. Without these restrictions, you might receive a lot of unwelcome mass mailings both at home and via e-mail.

> ➡ Note: E-mail sent to hundreds of people at ⬅ once for advertising is called *spam*. Spammers use e-mail addresses from stolen Internet lists, or they scan the Web for addresses. People who send spam pay very little for sending it and the ISPs are stuck processing it. If you respond to a spam message in any way (even to send a nasty-gram), the sender then knows there's a live person reading the message. Consequently, your e-mail address transfers to another, more valuable spam list.

Most auction sites forbid using personal user information for spam. Sending spam on the Internet is a sure gateway to unpopularity. Offenders usually find their cyber-mailboxes quickly filled with copies of site FAQs and not so cordial responses.

eBay

Launched in September 1995, the eBay auction site helps individual buyers and sellers, not large companies, sell items to one another over the Internet.

Seasoned Internet collectors know all about eBay. They lead the online auction business, with more than one million registered users and over 200 million completed auctions. The number will be larger when this book goes to print. In the time it took you to read this paragraph, about 95 new auctions started on eBay — it's *that* popular.

Each auction is assigned a consecutive serial number. When I last entered two auctions on eBay, the second auction's number was 441 numbers higher than the first one. I started them a little under one minute apart.

Information included on the site's "About eBay" page indicates that over 50 percent of the items listed on eBay are sold, which is apparently a better completion rate than any other electronic marketplace.

It costs around two dollars to start an auction. This can increase depending on what features you want for your auction. Auctions listed in featured categories, which come up first in search results, cost more to list. Featured listings that appear on the eBay home page are at premium rates.

Sellers pay an insertion fee of 25 cents to list an item that has a minimum bid under ten dollars, and 50 cents for items over that amount. The commission schedule is five percent of the sale amount up to 25 dollars, then 2.5 percent on the amount beyond that.

If your item doesn't sell, eBay returns your sales fee. If your item sells, the commission appears on your account. You can have up to ten dollars on your account or you can enter a credit card number that's retained on file. You then receive a statement of your account via e-mail.

The eBay Internet auction site receives more than 350 million hits each month. Suffice to say there's a tremendous amount of traffic on eBay. They were the first online auction site to use the peer-rating system, now known as feedback. Most other auction sites now also use a similar peer-rating system.

One of eBay's unique features is its "About Me" pages, where users can create something like a Web home page containing information they want other users to know, such as:

- Favorite Web links
- Currently running auctions
- Information about their business or livelihood
- Items they collect

Users can create and edit their About Me pages using any of several different formats.

For an additional charge, you can add your auction image to what eBay calls "The Gallery." Here, eBay presents a series of small pictures called *thumbnails,* listed by auction category. The photos appear in rows on numerous pages, ordered by the closing date of the auction. Potential bidders can browse the photos instead of looking at text versions of the listing or viewing the auctions one by one.

You can find eBay on the Web at www.ebay.com or look up the site representatives at the ICE shows.

Auctions.com

Auctions.com (www.auctions.com), formerly Auction Universe, is second only to eBay in terms of traffic. Its fee schedule and method of operation are very similar to eBay's. Membership is free. Listing an item for sale has a basic listing charge of 25 cents plus a 2.5 percent sales fee on the closing price.

Much like eBay, you register and establish a site ID and password. You have an initial account and if you exceed that amount, you must submit payment or a credit card number.

Auctions.com provides a flexible length of time for auctions to run, from one to 14 days. The auctions run with open-ended bidding. Auctions close at the scheduled closing time or five to 10 minutes after the last bid, whichever is later. As long as people are bidding within five minutes of each other, the auction doesn't end.

You'll find a very useful feature at Auctions.com — adjustable start and end times for auctions. You can schedule an auction to start and end at any time of the day. When you're entering the auction, the start time defaults to whatever time it is "now." You can adjust the time so the auction starts later.

If you attend an event that features Auctions.com's traveling road show, you can register and participate in one of their auctions right at the show. They also offer seminars on how to use the site.

CityAuction

City Auction (www.CityAuction.com) lets you browse live auctions in your own community. You can search for auctions listed by sellers in a specific radius relative to where you live.

Based in California, CityAuction is a user-friendly site. You'll find buying and selling rather simple. Their auction software is similar in concept and appearance to some of the other sites, so if you've bought or sold collectibles at an online auction site before, CityAuction will be even easier for you to use. For new users, there's also plenty of opportunity to learn about cyber-auctions at this site. CityAuction provides instructions for online listing and bidding.

CityAuction has some useful features. Sellers can designate their accounts as "merchant" or "private seller," so you know some key information about the seller before you bid. The Bidder Credit Card Requirement option allows sellers to accept credit card purchases.

Some of the other auction features you'll find are real-time countdown auction clocks, Falling Price listings, and Quick Win auctions. The site explains them all for you.

Other Online Auction Sites

Many auction sites operate on the Web; this table is only a sampling. You can use a search engine to find even more.

Uniform Resource Locator	Auction Site
auctions.amazon.com	Amazon.com Auctions
www.auctionaddict.com	Auction Addict
www.auctionanything.com	Auction Anything
www.auction2000.net	Auction Interactive 2000
www.auctions.com	Auctions.com
www.auctionware.com	AuctionWare
www.auctionworks.com	Auction Works
www.bidaway.com	BidAway
www.biddingtons.com	Biddington's
www.bidoncollectibles.com	Bid On Collectibles
www.BoxLot.com	Boxlot Online Auction
www.buffalobid.com	Buffalo Bid's Internet Auction
www.cityauction.com	CityAuction
www.collectex.com	CollectEx
www.collectibleonline.com	Collectible Online
www.collectit.net	Collectit.Net
www.comspec-marketing.com	Comspec Marketing
www.ebay.com	eBay
www.edeal.com	eDeal
www.ehammer.com	eHammer
www.ewanted.com	eWanted
www.global-auction.com	Global Auction Online
www.goldnage.com	Golden Age Auction
www.goldsauction.com	Gold's Auction
www.haggle.com	Haggle Online
www.interauction.com	interAUCTION
www.justglass.com	Just Glass
www.keybuy.com	Keybuy Auction House
www.liveauctiononline.com	Live Auction Online
www.ohioauction.com	The Ohio Auction & Classifieds
www.onewebplace.com	One Web Place
www.palmbeachauctions.com	Palm Beach Auctions
www.potteryauction.com	Pottery Auction
www.sellandtrade.com	SellAndTrade.com

```
www.sellathon.com . . . . . . . . .Sellathon Auction Services
www.sportsauction.com  . . . . . . . . . . . .Sports Auction
www.steinauction.com . . . . . . . . . . . . . .Stein Auction
www.up4bid.com . . . . . . . . . . . . . . . . . . . . .Up4Bid
www.utrade.com  . . . . . . . . . . . . . . . . . . . . .Utrade
```

➡️ Note: *Collector's Guide to Online Auctions* ⬅️
details the features available at all of these sites, and lists
many more auction sites of possible interest to collectors.

☛How Internet Auctions Work

Before you think about participating in any Internet auction, browse the site to get familiar with how it operates.

Read any information pages on the site:

- "Welcome" pages
- The FAQ
- Site guidelines
- Site tutorial
- Member services and help pages

If you can access current auctions as a guest (without a site ID and password), click on a few of them to see what they look like. Reload the page a few times to check for any bidding in progress. You're likely to see most bidding action when there are five or fewer minutes left on the clock.

If you've never used an auction site before, visit one and look around as much as possible. You should know your way around the site before you get started. Read all instructions before you bid or list an auction for the first time.

I made every attempt to present this material as generally as possible to cover the major auction sites. This section isn't a step-by-step instruction guide because auction sites vary. The guidelines here will familiarize you with the basic workings of most auction sites. If you encounter an auction site program that's different from what I describe here, refer to the instructions of that site.

Restrictions

You can't do certain things at online auction sites. Most sites contain strict policies to prevent users from conducting business that is illegal, unfair, or annoying for other users. This includes:

- Bidding on your own auction
- Selling illegal items or services
- Listing bogus auctions
- Refusing to honor sales or bids
- Calling back a bid
- Canceling an auction
- Building lists of user IDs for sending spam
- Shills

Most online auction sites take no responsibility for the sale or delivery of merchandise. They are simply a venue for a buyer and a seller. Though most have an e-mail address to which users can send site violation reports, they do not mediate if the buyer and seller cannot reach an agreement.

Some online auction sites, like eBay and Auctions.com, provide links to Internet third-party mediation services if anyone needs such resources to resolve an issue.

Registration

Before you can bid on items or start auctions, you must register at the site. You only need to register once, and it's free at most sites.

You're required to enter certain personal information that's maintained by the site in case someone needs to contact you. This information also puts the seller and buyer in contact when the auction closes.

Although the registration process varies from site to site, you can expect to provide the same type of information at all of them:

- E-mail address
- Site ID you'd like to use
- Full name
- Company name (if applicable)
- Street address
- City
- State or province
- Zip or postal code
- Country
- Daytime and evening phone numbers
- Fax number

At some auction sites, your e-mail address automatically becomes your site ID once you register.

Like many other registration processes on the Web, you might have to complete an online questionnaire. They usually include multiple-choice items you select with a mouse click. The people running the site want to know how you heard about it and how you plan to use it, plus your gender, marital status, education, household income, and other personal information. This section is usually optional.

Register Here to Bid and List Items!

Required Information	
E-mail address	
	Include your full e-mail name (name@email.com)
First and Last name	
Pick a User ID	
Street address	
City	
State	AL
Zip or Postal Code	
Phone number	
Optional Information	
Age	
Education	High School
Household Income	Under $25,000

Click here to Submit

Figure 6-1. Sample Registration Screen

Password

After you register, you need a password to participate. Some sites let you enter your own password, but others send you a temporary one in e-mail to use when confirming your registration. You can then change it to a password of your choice.

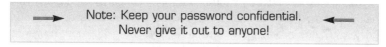
Note: Keep your password confidential. Never give it out to anyone!

Activate Your Registration

If the site sends your password via e-mail, it will include the URL for a page on which you must confirm your registration. Figure 6-2 shows a typical registration activation screen. You'll enter your site

ID and the password you received. Then you can change your password. Some sites require you to enter a new one right away.

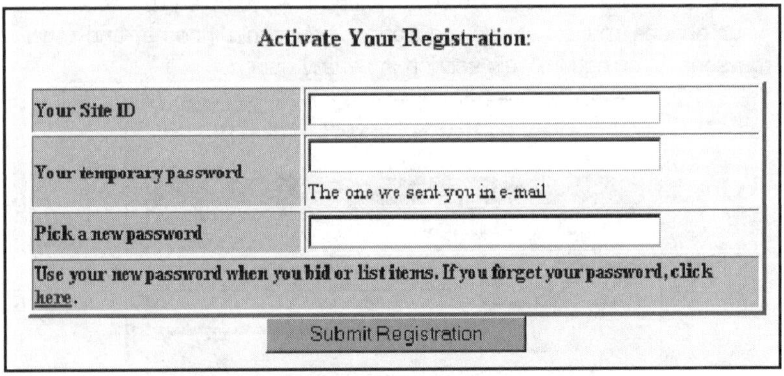

Activate Your Registration:

Your Site ID	
Your temporary password	
	The one we sent you in e-mail
Pick a new password	

Use your new password when you bid or list items. If you forget your password, click here.

Submit Registration

Figure 6-2. Registration Activation Screen

Most sites have a terms and conditions agreement and a button to click to indicate you understand and will adhere to the policies at that auction site. This procedure activates your user account.

Search

Once you're a registered user, you can buy and sell items at the site. Since the more popular auction sites have thousands of active auctions running at once, most have a built-in search function. The results of your search list as a new page in your browser.

You can search for items in different ways:

- Browse particular categories and sub-categories
- Enter a keyword search
- Search by seller
- Search by auction number
- Search completed auctions

Most Internet auction sites categorize listings by item type. This helps narrow down searches. When you browse a particular category, you'll see all listings in that category. The groupings, however, are usually very broad. If you're looking for a certain type of Czech vase and you search for the word "vase," you may see most of the art glass category. It would be quicker to narrow down your search by adding the word "Czech."

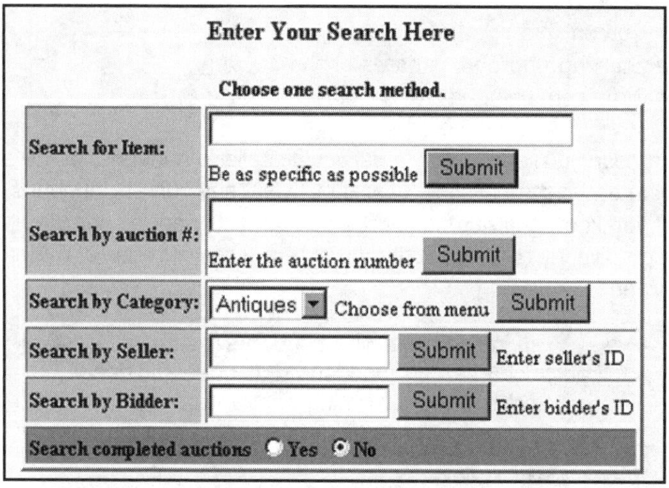

Enter Your Search Here

Choose one search method.

Search for Item:	_____ Be as specific as possible [Submit]
Search by auction #:	_____ Enter the auction number [Submit]
Search by Category:	[Antiques ▼] Choose from menu [Submit]
Search by Seller:	_____ [Submit] Enter seller's ID
Search by Bidder:	_____ [Submit] Enter bidder's ID
Search completed auctions ○ Yes ◉ No	

Figure 6-3. Typical Auction Search Screen

Auction sites have a feature that works like an Internet search engine except its index is limited to auctions in progress. You can type keywords into a search box and receive a page of all current listings that match any part of the text you entered.

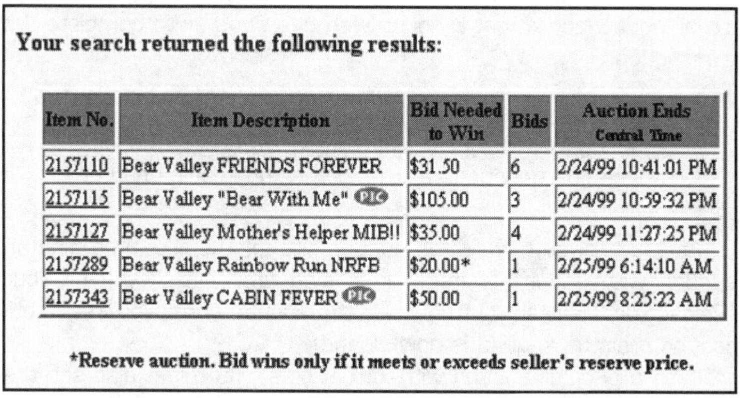

Your search returned the following results:

Item No.	Item Description	Bid Needed to Win	Bids	Auction Ends Central Time
2157110	Bear Valley FRIENDS FOREVER	$31.50	6	2/24/99 10:41:01 PM
2157115	Bear Valley "Bear With Me" 🖼	$105.00	3	2/24/99 10:59:32 PM
2157127	Bear Valley Mother's Helper MIB!!	$35.00	4	2/24/99 11:27:25 PM
2157289	Bear Valley Rainbow Run NRFB	$20.00*	1	2/25/99 6:14:10 AM
2157343	Bear Valley CABIN FEVER 🖼	$50.00	1	2/25/99 8:25:23 AM

*Reserve auction. Bid wins only if it meets or exceeds seller's reserve price.

Figure 6-4. Sample of Listings Returned by Search

A typical page of listings shows the following information:

- Auction number
- Title of the auction
- Type of auction
- Whether the auction contains a photo

- Current bid price
- Starting and ending dates of the auction
- Time remaining in the auction

In case you're following a particular seller's auctions, some sites let you enter the person's user ID to view any current auctions.

If you know the number of the auction you want to check on, you can go directly to that auction by entering the number in the space provided.

> ➡️ Note: Some online auction sites have ⬅️
> advanced search functions that offer additional
> criteria for searching auction listings.

Auction Duration

When listing an auction, the seller may decide how long it should run. Common auction lengths are seven, five, or three days. Some auction sites run auctions for up to 14 days, while others let you list auctions that last several hours or less.

The moment an auction begins, a clock starts. Users can enter bids only up until the last second before the auction closes. Then the auction is over and bidding ends. Both the buyer and seller receive e-mail notification to get in touch with one another to complete the transaction.

> ➡️ Note: Some auction sites keep auctions open ⬅️
> as long as there's active bidding. You'll read about
> open-ended auctions a little further on in this chapter.

As you browse through an auction site for the first time, find an auction with under a minute of bidding time left. If you hit your "Reload" or "Refresh" button when the auction ends, you'll see notification that the auction is now closed.

If it's a popular auction with lots of bids, you might also see the high bid increase during that last minute. Most bidding happens in the last hour of the auction.

Bidding

When you bid on an item, it means you agree to pay that amount in hopes of offering more than any other bidder. You have a "contract" with the seller that's upheld if you're high bidder when the auction ends.

Once you enter a bid, most auction sites send e-mail messages confirming your status at specific times during the auction:

- Each time you enter a bid
- When you're outbid by someone else
- When the auction closes
- If you're the high bidder at the end of the auction

If you win the auction, the site sends you and the seller an e-mail notification. It's then up to both of you to complete the transaction offline.

Bidding History

During the auction, users can usually see the number of bids and who made them. Most auction sites keep the amount of each bid hidden until the auction ends. The information appears either on the same Web page as the auction, or on a separate page that you access via a hyperlink.

Bidding History for Auction #435512957

Bidder	Bid Amount	Time of Bid
Sayshel	**	2/24/99 12:35:23 PM
Cobra430	**	2/24/99 11:34:08 AM
Moogie59	**	2/24/99 09:57:01 AM
Flying Vet	**	2/23/99 23:12:09 PM

**Bid amounts hidden until auction closes
or high bid meets reserve.**

Figure 6-5. Sample Bidding History for Open Auction

When the auction ends, the bid amounts will appear, as shown in Figure 6-6. Some sites show them for active auctions once the high bid meets the reserve price.

Bidding History for Auction #435512957

Bidder	Bid Amount	Time of Bid
Sayshel	23.50	2/24/99 12:35:23 PM
Cobra430	22.00	2/24/99 11:34:08 AM
Moogie59	6.50	2/24/99 09:57:01 AM
FlyingVet	5.00	2/23/99 23:12:09 PM

Auction closed.

Figure 6-6. Sample Bidding History for Closed Auction

Viewing the bidding history of a closed auction lets you track how often the same users bid. This gives you an idea of how eager someone is to get the piece and how likely they are to keep bidding down to the wire. You can also get an idea of the item's value in the eyes of other collectors.

Check the bidding history to familiarize yourself with how and when experienced participants place their bids. You can learn from their examples.

Selling

When you put an item up for auction, it means you agree to sell it to the highest bidder at the high bid price. You can decide the lowest acceptable price, or you can start the auction at a low amount and accept the highest bid.

You can list a single item or several items in a lot. Some sites let you enter multiples of the same item in something called a *Dutch auction*. However, every auction site runs somewhat differently.

Some sites send e-mail to the seller each time a person bids on one of his or her auctions. When you start an auction, you're usually notified of the following in e-mail:

- Confirmation of your auction listing
- Notice that someone has bid on your item
- End of auction summary

This chapter covers both selling and bidding in more detail.

Images and Hyperlinks

Most auction sites accept HTML tags within the item description. These tags allow sellers to include pictures of the item and hyperlinks to other Web sites offering more information about the piece. Since you'll probably be more inclined to bid on auctions that include photos, consider becoming a regular user at an auction site that allows them.

Later in this chapter, you'll learn how to include photographs in your auction descriptions.

☛Types of Auctions

Depending on the item listed, the seller may opt for a specific type of listing. The seller may choose from several auction types. Potential bidders should be aware of how each one works before they bid:

- Regular auction
- Featured and showcase auctions
- Dutch auction
- Private auction
- Reserve auction
- Open-ended auctions

Regular Auction

In this type of auction, the seller enters a minimum bid and the highest bid wins. As the seller, you're obligated to sell to the highest bidder for his or her high-bid price. As the buyer, you're obligated to purchase the item for your high-bid price. Contact between the buyer and seller is offline through e-mail.

Featured and Showcase Auctions

These auctions cost extra to run, anywhere from $4 to $100, depending on the site's guidelines. A featured auction usually has the title set in eye-catching boldface type and appears at the top of the list during a category search.

Showcase auctions, as the premier of the line, typically come up right on the main auction-site page in order to lure bidders immediately.

Dutch Auction

Dutch auctions are a special format only available at certain online auction sites. In a Dutch auction, a person has more than one of the same item up for sale. It doesn't matter if the seller has three or three hundred of them as long as it's a multiple of the exact same item.

The seller specifies the same starting bid for all items and indicates how many items are for sale. Buyers have the option of bidding at or above the starting bid for as many of the items as they wish to acquire. When the auction ends, the highest bidders purchase the goods at the lowest successful bid.

In a Dutch auction, it pays to bid early because the earliest successful bids win. Suppose that five of the same figurines are for sale at $25 each. Ten people bid $25 for one figurine. The first five bidders can each purchase an item since they all offered the winning amount.

If anyone bid over $25 for a figurine, that person would be among the winners for the item. The other four who bid $25 before any others would also win. Each of the five figurines would sell for $25.

If all 10 bids exceeded $25, then the five items would be sold to the high bidders at the lowest offer.

Or, let's say that a seller has five of the same Lilliput Lane cottages for sale and starts a Dutch auction with the minimum bid for each one at $50. At the end of the auction, the following bidding has taken place:

User	Amount of bid	Date of bid	Time of bid
Lorenzo	$51	Aug 22	12:55:05
Bigfish	$52	Aug 22	12:55:06
Krugman	$55	Aug 22	12:56:27
MarkoPolo	$52	Aug 23	03:29:03
Franko33	$65	Aug 23	22:25:46
Rey Man	$90	Aug 23	23:25:04
Hart2hart	$60	Aug 23	23:45:18
HeldOff	$55	Aug 24	04:03:55
Chowchow	$52	Aug 24	05:24:03
Jimbo50	$100	Aug 24	05:24:25

This auction would result in the following sales:

Winner	Amount paid
Krugman	$55
Franko33	$55
Hart2hart	$55
Rey Man	$55
Jimbo50	$55

Since the low successful bid for the item was $55, each of the high bidders only pays that amount for the item although their bids were higher.

Krugman and HeldOff tied for the low bid of $55. Because Krugman bid before HeldOff, Krugman is one of the winners.

If the number of bids is less than the amount of items offered in the Dutch auction, then only those items sell to the winning bidders. The same logic applies as shown in the example.

If a bidder chooses to bid on more than one item, his or her offer must exceed the other bids in order to win the number of items included in the bid.

When you list a Dutch auction, the site determines the winners and the winning amount for you. You'll receive this information in e-mail after the auction ends.

Auctions.com and eBay are two of the major auction sites that offer Dutch auctions. An advantage to sellers is they can list multiple items and pay only one insertion fee.

Private Auction

Not many Internet auction sites allow private auctions. Sellers typically use them when they think bidders might not want their identities known to others, such as when adult material is up for sale. Sellers also use them when they don't want anyone to "bid siphon" from their auction.

> ➡ Note: Bid siphoning is when a sneaky ⬅
> seller contacts a bidder and offers the same item
> for a lesser amount, offline.

Private auctions usually don't show up in searches. At the end of the auction, only the buyer and seller receive notification and the bidding history is not available to anyone.

Reserve Auction

Sellers may choose to set a *reserve price* for their auction. This represents the lowest price at which the person is willing to sell the item. The seller establishes a price at which bidding begins (the minimum bid), and then sets a reserve price. Bidders don't know the reserve price until the highest bid reaches that amount.

Some auction sites wait until the last hour of the auction to reveal if the bidding met the reserve price.

A reserve auction serves the best interest of the seller for two reasons:

- If system problems occur and bidders can't access the site, the clock sometimes keeps running. If the bidding was low when the system failed, the item may sell at a price much lower than its value if no reserve price was set.

> Note: Many auction sites will adjust all currently running auction clocks if a system failure exceeds two hours.

- The seller may want to induce more activity by setting a low minimum bid and then letting it bid up to the reserve. Auctions that are run this way usually get a lot more bidding action.

Buyers can benefit from reserve auctions as well:

- If you bid above your means, you aren't obligated to purchase the item if your bid didn't meet the reserve price.
- You can get a fair assessment for the item's value in the eyes of the seller.

Some auction sites don't allow reserve auctions, while others won't let you list an auction without a reserve price.

Open-Ended Auctions

Some auction sites use open-ended auctions, where the bidding remains open as long as bids enter. For each bid placed within a specific block of time before closing, like the final hour, a certain amount of time tacks onto the end of the auction. If the auction receives another bid within that time, the listing remains active for another stretch.

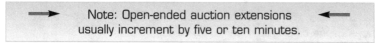

Note: Open-ended auction extensions
usually increment by five or ten minutes.

Auction sites that offer this feature do so to allow sellers to get the maximum amount for their item and to prevent last-minute bidding. It can be advantageous for sellers, but might discourage bidders who will hence need to watch an auction closing for an indefinite amount of time.

☛How To Bid On an Item

If the online auction site requires you to log in before you bid, you must enter your user ID and password on the log-in screen. You can then proceed to the auction page to bid.

Note: Most sites do not charge you to bid
on items. You have to pay the seller if you win,
but bidding is usually free.

The auction page where you place your bid will look something like Figure 6-7:

Enter Your Bid for Auction #435512957 !!

Your User ID [   ]

Your Password [   ]

Current minimum bid: **$76.50**

Your maximum bid
(include decimal point, i.e. 51.50): [   ]

[Review and place your bid]

NOTICE: By bidding on this item, you implicitly agree to buy it if you are the high bidder when the auction closes. Shill bids are illegal. By placing a bid, you give this auction site permission to release your name, address and phone number to the seller of this item.

Figure 6-7. Bid Entry Form

Bid entry forms may differ, depending on the auction site. You may not have to enter your user ID and password to bid if you previously logged in or the site knows you by a "cookie." Usually, you'll enter your bid the same way for all Internet auctions. If you encounter a site that does things differently, refer to its instructions.

Good Auctions To Bid On

Bidding on the item just by reading the title isn't advisable. You need to read the whole auction and look for more information:

- Does the auction include photos of the item from different angles?
- Does the description indicate the seller knows a lot about the collectible and can determine its quality and value?
- Does the seller clearly describe any flaws?
- If no flaws are mentioned, does the description indicate the product is in flawless condition?
- Do you know exactly what's included with the piece?
- Is the description easy to read and understand? Does it leave you with the impression that the seller is comfortable with the Internet auction process?
- Does the seller have a good feedback file?

The following paragraphs will walk you through the process of bidding on an item up for auction (user feedback is covered further in this chapter).

Enter Your Maximum Bid

Your maximum bid is the *most* you're willing to pay for an item, your self-imposed spending limit.

If you're the first bidder, the amount shown as your current bid will probably be lower than your maximum bid. The amount will match the minimum price set by the seller. The only exception is if your maximum bid meets the reserve price — then your current bid will reflect the reserve price, even if your maximum bid exceeds it.

Once you enter your bid, you can usually review it before confirming it with a mouse-click. This safeguards you in case you've made some wild error with the decimal point.

When you click on a link to confirm your bid, it takes effect. If you're the high bidder, the program returns a screen to notify you of this. Your user ID then appears on the auction page as the current high bidder.

E-mail will arrive with a recap of your bid, including the current offer and your maximum bid. Since there's no way to check your maximum bid amount from the auction page, refer to this e-mail as the auction clock starts to wind down.

Proxy Bidding

If another person attempts to outbid you, the program automatically *proxy bids* for you up to your maximum bid. If someone bids above your maximum, then he or she becomes the high bidder. You'll receive an outbid notice in e-mail.

Here is an example of how proxy bidding works:

1. The minimum bid is $5. You enter a maximum bid of $50.
2. You see that you are the current high bidder.
3. Your current bid is $5.
4. Another person bids $15.
5. Your bid automatically raises to $16 (or the next higher increment).
6. Someone else bids $28.
7. Your bid automatically raises to $29.
8. Another person bids $51.
9. You're no longer the high bidder and receive an outbid notice in e-mail.
10. You bid $52.
11. You're immediately outbid.
12. The high bidder's current offer is now $53.
13. You bid $60.
14. Your bid has exceeded the maximum bid of the current high bidder, so you are again the high bidder at $60.

The above can and often does go on numerous times during an auction, especially in the last hour before the auction closes if the item is highly desirable.

In case of a tie for the highest bid, the earlier bid wins. Proxy bidding usually won't work with Dutch auctions.

You Win!

You watched the last minute of the auction and see that you remained the high bidder at the close. So now what?

You can wait until you hear from the seller, or send an e-mail message right away. Indicate you're thrilled you won and are ready to send your payment to the specified address.

Sellers appreciate hearing from high bidders because it puts their mind at ease that the buyer is reliable and intends to pay.

Good communication usually guarantees that you get good feed-back.

Once you hear from the seller, be sure to send your payment within three days. The seller will let you know the preferred method of payment. *Never send cash.*

When the item arrives, inspect it carefully.

> • If it's in the condition you expected, notify the seller. He or she can enter positive feedback for you and then you can return the favor.
> • If it's not what you expected, you normally have three days to notify the seller that you're returning it.

If the item arrives in bad shape or doesn't match the description, contact the seller. Indicate that you're returning the item and expect a full refund.

When you need to return an item because you aren't happy with it, let the seller know right away. If he or she is agreeable and easy to deal with, leave the seller a positive feedback comment. This is a refreshingly honest seller and the rest of the auction community should know about it.

Auctions To Avoid

Similar to trading items with people you don't know, there are also things to watch for when you consider bidding at an Internet auction site.

Avoid bidding on anything absurd or outlandish, even if it's obviously a joke. I saw one auction where someone calling himself "god-almighty" had listed our entire planet (Earth) for sale. Another cyber-goofball auctioned a collection of his belly-button lint. There's nothing I'd rather do less than draw this type of person's attention by bidding on his bogus auction.

Be on the lookout for other auctions to avoid, usually entered by inexperienced sellers.

High Minimum Bid

Don't bid on items that start at the current market value. Since a lot of bidding usually occurs in the last few minutes, you might end up paying more for the item than it's worth.

The best auctions to bid on are those that start with a low minimum and have a reserve price set near the current market value. Since you don't know the reserve price, check the sec-ondary-price guides before you bid. This way you'll know when the bidding exceeds the item's actual value — then it's time to stop bidding.

Unclear Description

If the item description is unclear, the seller may not be familiar enough with the product to determine its quality and value.

Before you bid, read the description carefully. If something about it leaves you feeling unclear about what you'd be bidding on, do some investigating first:

- Send e-mail to the seller and ask for a better description or one or more pictures of the item.
- Check the seller's previous auctions.
- Check the seller's feedback file.
- Research the item in a secondary-market guide or on a collector Web site. Verify that it appears in the appropriate collectible line. It may be a product knock-off.

> ➡ Note: Some sneaky sellers of product ⬅ knock-offs will include the name of the better product in the auction title so their listing comes up in searches. Never bid on an item based on the title alone. Always be sure you read the auction description!

As with any Internet transaction, if your instincts leave you feeling unsure or uncomfortable about the item for sale, don't bid. Given the amount of auction traffic on the Internet, a better opportunity is bound to come along.

Don't Bid Too High!

Try to resist the competitive end of online bidding. One common mistake is to go for the win instead of the purchase. I confess to being guilty of this myself. The ten-dollar Erin Beanie Buddy that I ended up paying $32 for sits here now, nodding his fuzzy green head in agreement.

> ➡ Note: The best online auction practice is: ⬅ *bid to buy; don't bid to win.* If the item you're seeking goes up over the current market value, stop bidding.

If you lose this one, so what! Get a chuckle over the fool who paid too much for the item and look for another auction. You just might get a better deal the next time.

Bidding Frenzies

These drive the bidding up and compel people to put items up for auction on the Internet. Online auction sites have become the leading Internet business because of them.

Speculation states that online auctions escalate the secondary-market prices for collectibles. From what I've seen, this is definitely possible.

People are competitive by nature and play to win. Remember, though, that this kind of game can be costly. The bids you enter represent real money you have to dish out if you end up as high bidder. Try to use control. If the price goes up too high, let another bidder overpay.

The Internet is teeming with frenzied overspenders. While actively dueling for the high bid, some people send their contenders e-mail warnings to discourage competition. They claim they're going to keep bidding as high as they can in order to win.

If you receive e-mail like this, it's a good time to drop out of the auction and report this person to the auction-site administrator. Most of them frown on this practice.

Don't be tempted to place a maximum offer of $10,000 on an item so the overspender has to outbid you to win the auction. The person just may decide to stop bidding at $9,999.

Shill Bidding

When a seller uses another account or asks another user to increase the high bid, this is *shill bidding*. It's grossly unethical. Shills are illegal in all 50 states and strictly prohibited by the United States Uniform Commercial Code (U.S. UCC). Other countries may have similar laws. Auction sites strictly forbid it and will revoke offenders' accounts.

Unfortunately, shill bidding at online auction sites is not that easy to control or prevent. Sellers might be compelled to use shills to raise the bid to a "hidden reserve price," unaware the activity is forbidden. This is no reason to violate the law. It can happen, though, and you need to be on the lookout for it.

Aggressive or outlandishly high bidding often signifies shill bidding. Here are some other warning signs:

- Someone bids very aggressively and suddenly stops when the high bid reaches the reserve price.

- That person's ID shows up as an aggressive bidder in the seller's other auctions, even for non-related items.
- The aggressive bidder wins the auction, and the same seller immediately re-lists the item.
- Valid bidders typically hope to outbid someone by the least amount possible, so they'll enter a bid amount like $76.51. A shill bidder usually bids a whole number, like $80.00, to bump up the price.
- The seller has feedback from the aggressive bidder entered right after the account opened. This might indicate a friendship or family association.
- If the seller lists an Internet home page, check it to see if the aggressive bidder's e-mail address appears there as his or her spouse, partner, or friend.
- Send e-mail to the aggressive bidder and ask how long he or she has collected that line. Be personable. You might be able to judge by the reply if this is a genuine bidder or a shill.

None of the above is conclusive proof that shill bidding is going on. Sometimes friends honestly bid on each other's items, especially if that friendship formed between fellow collectors. Knowing the signs of shill bidding, though, can warn you that the high bid might be flagrantly out of line with the current market price.

If you suspect shill bidding, report it to the site administrator along with conclusive evidence and don't bid on that auction again. With any luck, the shill will make one last attempt to raise your bid and end up stuck with the high bid.

Last-Minute Bidding

Since winning means having the high offer at the end of an auction, the only way you can win is if nobody outbids you. Nobody can outbid you if you're the last bidder before the auction closes.

But this is not as easy as it sounds.

By now, you probably noticed that Web pages load in your browser faster at times and slower at others. The amount of Web traffic has a lot to do with page-loading speed. So does the content of the page.

> ⟹ Note: A page containing many images loads ⟸ more slowly. Learn how to turn off images on your browser so they don't have to load during the last minutes of an auction you're trying to win.

Since you can't predict how fast pages will load, watch the auction at least five minutes before it closes.

Beat the Clock

If you're the current high bidder, try this technique:

- Decide if you want to bid higher to secure the item. Increasing your bid when you're the current high bidder typically doesn't change the current price. The system simply updates your maximum bid to the new, higher amount.
- If you decide to take a chance and increase your maximum bid, access the bid entry screen when there's one minute left on the auction and submit your new maximum bid.
- Using a stopwatch or clock with a second hand, determine when the auction will be over.
- Position your mouse cursor over the "enter bid" or "activate bid" button, but *do not click*.
- Watch the second hand. When ten seconds remain on the clock, click to enter your bid.

By increasing your maximum at the last minute, you decrease the chances of losing to another bidder.

If you aren't the high bidder when the auction winds down to five minutes, check the current high bid and decide if you want to top it. If you do, then try this technique:

- Wait until there are three minutes left before the auction closes.
- Access the bid entry screen, enter your maximum bid, and activate the bid.
- If another person outbids you right away, decide if you want to bid higher.
- Go back to the bid entry screen and enter your new maximum bid. By now there should be under a minute left on the auction.
- Using a stopwatch or clock with a second hand, determine when the auction will be over.
- Position your mouse cursor over the "enter bid" or "activate bid" link but *do not click*.
- Watch the second hand. When ten seconds remain on the clock, click to enter your bid.

Each scenario offers two possible outcomes — you will win, or you will lose. Now that I've stated the obvious for you, let's talk about the odds.

When It *Will* Work

- Your bid enters in the last split second and nobody outbids you.
- The person you outbid has no time to get back to the auction site and bid after seeing the outbid notice in e-mail.
- The Web is running at optimum speed and your bid enters as soon as you click the bid-entry button.

When It *Won't* Work

- Someone else outbids you in the last super-split second.
- The current high bidder's maximum bid is still higher than your new maximum bid.
- Just as you're about to place your bid, the Web decides that it's naptime.

➡ Note: If you lose, contact the seller. He or ⬅ she may have several of the items and welcome the chance to make a sale without having to list another auction.

Sniping

The last-second bidding process I just described is called *sniping*. It's become an art for those who want to win online auctions. It's also very frustrating for those who haven't yet perfected the skill and end up outbid by a slight margin in the last second. Therefore, it's something you'll need to learn more about if you want to be a successful participant, especially as others hone their online auction sniping skills. The only way to beat a sniper is to snipe *better.* Perhaps you should practice last-second bidding on a few low-cost auctions before you try your luck at an auction for a more desirable item.

You can also get help with sniping right on the Web at eSnipe (www.esnipe.com). This site details what sniping is and how you can end up the high bidder with their automatic sniping program. With the information you provide, they actually place a last-second bid for you. Numerous bidders I interviewed have been happy with the results. Advertisements fund the site and there's no charge to use their sniping services.

There's also no guarantee you'll win, even with special bidding software. You have a better chance of winning, however, if you at least attempt to place a last-minute bid. And of course, in the midst of all this, remember not to outbid your pocketbook.

☞How To List an Auction

Listing an auction constitutes an agreement with both the auction site and your potential customer. Before you put your item up for auction, you need to do a few things:

- Check the item carefully for flaws. You must note these in the auction description.
- Know the item's current market value.
- Decide on a reserve price (if any) for the auction.
- Have a GIF or JPEG image file (digital photograph) of the piece (discussed further in this chapter).
- Have the image file stored in a Web directory and know its URL.
- Activate Notepad or a word processing program so you can enter and edit the description offline.
- Be sure you've activated your account and have enough credit left to cover the auction fees. If you have a credit card number on file, this won't be a problem.

Writing the Description

The item description is the most important part of your auction. It can mean the difference between getting a lot for the piece and not selling it at all. This is why I devoted an entire chapter to auction descriptions. Give a lot of thought to how you write and format them.

Until you have the hang of listing auctions, call up Notepad or another word processing program and write the description. This will acquaint you with how the description-entry area on an auction site works.

Now write the description. Be sure to list the terms of sale. This includes:

- Who pays for shipping and insurance
- Method of payment
- How soon you expect payment
- Expectations of the buyer

State all this clearly in the item description. *Collector's Guide to Online Auctions* details additional important information to include when you write your auction descriptions.

Bare-Bones Basic Description

If you don't mind entering a plain-text auction description, simply type in the description as you see fit. Here's an example:

> BEAR VALLEY "GIMME SOME LOVE" MIB!
> This lovely bear from the "Bear Valley" line is in perfect condition — no missing fur, all tags attached, no bends or creases. She would love to live at your house!
> Buyer pays postage and insurance, and seller reserves the right not to sell to anyone with excessive negative feedback. Payment with money order or bank check ships right away. Payment with personal check ships after 10 business days.
> Have fun bidding!

When you type or copy this text into the description-entry area, it will format exactly the way you typed it. Some sites will ignore your line returns and format your text as one text block unless you skip a line between paragraphs or use HTML tags.

Adding a Picture

Typically, auction sites contain a separate area to enter the URL for a photograph you want included in your listing. Auctions with pictures usually close higher than ones without them.

This is because a picture is worth ... well, you know the saying. Photos lend an aura of authenticity to your auction because the buyer can actually see what he or she is bidding on.

> ➡ Note: If you only have one picture to go ⬅ with your auction, use the "image URL" entry line. This will cause a little icon to appear by your listing indicating that it includes a photograph. Users see this when they do an auction search.

If you have other pictures of the item to include with your auction, you'll need to code the URL of any extra images into your description using the HTML code.

Wait a minute. HTML code? To auction something on the Internet?

Please don't worry. Chapter 7 provides you with everything you need to know about HTML code to enter auction descriptions. You'll make files to use over and over, giving you the best auctions on the block every single time. Keep this book handy — it will be your online auction friend.

Before you can add a picture to your auction, you must first know where on the Web the image file for that picture "lives."

> ➤ Note: The image you want to use *must* have ⬅
> a location on the Web. It cannot be on your hard drive. Although you can see it in your browser, nobody else can. If you don't have space on the Web, contact an image-hosting service to set up a URL. Chapter 7 lists a few image-hosting services. Chapter 8 includes Web sites that offer free space for home pages where you can upload and host your own images.

Image Files

The best file format for photographs is something called JPEG (pronounced "jay-peg"). JPEG stands for Joint Photographic Experts Group, the people who designed the format. A JPEG file has the extension "jpeg" or "jpg," as in cobra.jpg.

Another common image format is GIF (pronounced "jiff"). GIF stands for Graphic Interchange Format. CompuServe developed it to establish a standard. Photographs can be GIF files but they aren't as clear as JPEG files because the manner of compression for the image is different. GIF files, on the other hand, are far better for non-photographic images such as arrows, drawings, animated icons, and those little "We Accept VISA" images. A GIF file has the three-letter extension "gif," as in arrow.gif.

Though many other image formats exist, JPEG and GIF are the two most commonly used on the Web.

Image Host

An image host stores your image and allows it to be accessible by any-one using the Internet. If you have a home page on the Web, you can use that area as your image host. Just upload your picture to the Internet directory in which you keep your page code files, and make note of the directory path to the image. This will form the image's URL. For example:

http://www.domain.com/homepage/images/bear.jpg

A hosting site usually charges a small fee to host your image file. Chapter 7 includes links to many image-hosting sites.

Some auction sites now offer an image-uploading feature. You can upload an image to the auction site from your hard drive and they will host it for you, either as an auction service included in the listing fee, or for an additional charge. Check the auction site to see if they include this feature.

Enter the Auction

Once you're satisfied with the description, it's time to start the auction. Leave your Notepad screen up so you can copy the text when you get to the description-entry area.

Call up the online auction Web site and access the auction-entry screen. Enter your user ID and password wherever the site calls for them.

Most auction-entry programs are similar. Some of them contain less information, and others may ask for information that isn't included here. If so, refer to the site tutorial.

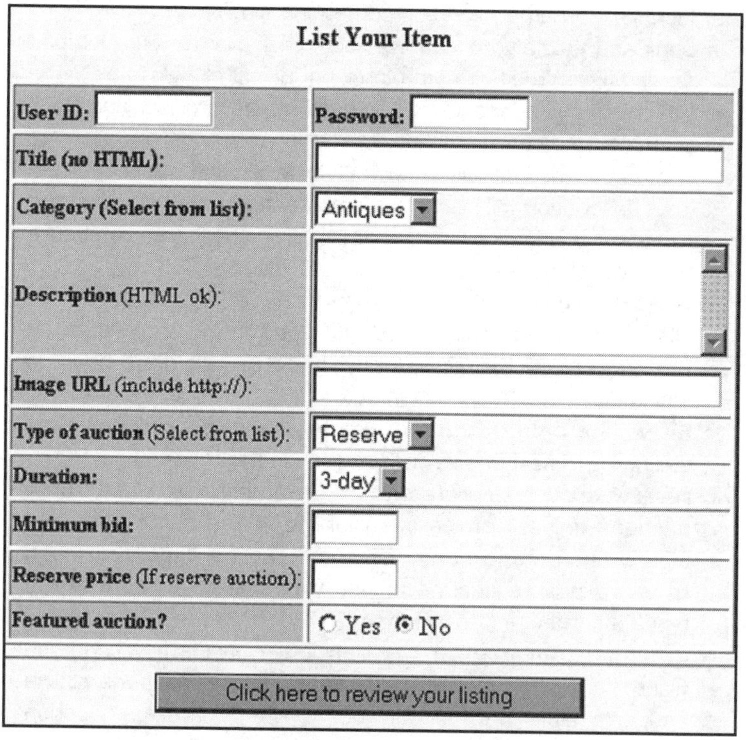

List Your Item

User ID:		Password:	
Title (no HTML):			
Category (Select from list):	Antiques		
Description (HTML ok):			
Image URL (include http://):			
Type of auction (Select from list):	Reserve		
Duration:	3-day		
Minimum bid:			
Reserve price (If reserve auction):			
Featured auction?	○ Yes ● No		

Click here to review your listing

Figure 6-8. Sample Auction-Entry Screen

Now let's get that auction running!

- **Enter a title** – Use the name of both the item and the collectible line in your title. This will ensure that bidders see your auction when they do a text search. You're usually limited to the number of characters you can put in your title, but no HTML tags. Choose your words wisely. Abbreviate to make room.

Good Title: Precious Moments Someone's Sleeping MIB!
Not-So-Good Title: Popular Bunny Figurine in Great Shape!

- **Pick a category** – Highlight or use a pull-down menu to select your item's category. Since some auction sites have sub-categories, try to narrow down the category as much as possible. If your collectible line has its own grouping, great. This will make it easier for your buyers to find your auction with a category search. If there isn't a category for your item, use "Collectible, Contemporary," or something similar.

- **Copy and paste your description** – Click over to your Notepad screen. From the Edit menu, click on "Select all." Go back to the Edit menu and select "Copy." Go back to your browser and place your mouse cursor in the box where you enter the item description. Go to the Edit menu on your browser and select "Paste." Your description will load into the text entry area. Proofread the text after you load it into the description-entry area to ensure that everything copied over.

- **Add the picture URL** – There's usually a field for the image URL. Enter it into this space and don't forget to include the http:// unless the site clearly indicates you don't need to include it. It might be assumed.

- **Enter the type of auction you're running** – Unless you're selling an inexpensive item, I recommend you enter a reserve auction to protect your investment. Don't use Dutch auctions unless you have a multiple of the same item and clearly understand how they work. There's usually no need to use a private auction unless your collectible item is the type I'd rather not mention.

- **Enter the duration of the auction** – Decide how long you want the auction to run. Since most bidding happens at the end, you might want to consider a five- or three-day auction for popular items.

➡ Note: For low-priced popular items, ⬅
use three-day auctions.

- **Enter your minimum bid** – The bidding starts at this amount. Start your auctions with a low minimum. This attracts buyers.

- **Enter your reserve price** – Make sure it's close to the item's current market value so people don't stop bidding before the auction hits the reserve price. They're under no obligation to purchase the item if the high bid is lower than your reserve price.

- **Decide if you want a featured or showcase auction** – If you want your auction to attract attention, make it featured or showcase. The additional fee appears on the auction entry form. If you want to list a regular auction, leave those fields blank or choose "N/A" if an option exists.

- **All set?** Click the "Enter" button. Proofread the entire form to ensure it's correct. Most auction sites let you review your auction before you start it running. If the site doesn't have this feature, go back and check the form one more time. Review it carefully. Does it look right? Is the title okay? Did you select the right category? Are the minimum bid and reserve price correct? Did you format your description right and do your pictures show up? If not...

- **Edit if necessary** – Hit the Back button on your browser and return to the auction-entry page if you need to correct anything. You might have to re-enter your site ID and password because some browsers erase them when you hit your Back button. When you're done, preview the auction again to be sure it's correct this time.

- **Hit the start button and let the bidding begin!**

While this might seem like a lot of work just to list an item for auction, it does get easier after you do it a few times.

Bear Valley "Gimme Some Love" MIB !!

Item #435512957

Current Bid: **$20.00** (not at reserve)   Number of bids: 0
Quantity: 1   First bid: $20.00
Time left: **2 days + 23:59:09**   Seller: **Tippycanu**
Location: Slidell, LA   High bidder: no bids

BEAR VALLEY "GIMME SOME LOVE" MIB! This lovely bear from the "Bear Valley" line is in perfect condition - no missing fur, all tags attached, no bends or creases. She would love to live at your house! Buyer pays postage and insurance, and seller reserves the right not to sell to anyone with excessive negative feedback. Payment with money order or bank check ships right away. Payment with personal check ships after 10 business days. Have fun bidding!

Click here to enter a bid

Figure 6-9. Sample Auction Page

When you start the auction, the program takes you right to the auction page or to a link for it. Go check it out!

Figure 6-9 depicts a sample auction screen without a picture. Normally the picture would show under the description. If you used HTML to add another picture, it appears within the description. There are examples of this in Chapter 7.

Notice the auction clock has started running. Registered users can now bid on your auction. It may take a while for the auction to appear listed with its category, but it will show up in text searches almost right away. A search by auction number or seller also brings it up.

Remember, never bid on your own item with another user ID. This is shilling.

As the clock winds down, you'll see bidding action. Toward the end of the auction, the page might look like this:

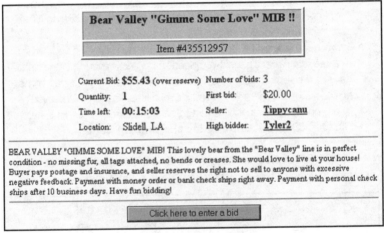

Bear Valley "Gimme Some Love" MIB !!

Item #435512957

Current Bid: **$55.43** (over reserve)	Number of bids: 3		
Quantity: 1	First bid:	$20.00	
Time left: **00:15:03**	Seller:	**Tippycanu**	
Location: Slidell, LA	High bidder:	**Tyler2**	

BEAR VALLEY "GIMME SOME LOVE" MIB! This lovely bear from the "Bear Valley" line is in perfect condition - no missing fur, all tags attached, no bends or creases. She would love to live at your house! Buyer pays postage and insurance, and seller reserves the right not to sell to anyone with excessive negative feedback. Payment with money order or bank check ships right away. Payment with personal check ships after 10 business days. Have fun bidding!

Click here to enter a bid

Figure 6-10. Auction Nearing Closing

You'll probably see most of the bidding in the last 15 minutes, and even more in the last minute as people try to outbid each other.

☞User Feedback

Almost every auction site provides some kind of system where users can report on one another when a transaction completes.

To leave feedback for another user, follow the appropriate link. It's usually called feedback, user rating, or something similar. You'll enter your user ID and that of the person you're rating and whether the comments are positive or negative. Some sites allow neutral feedback.

There's usually a character limit to prevent people from making it a sounding board. The best type of feedback gets right to the point:

Quick pay, nice e-mail, would be happy to deal with anytime! A+++

Leaving positive comments for another user is similar to giving that person a good reference.

When To Leave Positive Feedback

Post positive comments when you complete a successful transaction with someone. Here are a few other situations where positive feedback might be in order:

- You weren't happy with an item and returned it, and the seller cheerfully refunded your money.
- Your buyer returned an item to you and left you good feedback for cheerfully issuing a refund.

Browse through other feedback files to see the comments that reliable users usually receive. Normally, the seller enters feedback first after the buyer has sent payment.

> Note: Some users prefer to wait until the transaction is finished before posting feedback. You never know what might happen.

Only give feedback for people who have transacted with you on that auction site. Although it's tempting to leave comments for your friends who just established their site IDs, this may be a form of shilling and is policy violation on most online auction sites.

When To Leave Negative Feedback

Be sure any negative feedback you submit reflects *your* experience with the person. Since you can't withdraw comments, enter negative feedback as a last resort. Try to settle the matter first on the phone or in e-mail.

Users with too many negative comments may have their site privileges revoked. Here are some instances where posting negative feedback about a user, as either the seller or winner, may be necessary:

- Winner refuses to buy
- Seller refuses to sell

- Seller fails to send item after receiving payment
- Seller sends an item that doesn't match the description and refuses to refund
- Seller refuses to accept return of an item within the three-day review period
- Any dishonest or illegal behavior

Remember that the decision to enter comments is up to the person doing it. If someone refuses to enter positive feedback for you, don't retaliate with negative comments. Some users choose to leave feedback only when they feel the person they dealt with went above and beyond the call of duty.

If another user posts positive comments for you, you are under no obligation to reciprocate. If the transaction completed with no problems, though, you should leave a good report for that person as well. You never know when you may be dealing with him or her again.

I hope your auctions attract good people and your items sell for your desired amount. The next chapter includes auction description formats that may help facilitate both.

Chapter 7 — Entering Eye-Catching Auctions

They say presentation is everything. It's another one of those perception things. Buyers on the Web can't see you — only how you represent both yourself and what you're selling. You have a very small space in which to accomplish a very large job.

The more you appear to know your way around the auction site, the more confidence your bidders will have that you're a reliable seller. This chapter will help you accomplish this by entering eye-catching auctions using HTML code:

- Basic HTML formatting tags
- Coding auction descriptions
- Fancy auction description templates
- Sites that have auction software

☞Basic HTML Formatting Tags

The information you enter in the item description area usually defaults to some ordinary text. You probably want your auction to stand out among the rest. Who doesn't? This section provides some simple HTML tags that allow you change the color, font, and size of your descriptive text.

As you read about in Chapter 2, HTML stands for Hyper-Text Markup Language. HTML is a document-layout language with which we make pages for the World Wide Web.

> ➡ Note: This is in no way a definitive HTML ⬅
> user guide! The HTML code provided here is only a subset of
> the formatting language, but contains everything you need
> to know to format great auction descriptions.

Conventions Used

In these HTML coding examples, I use boldface to indicate text that's not part of the code. When you do your coding, replace my bold text with your own information.

Where you see double quotes, slashes, or arrow brackets, those are important elements of the HTML code. Be sure you include those when you write your code.

You Are Entering Tagville

The HTML markup language consists of code elements, or *tags*. They remind me of the signs you'll see in the Czech Republic when you enter and leave towns. One sign bears the name of the town as you enter, and an identical sign has a slash through the name as you leave. The stretch of road between the two signs is within the town.

HTML tags are similar. Most of them come in sets — a start tag and an end tag. The start tag indicates that a certain directive occurs after the tag, and the end tag stops the directive. The effected text is between the two tags.

Tags appear inside arrow brackets (< and >). The end tag is the same as the start tag, except the first character after the < is a slash (/) to indicate the tag's directive stops there.

> ➡ Note: HTML end tags are rather like ⬅
> road signs that show a slash through something you can't do, such as a large P with a slash through it means "no parking." HTML end tags mean "no more of whatever you had going with the start tag."

Physical Tags

Tags that change the appearance of the text are *physical tags*. Each one has an open and close directive. The tags that start and stop bold text are <B> and </B>. Any text you put between the two tags will appear in boldface font when you view the page in your browser.

The following tags create italicized and underlined text, and text that's smaller or larger than the current default size.

> ➡ Note: Underlined text can be mistaken for ⬅
> hyperlink text. Use underlining sparingly!

HTML Code	Function
<B> </B>	Bold faced text
<I> </I>	Italic text
<U> </U>	Underlined text
<BLINK> </BLINK>	Blinking text
<SMALL> </SMALL>	Text one size smaller than the default
<BIG> </BIG>	Text one size larger than the default

> ➡ Note: The blinking text tag may not work ⬅
> on all browsers and may go away altogether in the future. When blinking text appears on a home page, it tends to annoy the reader very quickly but for auction descriptions, it might be a great eye-catcher. Of course, I can't demonstrate blinking text on this static hardcopy, so you'll have to take my word for it.

Here's how the physical tags work:

HTML Code   **Output**

`<B>`**For Sale!**`</B>` . . . .**For Sale!**

`<I>`**For Sale!**`</I>` . . . . *For Sale!*

`<U>`**For Sale!**`</U>` . . . . <u>For Sale!</u>

`<BLINK>`**For Sale!**`</BLINK>` . . . . . . For Sale (blink! blink!)

`<SMALL>`**For Sale!**`</SMALL>` . . . . For Sale!

`<BIG>`**For Sale!**`</BIG>` . . . . .For Sale!

> ➡ Note: Each coding example uses the start ⬅ and end tags. One of the most common coding mistakes in HTML is to forget to close a tag. This can cause the rest of the text on the page to be in bold face if you forgot to close your `<B>` tag with `</B>`.

You can combine tags for more than one effect. Notice that the tags open and close in mirrored order:

HTML Code   **Output**

`<B><I>`**Text that is both bold and italic**`</I></B>` ***Text that is both bold and italic***

HTML tags are not case sensitive. You can use `<B>`, `<b>`, or any combination for start and end tags. It's a good idea to pick one case and stick with it because it makes it easier to spot the code from your text when you edit the HTML file later.

Attributes and Values

An *attribute* gives more direction to the function of the tag. Attributes must be included within the main tag and some of them have a *value* attached to them with an equal (=) sign.

`<TAG ATTRIBUTE=VALUE>`**text**`</TAG>`

Don't put any spaces between the attribute, the equal sign, or the value.

Assigning Text Color and Font Style

You change the color and font style of the text a little differently. Here you have to use the `<FONT>` tag. You can use three attributes within the `<FONT>` tag:

• COLOR – uses any of a hundred or so color names to change the color of the text. You can also use hexadecimal RGB codes if you are familiar with them, but color names are easier. The table below lists many color names you can use with the COLOR attribute.

• FACE – indicates what typeface you want the text to be. If the name of the font has more than one word, include spaces between the words but enclose the name in double quotes.

• SIZE – changes the size of the text. Your text size can be from 1 to 7 points.

Color

A six-digit hexadecimal code after a pound sign (#) used with the COLOR attribute changes the color of the text. This coding example switches the text color to red:

<FONT COLOR=#CC0000>**This will be red text.**</FONT>

Many Web designers include hex codes for colors so they can clearly define hues, but you don't have to. You can use colors by their name instead of trying to figure out hexadecimal codes. It works like this:

<FONT COLOR=red>**This also will be red text.**</FONT>

Here's a list of color names recognized by most browsers. Notice there are no spaces in the names, so you don't need to enclose the name in quotes.

aliceblue	darkviolet	lightskyblue	paleviolet
antiquewhite	deeppink	lightslateblue	papayawhip
aquamarine	deepskyblue	lightslategray	peachpuff
azure	dimgray	lightsteelblue	peru
beige	dodgerblue	lightyellow	pink
bisque	firebrick	limegreen	plum
black	floralwhite	linen	powderblue
blanchedalmond	forestgreen	magenta	purple
blue	gainsboro	maroon	red
blueviolet	ghostwhite	mediumaquamarine	rosybrown
brown	gold	mediumblue	royalblue
burlywood	goldenrod	mediumorchid	saddlebrown
cadetblue	gray	mediumpurple	salmon
chartreuse	green	mediumseagreen	sandybrown

chocolate	greenyellow	mediumslateblue	seagreen
coral	honeydew	mediumspringgreen	sienna
cornflowerblue	hotpink	mediumturquoise	skyblue
cornsilk	indianred	mediumvioletred	slateblue
cyan	ivory	midnightblue	slategray
darkblue	khaki	mintcream	snow
darkcyan	lavender	mistyrose	springgreen
darkgoldenrod	lavenderblush	moccasin	steelblue
darkgray	lawngreen	navajowhite	tan
darkgreen	lemonchiffon	navy	thistle
darkkhaki	lightblue	navyblue	tomato
darkolivegreen	lightcoral	oldlace	turquoise
darkorange	lightcyan	olivedrab	violet
darkred	lightgoldenrodyellow	orange	violetred
darksalmon	lightgray	orangered	wheat
darkseagreen	lightgreen	orchid	white
darkslateblue	lightpink	palegoldenrod	whitesmoke
darkslategray	lightsalmon	palegreen	yellow
darkturquoise	lightseagreen	paleturquoise	yellowgreen

Table 7-1. Color Names That Can be Used with the COLOR Attribute

You might prefer using hexadecimal codes. Lynda Weinman includes full-color hexadecimal charts in *Designing Web Graphics — How to Prepare Images and Media for the Web* [New Riders Publishing, 1996]. Weinman's series on Web graphics is excellent for anyone creating images for the Internet.

If you want to view colors and their hexadecimal codes right in your Web browser, check out Weinman's "Non-Dithering Colors by Hue" page at www.lynda.com/hexh.html.

Face

Within the <FONT> tag, the FACE attribute means typeface. If the typeface includes more than one word, like Comic Sans MS, you must include the name in double quotes to indicate that it's one value.

In order for a particular typeface to show up in the viewer's browser, it needs to be loaded on his or her PC. To ensure that your text displays the way you want it, you can include several font names, separated by commas, with the FACE attribute. When the file loads in the browser, it looks at each font name in order until it sees one that it recognizes, and then displays the text in that typeface.

Here's an example:

<FONT FACE="Verdana, Arial, Helvetica">

Each of these fonts, Verdana, Arial, and Helvetica, is a standard sans serif font. Most PCs are bound to have at least one of them installed. If not, the text displays in the default style.

Size
The SIZE attribute needs a value from 1 to 7, relative to the default font size.

> ➤ Note: Seventy-two points equal one inch in ◄═══
> print matter but not in a Web browser. Point size is
> relative to factors like the browser version, the software,
> and the monitor size.

In the following examples, I used the COLOR, FACE, and SIZE attributes and corresponding values to change the color, typeface, and text size:

HTML Code	Output
<FONT FACE=Tekton>**Text in the Tekton font is cool!**</FONT>	Text in the Tekton font is cool!
<FONT SIZE=3>**This text is a size 3!**</FONT>	This text is a size 3!
<FONT COLOR=GREEN FACE="Lemonade ICG">**You can also combine attributes within a tag!**</FONT>	You can also combine attributes within a tag!

> ➤ Note: When using HTML code, be sure you ◄═══
> don't add any spaces or unnecessary characters where
> you don't see any in my examples. Use the code just as
> shown, except insert your own text between the start tag
> and the end tag.

Text Formatting
Formatting tags allow you to space and center your text, include vertical spacer lines, and add pictures and tables on the page. The first three tags shown in the following table are single tags and don't need an end tag:

HTML Code	Function
<P>	Start a new paragraph. Adds a blank line between the text blocks
 	Line break with no space between the lines of text
<HR>	Makes a horizontal line, usually used in an auction description to set off a photograph
<CENTER> </CENTER>	Centers anything between the start and end tags.

Lists

You can create ordered and unordered lists with HTML. Ordered lists contain numbers or letters by each list item. Unordered items have bullets by each item.

HTML allows you to nest any type of list within another list.

Ordered Lists

Use an ordered list when the order of the items listed is important. Ordered lists start with the <OL> tag and end with </OL>. Indicate list items with <LI>, which is a single-ended tag.

HTML Code	Output
<OL>	
<LI>**This is Item 1.**	1. This is Item 1.
<LI>**This is Item 2.**	2. This is Item 2.
<LI>**This is Item 3.**	3. This is Item 3.
</OL>	

The items in an ordered list are automatically ordered starting with the Arabic numeral 1. You can change that value with the START attribute in the <OL> tag.

HTML Code	Output
<OL START=4>	
<LI>**This is Item 4.**	4. This is Item 4.
<LI>**This is Item 5.**	5. This is Item 5.
<LI>**This is Item 6.**	6. This is Item 6.
</OL>	

Use the TYPE attribute within the <OL> tag to change the numbering style. Four values are accepted with the TYPE attribute:

- A – A, B, C, etc.
- a – a, b, c, etc.
- I – I, II, III, etc.
- i – i, ii, iii, etc.

HTML Code	Output

`<OL TYPE=I>`
`<LI>`**This is the first item.**
`<LI>`**This is the second item.**
`<LI>`**This is the third item.**
`</OL>`
	I. This is the first item.
	II. This is the second item.
	III. This is the third item.

Combine attributes within the `<OL>` tag. In other words, make your list item start with Roman numeral IV this way:

HTML Code	Output

`<OL TYPE=I START=4>`
`<LI>`**This is item 4.**
`<LI>`**This is item 5.**
`<LI>`**This is item 6.**
`</OL>`
	IV. This is item 4.
	V. This is item 5.
	VI. This is item 6.

Unordered Lists

Use an unordered list when the order of the items isn't important. Unordered lists start with the `<UL>` tag and end with `</UL>`. Indicate list items with `<LI>`. Items are set off with a bullet.

HTML Code	Output

`<UL>`
`<LI>`This is an item.
`<LI>`This is an item too.
`<LI>`This is another item.
`</UL>`
	• This is an item.
	• This is an item too.
	• This is another item.

Tables

Tables are a little more complex than lists, but you can do a lot with them, such as:

- Specify the height and width of table cell
- Include photos

• Add borders around text and photos
• Include hyperlinks
• Use color backgrounds
• Use textured backgrounds
• Span multiple rows or columns

Define a table with the <TABLE> and </TABLE> tags. Just about anything can appear in a table cell — photos, lists, or another table. What's more, you can even give table cells their own background color.

The <TABLE> tag has a few attributes. A set of special table tags defines parts of the table.

Table Tags

• The <TR> tag defines a table row.
• The <TH> tag defines a table header. This may default to bold face type. You don't need to include headers in your tables if you don't want to.
• The <TD> tag defines a cell of table data.

Each of the above uses a corresponding end tag.

Basic Table Coding

Here is the HTML coding for a basic borderless table:

HTML Code	Output	
<TABLE>		
<TR>	**Heading 1 Heading 2**	
<TH>**Heading 1**</TH>	Data 1	Data 2
<TH>**Heading 2**</TH>	Data 3	Data 4
</TR><TR>		
<TD>**Data 1**</TD>		
<TD>**Data 2**</TD>		
</TR><TR>		
<TD>**Data 3**</TD>		
<TD>**Data 4**</TD>		
</TR></TABLE>		

Borders

As shown in the example above, the border default for <TABLE> is "none," or zero. To get a nice chiseled border around your table and the rows and cells, use the BORDER attribute within the <TABLE> tag. Use a value of from 1 to 5 with the BORDER attribute to alter the thickness.

> ➡️ Note: The value numbers represent pixels. ⬅️
> A pixel is a picture element or the smallest unit of
> measure on the computer screen.

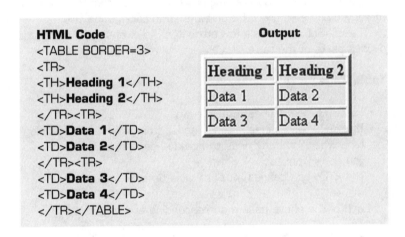

HTML Code

```
<TABLE BORDER=3>
<TR>
<TH>Heading 1</TH>
<TH>Heading 2</TH>
</TR><TR>
<TD>Data 1</TD>
<TD>Data 2</TD>
</TR><TR>
<TD>Data 3</TD>
<TD>Data 4</TD>
</TR></TABLE>
```

Output

Heading 1	Heading 2
Data 1	Data 2
Data 3	Data 4

Cell Spacing and Padding

Use the CELLSPACING attribute in the <TABLE> tag to control the space between the adjacent cells in a table that are along the outer edges of the cells. The value for the CELLSPACING attribute is a number in pixels.

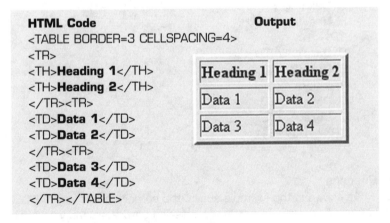

HTML Code

```
<TABLE BORDER=3 CELLSPACING=4>
<TR>
<TH>Heading 1</TH>
<TH>Heading 2</TH>
</TR><TR>
<TD>Data 1</TD>
<TD>Data 2</TD>
</TR><TR>
<TD>Data 3</TD>
<TD>Data 4</TD>
</TR></TABLE>
```

Output

Heading 1	Heading 2
Data 1	Data 2
Data 3	Data 4

The CELLPADDING attribute in the <TABLE> tag controls the space between the edge of a cell and its content. The value for the CELLPADDING attribute is a number in pixels.

HTML Code   **Output**

```
<TABLE BORDER=3 CELLPADDING=4>
<TR>
<TH>Heading 1</TH>
<TH>Heading 2</TH>
</TR><TR>
<TD>Data 1</TD>
<TD>Data 2</TD>
</TR><TR>
<TD>Data 3</TD>
<TD>Data 4</TD>
</TR></TABLE>
```

Heading 1	Heading 2
Data 1	Data 2
Data 3	Data 4

Placement Inside a Cell

The cells used in the examples above are very small. As you enter text, images, and links into the table cells, they expand to accommodate the contents. If you have one cell that has a small image or just a few words, you may want that to appear in the center of the cell. You can control this.

The ALIGN and VALIGN attributes of the <TH> and <TD> tags allow you to control the alignment of the cell contents. The ALIGN attribute controls it horizontally, while VALIGN controls it vertically.

The ALIGN attribute has three values:

- LEFT
- CENTER
- RIGHT

The VALIGN attribute has three values:

- TOP
- MIDDLE
- BOTTOM

The following figure shows a table formatted using the ALIGN and VALIGN attributes within <TD> tags. Notice that I used the <BR> tag within the "Data Number 1" cell just to expand it. This won't be necessary when you have a lot of text there

HTML Code
```
<TABLE BORDER=3>
<TR>
<TH>Heading 1</TH>
<TH>Heading 2</TH>
<TH>Heading 3</TH>
</TR><TR>
<TD>Data<BR>Number<BR>1</TD>
<TD ALIGN=RIGHT>Data 2</TD>
<TD VALIGN=TOP>Data 3</TD>
</TR></TABLE>
```

Output

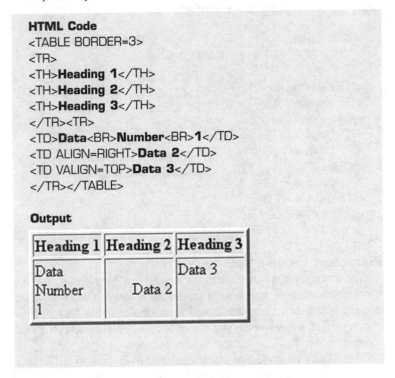

Spanning Rows and Columns

Let's say you want one cell to span two rows and another to span two columns. Control this with the COLSPAN and ROWSPAN attributes within the <TH> and <TD> tags. The value for each is a number greater than one, not to exceed the number of rows or columns (depending on what you're spanning) in the table.

This example illustrates a header spanning two columns in the table:

HTML Code
```
<TABLE BORDER=3>
<TR>
<TH COLSPAN=2>Heading 1</TH>
<TH>Heading 2</TH>
</TR><TR>
<TD>Data One</TD>
```

```
<TD>Data Two</TD>
<TD>Data Three</TD>
</TR></TABLE>
```

Output

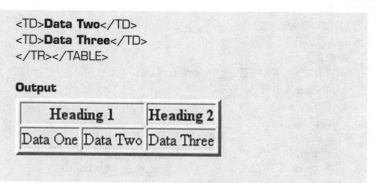

Heading 1		Heading 2
Data One	Data Two	Data Three

Here's an example of a cell that spans two rows in the table:

HTML Code
```
<TABLE BORDER=3>
<TR>
<TH>Heading 1</TH>
<TH>Heading 2</TH>
<TH>Heading 3</TH>
</TR><TR>
<TD ROWSPAN=2>Data 1</TD>
<TD>Data 2</TD>
<TD>Data 3</TD>
</TR><TR>
<TD>Data 4</TD>
<TD>Data 5</TD>
</TR></TABLE>
```

Output

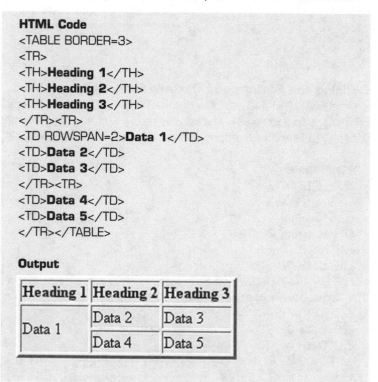

Heading 1	Heading 2	Heading 3
Data 1	Data 2	Data 3
	Data 4	Data 5

Defining the Color of a Cell

If you want to highlight certain cells or just add a little life to your table, try changing the background color of one or more of the cells. Use the BGCOLOR attribute in the <TH> or <TD> tags with a color name or a hex code:

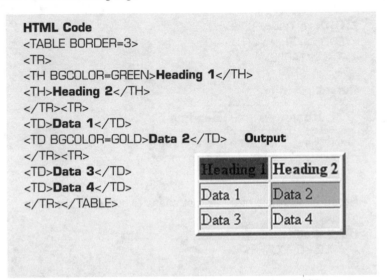

```
HTML Code
<TABLE BORDER=3>
<TR>
<TH BGCOLOR=GREEN>Heading 1</TH>
<TH>Heading 2</TH>
</TR><TR>
<TD>Data 1</TD>
<TD BGCOLOR=GOLD>Data 2</TD>    Output
</TR><TR>
<TD>Data 3</TD>
<TD>Data 4</TD>
</TR></TABLE>
```

Heading 1	Heading 2
Data 1	Data 2
Data 3	Data 4

Defining the Background Pattern for a Cell

The BACKGROUND attribute of the <TH> or <TD> tag adds a pattern image to a table cell. The value is the URL of an image file that will "tile" to fill the background of the table cell. Here's an example:

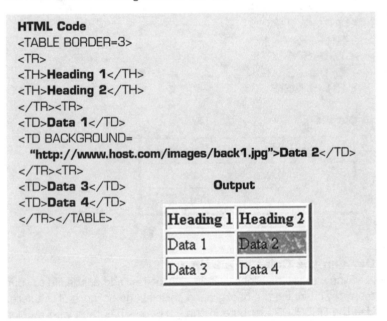

```
HTML Code
<TABLE BORDER=3>
<TR>
<TH>Heading 1</TH>
<TH>Heading 2</TH>
</TR><TR>
<TD>Data 1</TD>
<TD BACKGROUND=
  "http://www.host.com/images/back1.jpg">Data 2</TD>
</TR><TR>
<TD>Data 3</TD>                    Output
<TD>Data 4</TD>
</TR></TABLE>
```

Heading 1	Heading 2
Data 1	Data 2
Data 3	Data 4

Adding an Image

The <IMG> tag lets you include a picture within your auction description. Use the SRC attribute with the image URL as the value.

Decide where you want your image to appear. At that point, insert the following code just as it appears here:

<IMG SRC= "**http://www.domain.com/homepage/images/cobra.jpg**">

I use http://www.domain.com/homepage/images/cobra.jpg as an example. You'll use the image URL you want in your auction description. Note that when you enter the URL, it must contain the full path, including the http:// part.

Positioning an Image

You can control the position of an image with the ALIGN attribute in the <IMG> tag. Use this only when the image is not inside a table. Without this attribute, the image aligns to the left. The values for ALIGN are LEFT, RIGHT, TOP, MIDDLE, and BOTTOM.

The LEFT and RIGHT values flow subsequent text around the image. The others align the image vertically with respect to the surrounding text.

The TOP, MIDDLE, and BOTTOM attribute values only apply to the image relative to any text on the page.

Here's an example of the ALIGN attribute used to position an image to the right of an adjacent paragraph:

HTML Code
<IMG SRC="**http://www.host.com/images/bearcp.jpg**"
    ALIGN=RIGHT> **This one-of-a-kind chocolate brown bear is soft and fuzzy from his head to his hand-stitched feet.**
<P>
He proudly sports a gold bow around his neck. What a perfect addition to your teddy bear gallery!
Output

This one-of-a-kind chocolate brown bear is soft and fuzzy from his head to his hand-stitched feet.

He proudly sports a gold bow around his neck. What a perfect addition to your teddy bear gallery!

Of course, this example is on a small scale, as it would appear in a very small browser. You'll need much more text for it to wrap around the aligned image. Some of the auction description examples further in this chapter use the ALIGN attribute within the <IMG> tag.

Animated GIFs

Since animated icons are GIF files, you add them the same way you do any other image file. You just need to know the URL of the image.

Remember that large animated images, or those with many frames, take a long time to load. Stick with small, simple animation to dress up your auction description, or to populate the image URL field on the auction-entry form.

Adding Hypertext Links

If you want bidders to visit your home page, include a hyperlink in your auction description. All you need is the URL to your home page.

Hypertext links start with the <A> (anchor) tag and end with </A>. Use the HREF attribute with the page URL as the value. Whatever you enter between <A> and </A> will appear underlined in the browser. When you pass your mouse cursor over it, the arrow will change into a little hand, indicating the text is a *hot spot.* If you click on a hot spot, the hyperlinked page loads in your browser.

HTML Code
<A HREF="http://www.domain.com/~jennyB">See Jenny's Page!</A>
Output   See Jenny's Page!

The underlined text appears as hyperlink text, or a hot spot.

> → Note: Be certain to close the <A> tag ⟵ because if you don't, the rest of the text (and everything else) on the page might become part of your hyperlink.

Opening Your Link in a New Browser

If your link is within your auction description, you might not want to draw your bidder's attention away from your auction.

To make the link open up a new browser, leaving the host browser undisturbed, include the TARGET attribute with _NEW as the value within your <A> tag.

HTML Code
<A HREF="**http://www.domain.com/~jennyB**"
  TARGET="_NEW">**See Jenny's Page!**</A>

Result

The link opens in a new browser when clicked on, leaving the original browser undisturbed.

Making Your E-mail Address a Hyperlink

If you want your viewers to send you e-mail by clicking on your e-mail address, use the <A> tag with the HREF attribute. The value is MAILTO:**address**, as in this example:

HTML Code
<A HREF="MAILTO:**user@email.com**">**user@email.com**</A>

Output   u̲s̲e̲r̲@̲e̲m̲l̲h̲m̲.̲c̲o̲m̲

The e-mail address will appear as hyperlink text. Though not all browsers support e-mail links, the ones that do make it very easy for your viewers to contact you.

Including your e-mail address between the start and end <A> tags causes it to be a hypertext link. When clicked on, it brings up an e-mail screen addressed to you.

Making an Image a Hyperlink

If you want your reader to be able to click on a picture to access another site, you must code the <IMG> tag information between the starting and ending <A> tags. This causes a two-pixel wide border to appear around the image by default. If you want a borderless image, use the BORDER attribute with a value of zero. For a thicker border, increase the value to a number larger than two.

HTML Code:
<A HREF="**http://www.domain.com/~jennyB**">
<IMG SRC="**http://www.host.com/images/bear.jpg**"
  BORDER=0>
</A>

Result:

The image is a borderless hyperlink.

Learning More About HTML

HTML is a vast and comprehensive coding language. It provides many, many more capabilities than what I describe here. This is enough to help you format some great auction descriptions, though. If you decide to design Web pages, you may want to invest in an HTML reference book or two.

Many great books can to teach you to become an expert at HTML coding and Web page design. My personal favorite is *HTML: The Definitive Guide* by Chuck Musciano and Bill Kennedy (O'Reilly & Associates, Inc.).

Writing Your Auction Description with HTML

Open Notepad or a word-processing program where you can enter and save plain text. Type in your description along with the URL to any additional image files you want to appear with your item description.

> **Note:** If your favorite collectible bulletin board allows HTML in the message entry area, use any of the HTML coding examples in this book to add some life to your bulletin board posts.

It might be easier to work with Notepad if you select "Word wrap" from the edit menu. This way you don't have to keep using the scroll bars when you want to view text that extends beyond the screen.

Save your description in a file called *practice.html* (or any name you choose) and open it in your browser to see how it looks. You can do this with the File menu on your browser.

Select "Open" and type in the path to the *practice.html* file you just saved. You can also use the "Browse" button to find the file with a user interface.

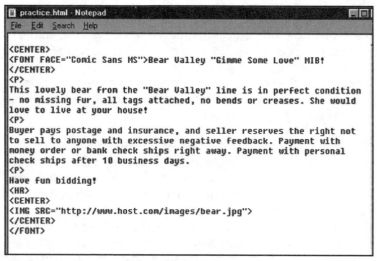

practice.html - Notepad

File Edit Search Help

```
<CENTER>
<FONT FACE="Comic Sans MS">Bear Valley "Gimme Some Love" MIB!
</CENTER>
<P>
This lovely bear from the "Bear Valley" line is in perfect condition
- no missing fur, all tags attached, no bends or creases. She would
love to live at your house!
<P>
Buyer pays postage and insurance, and seller reserves the right not
to sell to anyone with excessive negative feedback. Payment with
money order or bank check ships right away. Payment with personal
check ships after 10 business days.
<P>
Have fun bidding!
<HR>
<CENTER>
<IMG SRC="http://www.host.com/images/bear.jpg">
</CENTER>
</FONT>
```

Figure 7-1. Microsoft Notepad Used to Format an Auction Description

> Note: All HTML files must end with a file extension of either .html or .htm so your browser software recognizes them.

The formatted file will open in your browser. Keep the file open in Notepad in case you need to make changes or corrections to the description. If you change the file, be sure to save it from the File menu. Hit the Reload or Refresh button in your browser to view the changes.

> Note: When previewing an auction description in your browser, size the browser down to the approximate size of the space in which the description appears on an auction page. While everyone has his or her browser set differently when viewing auction pages, this will give you an idea of what the description will look like in a smaller space.

Browser Differences

Speaking of browsers, this is a good time to mention that Netscape and Internet Explorer occasionally interpret and display HTML code differently from one another. I used Internet Explorer for all the examples in this book. For Netscape, you may need to adjust the HTML code somewhat to get the desired effect.

You'll see most of the differences where physical tags or specific typefaces are used. Internet Explorer will apply your <FONT> tag to a table or list that follows it, whereas Netscape usually requires the <FONT> tag at the beginning of the text to which it applies in order to carry out the function. Users of both browsers will see your auction, so it might be a good idea to open your code file in both of them to check the results. Nevertheless, the following examples will produce a passable result in either browser and will look much better than the boring default text.

☞Coding Auction Descriptions

This section includes examples of auction descriptions coded in simple HTML. I coded them in Microsoft's Notepad and then pasted them into the description area of the auction entry screen. That little space (shown in the Chapter 6 example) to add the description may look like it's too tiny to fit all this code. Most auction sites, however, don't limit the number of characters you can enter in that field.

Just copy, point, and paste. Then feed your HTML code right into the description area.

> ➡ Note: Some auction sites include horizontal ⬅ lines between the auction description and the picture you include. Watch for any automatic formatting done by the site program. Look carefully at other active auction pages, and review your description before you submit it so the page doesn't end up being cumbersome with lines and spaces.

The following examples show both the HTML code and the result that displays in your browser. Boldface type represents data you have to supply, such as your item description, a file name, or a URL.

You might want to make a few practice files before you use the HTML code for auction descriptions. They may take a while to type in, but once you've saved the text to a file, you can reuse the code just by replacing the old text with the new text when it comes time to list another auction.

> ➡ Note: When you find a description style ⬅ you like, type it in one time and save it to use as a template file. Whenever you list an auction, simply replace the previous information with new information, change a background color or two, and your auction will look great.

By the way, these descriptions will look much better in your browser!

Auction Description Formats

Example 1

This example uses the Comic Sans MS typeface, formatting tags, and image inclusion. In the code for Example 1 (p. 218), notice how and where the HTML tags are placed to achieve the exact results I want:

Bear Valley "Gimme Some Love" MIB!

This lovely bear from the "Bear Valley" line is in perfect condition - no missing fur, all tags attached, no bends or creases. She would love to live at your house!

Buyer pays postage and insurance, and seller reserves the right not to sell to anyone with excessive negative feedback. Payment with money order or bank check ships right away. Payment with personal check ships after 10 business days.

Have fun bidding!

Figure 7-2. Example 1. Auction Description.

Example 2

In this example, I used an unordered list to accentuate what I feel are the selling points of the bear. See the code for Example 2 (p. 218).

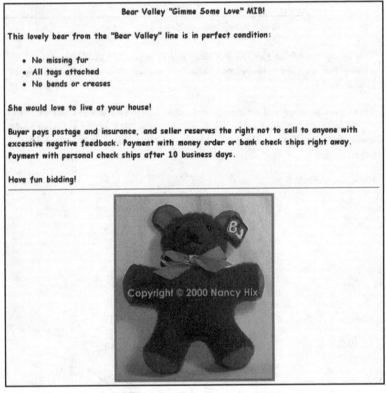

Bear Valley "Gimme Some Love" MIB!

This lovely bear from the "Bear Valley" line is in perfect condition:

- No missing fur
- All tags attached
- No bends or creases

She would love to live at your house!

Buyer pays postage and insurance, and seller reserves the right not to sell to anyone with excessive negative feedback. Payment with money order or bank check ships right away. Payment with personal check ships after 10 business days.

Have fun bidding!

Figure 7-3. Example 2. Auction Description.

Example 3

This description uses a table and adds a bar icon. In the code for Example 3 (p. 219), notice that for the bar icon, the full-path URL is included within the <IMG> tag.

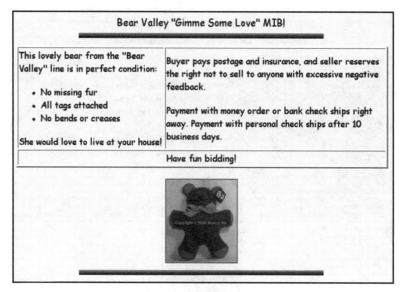

Figure 7-4. Example 3. Auction Description.

Example 4

This next example shows table cell shading. In the code for Example 4 (p. 220), notice how the <CENTER> tag is used to position the images outside the table.

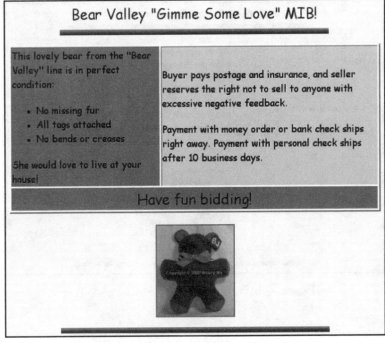

Figure 7-5. Example 4. Auction Description.

Example 5

This example adds a photograph inside a table cell. The color shading and image positioning are accomplished using the BGCOLOR and ALIGN attributes within the <TD> tag. See the code for Example 5 (p. 221).

Bear Valley "Gimme Some Love" MIB!

This lovely bear from the "Bear Valley" line is in perfect condition:

- No missing fur
- All tags attached
- No bends or creases

She would love to live at your house!

Buyer pays postage and insurance, and seller reserves the right not to sell to anyone with excessive negative feedback.

Payment with money order or bank check ships right away. Payment with personal check ships after 10 business days.

Have fun bidding!

Figure 7-6. Example 5. Auction Description.

Example 6

This example adds a border around the picture and includes the title within the table. I used a nested table within another table cell to achieve the border around the picture. Since the title is in a table cell, the <FONT> tag has to appear outside the table to affect the entire table. See the code for Example 6 (p. 222).

Figure 7-7. Example 6. Auction Description.

Example 7

This example displays table cells with a patterned background by using the BACKGROUND attribute within the <TD> tag. I added a hyperlink so viewers can visit my home page. See the code for Example 7 (p. 223).

Figure 7-8. Example 7. Auction Description.

Auction Description Code

The following pages include the HTML code for the auction description samples in Examples 1-7, pgs. 211 – 217. The text in regular font is the necessary HTML code that must be entered exactly as it's shown here. You will replace the boldface text with your own information.

Code for Example 1

```
<CENTER>
<B><FONT FACE="Comic Sans MS">Bear Valley "Gimme Some Love" MIB!
</CENTER>
<BR>
This lovely bear from the "Bear Valley" line is in perfect condition — no missing fur, all tags attached, no bends or creases. She would love to live at your house!
<P>
Buyer pays postage and insurance, and seller reserves the right not to sell to anyone with excessive negative feedback. Payment with money order or bank check ships right away. Payment with personal check ships after 10 business days.
<P>
Have fun bidding!</B>
<HR>
<CENTER>
<IMG SRC="http://www.host.com/images/bear.jpg">
</CENTER>
</FONT>
```

Code for Example 2

```
<CENTER>
<B><FONT FACE="Comic Sans MS">Bear Valley "Gimme Some Love" MIB!
</CENTER>
<BR>
This lovely bear from the "Bear Valley" line is in perfect condition:
<UL>
<LI>No missing fur
<LI>All tags attached
```

```
<LI>No bends or creases
</UL>
She would love to live at your house!
<P>
Buyer pays postage and insurance, and seller reserves the
    right not to sell to anyone with excessive negative feed-
    back. Payment with money order or bank check ships
    right away. Payment with personal check ships after 10
    business days.
<P>
Have fun bidding!</B>
<HR>
<CENTER>
<IMG SRC="http://www.host.com/images/bear.jpg">
</CENTER>
</FONT>
```

Code for Example 3

```
<CENTER>
<FONT FACE="Comic Sans MS" SIZE=4>Bear Valley "Gimme
    Some Love" MIB!
<IMG SRC="http://www.host.com/images/bluebar.gif">
<BR>
<TABLE BORDER=2>
<TR>
<TD>This lovely bear from the "Bear Valley" line is in per-
    fect condition:
    <UL>
    <LI>No missing fur
    <LI>All tags attached
    <LI>No bends or creases
    </UL>
</TD>
She would love to live at your house!
<TD>
Buyer pays postage and insurance, and seller reserves the
    right not to sell to anyone with excessive negative feed-
    back.</TD>
<P>
Payment with money order or bank check ships right away.
    Payment with personal check ships after 10 business days.
```

```
</TR><TR>
<TD COLSPAN=2 ALIGN=CENTER><FONT SIZE=5>Have fun
   bidding!</FONT></TD>
</TR>
</TABLE>
<P>
<IMG SRC="http://www.host.com/images/bear.gif">
<BR>
<IMG SRC="http://www.host.com/images/bluebar.gif">
</CENTER>
</FONT>
```

Code for Example 4

```
<CENTER>
<FONT FACE="Comic Sans MS" SIZE=5>Bear Valley "Gimme
   Some Love" MIB!
<IMG SRC="http://www.host.com/images/bluebar.gif">
<TABLE BORDER=2>
<TR>
<TD BGCOLOR=darkgoldenrod>This lovely bear from the
   "Bear Valley" line is in perfect condition:
   <UL>
   <LI>No missing fur
   <LI>All tags attached
   <LI>No bends or creases
   </UL>
</TD>
She would love to live at your house!
<TD BGCOLOR=gold>Buyer pays postage and insurance, and
   seller reserves the right not to sell to anyone with exces-
   sive negative feedback.</TD>
<P>
Payment with money order or bank check ships right away.
   Payment with personal check ships after 10 business
   days.
</TR><TR>
<TD COLSPAN=2 ALIGN=CENTER BGCOLOR=darkgoldenrod>
<FONT SIZE=5>Have fun bidding!</FONT></TD>
</TR>
</TABLE>
<P>
```

```
<IMG SRC="http://www.host.com/images/bear.jpg">
<BR>
<IMG SRC="http://www.host.com/images/bluebar.gif">
</CENTER>
</FONT>
```

Code for Example 5

```
<CENTER>
<FONT FACE="Comic Sans MS"><FONT SIZE=5>Bear Valley
   "Gimme Some Love" MIB!
<TABLE BORDER=2>
<TR>
<TD BGCOLOR=gold ALIGN=CENTER>
<IMG RC="http://www.host.com/images/bear.jpg"></TD>
<TD BGCOLOR=gold>This lovely bear from the "Bear Valley"
   line is in perfect condition:
   <UL>
   <LI>No missing fur
   <LI>All tags attached
   <LI>No bends or creases
   </UL>
</TD>
She would love to live at your house!
</TR><TR>
<TD COLSPAN=2 BGCOLOR=gold>Buyer pays postage and
   insurance, and seller reserves the right not to sell to
   anyone with excessive negative feedback.</TD>
<P>
Payment with money order or bank check ships right away.
   Payment with personal check ships after 10 business
   days.
</TR><TR>
<TD COLSPAN=2 ALIGN=CENTER BGCOLOR=darkgoldenrod>
<FONT SIZE=5>Have fun bidding!</FONT></TD>
</TR>
</TABLE>
</CENTER>
</FONT>
```

Code for Example 6

```
<CENTER>
<FONT FACE="Comic Sans MS">
<TABLE BORDER=2>
<TR>
<TD COLSPAN=2 ALIGN=CENTER BGCOLOR=darkgoldenrod>
<FONT SIZE=5>Bear Valley "Gimme Some Love" MIB!
</TR><TR>
<TD BGCOLOR=darkgoldenrod ALIGN=CENTER>
  <TABLE BORDER=3>
  <TR>
<TD BGCOLOR=gold> <IMG SRC=
  "http://www.host.com/images/bear.jpg"></TD>
  </TR>
  </TABLE>
</TD>
<TD BGCOLOR=gold>This lovely bear from the "Bear Valley"
  line is in perfect condition:
  <UL>
  <LI>No missing fur
  <LI>All tags attached
  <LI>No bends or creases
  </UL>
</TD>
She would love to live at your house!
</TR><TR>
<TD COLSPAN=2 BGCOLOR=gold>Buyer pays postage and
  insurance, and seller reserves the right not to sell to
  anyone with excessive negative feedback.</TD>
<P>
Payment with money order or bank check ships right away.
  Payment with personal check ships after 10 business
  days.
</TR><TR>
<TD COLSPAN=2 ALIGN=CENTER BGCOLOR=darkgoldenrod>
<FONT SIZE=5>Have fun bidding!</FONT></TD>
</TR>
</TABLE>
</CENTER>
</FONT>
```

Code for Example 7

```
<CENTER>
<FONT FACE="Comic Sans MS">
<TABLE BORDER=3>
<TR>
<TD COLSPAN=2 ALIGN=CENTER BGCOLOR=slateblue><FONT
   SIZE=5>Bear Valley "Gimme Some Love" MIB!</TD>
</TR><TR>
<TD BGCOLOR=rosybrown ALIGN=CENTER>
   <TABLE BORDER=3 CELLPADDING=2>
   <TR>
   <TD BGCOLOR=royalblue>
<IMG SRC="http://www.host.com/images/bear.jpg">
</TD>
</TR>
</TABLE>
</TD>
<TD BACKGROUND=
   "http://www.host.com/images/pinkbg.gif">This lovely
   bear from the "Bear Valley" line is in perfect condition:
   <UL>
   <LI>No missing fur
   <LI>All tags attached
   <LI>No bends or creases
   </UL>
She would love to live at your house!</TD>
</TR><TR>
<TD COLSPAN=2 BACKGROUND=
   "http://www.host.com/images/pinkbg.gif">
Buyer pays postage and insurance, and seller reserves the
   right not to sell to anyone with excessive negative feed-
   back.
<P>
Payment with money order or bank check ships right away.
   Payment with personal check ships after 10 business
   days. Please check out our
<A HREF="http://www.host.com/ourhome.html">HOME
   PAGE</A> for other items that we have for sale!</TD>
</TR><TR>
<TD COLSPAN=2 ALIGN=CENTER BGCOLOR=slateblue><FONT
   SIZE=5>
```

Have fun bidding!</FONT></TD>
</TR>
</TABLE>
</CENTER>
</FONT>

☞Fancy Auction Description Templates

These next few examples are more detailed than the previous ones. Once you get the hang of coding in HTML, designing your own auction descriptions will be easy.

As I mentioned before, you'll only have to type in the code file once, and test it by opening it in your browser. Then, you can save it to a file and reuse it each time you enter an auction. Just replace the previous auction's information with the new data.

> ➡ Note: Don't want to type all this in from ⬅
> scratch? I don't blame you! Send me e-mail at
> Marble90@aol.com and let me know which auction
> description you want. I'll send you the HTML code file. Be
> sure to tell me the example number and the title of this book!

Again, these examples will show up better in your browser. The background colors I chose looked fine to me when I tested them, but others may find them enough to induce a migraine. If you decide to use other colors, simply replace the names within the appropriate tag.

Color Schemes

Since this book is in grayscale, I tried to use background colors and backgrounds that would contrast well. In doing so, I discovered some color combinations of dark and light that go well together. This table lists some suggestions:

Light Color	Dark Color
cyan	darkcyan
salmon	orangered
violet	darkviolet
skyblue	royalblue
lightpink	indianred
peachpuff	salmon
palegreen	forestgreen
gold	darkgoldenrod

tan	sienna
violet	darkviolet
royalblue	lightslateblue
lightskyblue	darkblue
burlywood	maroon
turquoise	cadetblue
tomato	firebrick
springgreen	seagreen
dodgerblue	lightslateblue
lightslategray	darkslategray

Table 7-2. Contrasting Colors

> ➡ Note: With very dark backgrounds, be sure ⬅
> to use a lighter color for your text.

Icons Used in These Examples

Though I show the URL to icons and background patterns used in these examples, they are not actual URLs to those icons. I simply included them in the HTML code to illustrate how to include images with the descriptions.

You can find many of the icons that appear in these examples at the image bank sites listed toward the end of this chapter.

Adding a Link to Your Current Auctions

If you have other auctions running, you may want to code a link to them in your auction descriptions. Bidders can save on shipping charges if they buy several items from you at the same time.

To get the URL for your current auctions, do a seller search on yourself. Copy the URL of the result page into an auction description code file, and include that URL within the <A> tag.

Fancy Auction Description Formats

The next five auction description examples add more flair to your listing. Remember, you can experiment with these by opening the HTML code file in your browser.

Example 8

This example adds some fancy text symbols to dress up the title. These won't slow the page loading since they're text instead of image files. See the code for Example 8 (p. 230).

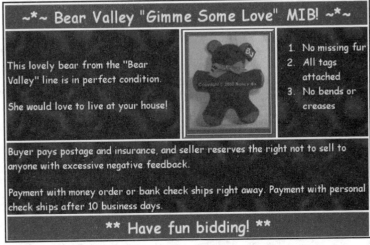

Figure 7-9. Example 8. Auction Description.

Example 9

The code for Example 9 (p. 231) will show you how to place the picture in the same frame as the title.

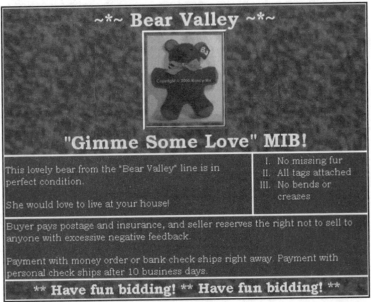

Figure 7-10. Example 9. Auction Description.

Example 10

This example uses background patterns and table-cell shading to make the picture, title, and descriptions stand out from each other. Notice the link to my other auctions. See the code for Example 10 (p. 232).

Figure 7-11. Example 10. Auction Description.

Example 11

This example uses border images and text formatting to achieve the desired result. In the code for Example 11 (p. 233), notice the use of the BORDER attribute set to zero within the <IMG> tag to prevent a border around the hyperlink image.

Figure 7-12. Example 11. Auction Description.

Example 12

This example uses double bar images and puts some of the descriptive text and the picture into a borderless table. You can find bars like these in many image banks on the Web. See the code for example 12 (p. 234).

Figure 7-13. Example 12. Auction Description.

Fancy Auction Description Code

The following pages include the HTML code for the auction description samples in Examples 8-12 (pgs. 226 – 229). The text in regular font is the necessary HTML code that must be entered exactly as it's shown here. You will replace the boldface text with your own information.

Code for Example 8

```
<CENTER>
<FONT FACE="Comic Sans MS">
<TABLE BORDER=4>
<TR>
<TD COLSPAN=3 ALIGN=CENTER BGCOLOR=slateblue>
<FONT SIZE=5 COLOR=antiquewhite><B> ~*~ Bear Valley
   "Gimme Some Love" MIB! ~*~</TD>
</TR><TR>
<TD BACKGROUND=
   "http://www.host.com/images/back1.jpg">
<FONT COLOR=beige>This lovely bear from the "Bear Val-
   ley" line is in perfect condition.</TD>
<P>
She would love to live at your house!
<TD BGCOLOR=royalblue ALIGN=CENTER>
   <TABLE BORDER=3 CELLPADDING=2>
   <TR>
   <TD BGCOLOR=royalblue>
   IMG SRC="http://www.host.com/images/bear.jpg">
   </TD></TR>
   </TABLE>
</TD>
<TD BACKGROUND=
   "http://www.host.com/images/back1.jpg">
<FONT COLOR=beige>
   <OL>
   <LI>No missing fur
   <LI>All tags attached
   <LI>No bends or creases
   </OL>
</TD>
</TR><TR>
<TD COLSPAN=3 BACKGROUND=
   "http://www.host.com/images/back1.jpg">
<FONT COLOR=beige>Buyer pays postage and insurance,
```

and seller reserves the right not to sell to anyone with
excessive negative feedback.

```
<P>
```

Payment with money order or bank check ships right
away. Payment with personal check ships after 10 business days.</TD>

```
</TR><TR>
<TD COLSPAN=3 ALIGN=CENTER BGCOLOR=slateblue>
<FONT SIZE=5 COLOR=antiquewhite><B>** Have fun bid-
   ding! **</B></FONT></TD>
</TR></TABLE></CENTER></FONT>
```

Code for Example 9

```
<CENTER>
<FONT FACE="Bookman">
<TABLE BORDER=4>
<TR>
<TD COLSPAN=2 ALIGN=CENTER
BACKGROUND="http://www.host.com/images/back2.jpg">
<FONT SIZE=6 COLOR=antiquewhite><B> ~*~ Bear Valley ~*~
   <TABLE BORDER=3>
   <TR>
   <TD><IMG
   SRC="http://www.host.com/images/bear.jpg"></TD>
   </TR></TABLE>
</TD>
"Gimme Some Love" MIB!
</TR><TR>
<TD BGCOLOR=darkviolet>
<FONT COLOR=white>This lovely bear from the "Bear Val-
   ley" line is in perfect condition.
<P>
She would love to live at your house!</TD>
<TD BGCOLOR=darkviolet><FONT COLOR=white>
   <OL TYPE=I>
   <LI>No missing fur
   <LI>All tags attached
   <LI>No bends or creases
   </OL>
</TD>
</TR><TR>
<TD COLSPAN=2 BGCOLOR=darkviolet><FONT
```

```
COLOR=white>Buyer pays postage and insurance, and
seller reserves the right not to sell to anyone with
excessive negative feedback.
<P>
Payment with money order or bank check ships right
   away. Payment with personal check ships after 10 busi-
   ness days.</TD>
</TR><TR>
<TD COLSPAN=2 ALIGN=CENTER
BACKGROUND="http://www.host.com/images/back2.jpg">
<FONT SIZE=5 COLOR=antiquewhite><B>** Have fun bid-
   ding! ** Have fun bidding! **</B></FONT></TD>
</TR>
</TABLE>
</CENTER>
</FONT>
```

Code for Example 10

```
<CENTER>
<FONT FACE=Arial>
<TABLE BORDER=4>
<TR>
<TD COLSPAN=2 ALIGN=CENTER
BACKGROUND="http://www.host.com/images/pinkbg.gif">
<FONT SIZE=6 COLOR=maroon><B> ~*~ Bear Valley ~*~
<BR>
"Gimme Some Love"
<BR>
Mint In Box!</B></TD>
</TR><TR>
<TD ALIGN=CENTER
BACKGROUND=indianred>
<TABLE BORDER=3 CELLPADDING=5>
   <TR>
   <TD><IMG SRC=
   "http://www.host.com/images/bear.jpg"></TD>
   </TR></TABLE>
</TD>
<TD BGCOLOR=indianred ALIGN=CENTER>
<FONT COLOR=antiquewhite><B>This lovely bear from the
   "Bear Valley" line is in perfect condition.
<P>
```

She would love to live at your house!

```
<UL>
  <LI>No missing fur
  <LI>All tags attached
  <LI>No bends or creases
  </UL>
</TD>
</TR><TR>
<TD COLSPAN=2 BGCOLOR=lightpink><FONT
  COLOR=maroon><B>Buyer pays postage and insurance,
  and seller reserves the right not to sell to anyone with
  excessive negative feedback.
<P>
Payment with money order or bank check ships right
  away. Payment with personal check ships after 10 busi-
  ness days. Please check out our
<A HREF="http://www.site.com/auction/allmine">OTHER
  AUCTIONS</A>
to save on shipping!</B></TD>
</TR><TR>
<TD COLSPAN=2 ALIGN=CENTER
BACKGROUND="http://www.host.com/images/pinkbg.gif">
<FONT SIZE=5 COLOR=maroon><B>* * Have fun bidding! * *
  Have fun bidding! * *</B></FONT></TD>
</TR></TABLE>
</CENTER></FONT>
```

Code for Example 11

```
<CENTER>
<A HREF="http://www.host.com/ourhome.html">
<IMG SRC="http://www.host.com/images/bearvalley.gif"
  BORDER=0></A>
<BR>
<FONT FACE="Comic Sans MS"><BIG>"Gimme Some Love"
  MIB!</BIG>
<BR>
<SMALL><I>Click on the Bear Valley image to visit our
  home page!</I></SMALL>
<BR>
<IMG SRC="http://www.host.com/images/flowers.gif">
</CENTER>
<P>
```

This lovely bear from the "Bear Valley" line is in perfect condition!

```
<UL>
<LI>No missing fur
<LI>All tags attached
<LI>No bends or creases
</UL>
```

She would love to live at your house!

```
<P>
```

Buyer pays postage and insurance, and seller reserves the right not to sell to anyone with excessive negative feedback. Payment with money order or bank check ships right away. Payment with personal check ships after 10 business days.

```
<P>
```

Have fun bidding!

```
<P>
<CENTER>
<IMG SRC="http://www.host.com/images/flowers.gif">
<P>
<IMG SRC="http://www.host.com/images/bear.jpg">
</CENTER>
</FONT>
```

Code for Example 12

```
<CENTER>
<A HREF="http://www.host.com/ourhome.html">
<IMG SRC="http://www.host.com/images/bearvalley.gif"
  BORDER=0></A>
<BR>
<FONT FACE="Comic Sans MS"><BIG>"Gimme Some Love"
  MIB!</BIG>
<BR>
<SMALL><I>Click on the Bear Valley image to visit our
  home
  page!</I></SMALL>
<BR>
<IMG SRC="http://www.host.com/images/emboss.gif">
<BR>
<IMG SRC="http://www.host.com/images/rainbow.gif">
</CENTER>
<P>
```

```
<B>This lovely bear from the "Bear Valley" line is in per-
   fect condition!</B>
<BR>
<TABLE CELLPADDING=10 WIDTH=500>
<TR>
<TD>
   <UL>
   <LI>No missing fur
   <LI>All tags attached
   <LI>No bends or creases
   </UL>
</TD>
<TD>
   <TABLE BORDER=2>
   <TR>
   <TD BGCOLOR=BLUE><IMG
      SRC="http://www.host.com/images/bear.jpg"></TD>
      </TR>
   </TABLE>
</TD>
</TR>
</TABLE>
<B>She would love to live at your house!
<P>
Buyer pays postage and insurance, and seller reserves
   the right not to sell to anyone with excessive negative
   feedback. Payment with money order or bank check
   ships right away. Payment with personal check ships
   after 10 business days.
<P>
<CENTER>
<BIG><FONT COLOR=BLUE>Have fun
   bidding!</FONT></BIG></B>
<P>
<IMG SRC="http://www.host.com/images/rainbow.gif">
<BR>
<IMG SRC="http://www.host.com/images/emboss.gif">
</CENTER></FONT>
```

☛Sites That Have Auction Software

Certain Web sites offer special auction tools and software you can download. The programs are designed to help manage your on-line auctions. Some of them offer information about the status of all auctions that you have listed on all online auction sites. Others help you format your auction descriptions.

You'll find a comprehensive directory of sites that offer auction tools in *Collector's Guide to Online Auctions*. In the meantime, you can check out a few:

Uniform Resource Locator	Site Name
www.auction-network.com/html/scripts.html	Auction Network.
auctioneer.vtrader.com	Auctioneer v2.0
home.cyber-quest.com/jslocum/bt . . .	Blackthorne Software
www.everysoft.com	EveryAuction

Image Hosting

These sites offer image hosting for auctions. Some charge a fee to host your image, while others offer free space. A few of them have other auction tools available as well.

Uniform Resource Locator	Site Name
www.auctionpix.com . . .	Auction Pix Image Hosting Service
www.easyauction.com	EasyAuction
www.meteors.com	Imagehost by Meteors Design
www.imagehosting.com/general/hosting.html	Imagehosting.com
www.kathost.com	Kat's Image Hosting
www.pixplus.com	Lynnie's PixPlus
www.mrpics.com	MrPics.com
www.vistanet.net/pics	Pics+Plus
www.javanet.com/~markr	Picture This
www.images4u.net	Service For You Inc.
www.traderjax.com	Traderjax.com
www.pixelhost.com	PixelHost
www.witchywoman.com	Witchywoman.com

Image Banks

These Web sites have collections with hundreds of images and icons to use on your home pages or in your auction descriptions. To maintain control over images you want to use (site owners can and often do move files around), copy the picture to your hard drive and upload it to your Web directory later. You can then use the image on your Web pages.

Remember that linking images back to another host puts a lot of traffic on that server.

Uniform Resource Locator	Site Name
pixelplace.com	The Icon Factory
www.hlt.uni-duisburg.de/Icons	Anthony Thyssen's Icon Library
www.animationlibrary.com/	Animation Library
www.andyart.com	Andy's Art Attack
www.iconbazaar.com	IconBAZAAR
www.clipartconnection.com	The Clip Art Connection
www.arttoday.com	ArtToday
www.barrysclipart.com	Barry's Clip Art Server
people.delphi.com/nlopez/anim.htm	Cat GIF Animations
www.netmegs.com/~animate	Animation Shack
www.rewnet.com/bbb	Buttons, Bullets, and Backgrounds
www.specialweb.com/original	Celine's Original .GIFs
www.efn.org/~trentj/useless1.html	The Useless Button Universe
web2.airmail.net/lrivera	FOUR bEES Free Web Graphics
members.tripod.com/~nutty747	Free Web Art
www.theshockzone.com	TheShockzone

Copying an Icon

The Web gives us a great function for "borrowing" icons from other pages. You can copy and save any icon on any page, unless the image is part of a program. Just place your mouse cursor over the picture, right-click, select "Save Image As" or "Save Picture As" from the menu, and tell your computer where to keep the file.

> ➡ Note: Be sure you don't reuse any ⬅
> copyrighted images. Include credits for any images
> if the host site specifies that you should.

To keep track of your image files, build a "web-pix" directory (or something similar) for storing them. Then you won't have to hunt them down later.

Collector and Auction Portals

Many Web portals, like some of those listed in Chapter 4, include hyperlinks to online auction sites. You can also find free auction software tools, like item counters, HTML tutorials, and programs that generate auction descriptions that you can copy and paste as you enter the auction.

Now that you're familiar with HTML and have plenty of resources to work with, you might be thinking about making your own home page on the Web.

Chapter 8 — Home, Home on the Web

Nothing makes you feel more at home on the Web than having your own home page. Your Web soul needs somewhere to live, and a home page is the perfect place. In addition, you can be of great service to your fellow collectors by building a site that offers information about your favorite line, or contains links to other sites made by folks who enjoy collecting the same items you do.

Now that you've mastered coding great auction descriptions in HTML, making your own Web pages will be a breeze.

This chapter gets you started making your personal home page. With a Web page, you can meet other collectors by being part of a Web ring or link exchange, list any collectibles you may want to sell or trade, or just tell the world a little about yourself. You can also add your favorite links to other sites in order to keep the Web spinning.

Here's what we'll cover in this chapter:

- What's a home page?
- Creating your page
- Web sites that offer free home pages
- Web sites with links to free stuff
- Tying this in with collecting
- How do you DO that?

☛ What's a Home Page?

A home page is actually the main page in a set of Web documents. Your home page should be in a file called *index.html*. Most servers will default to that page if no file name appears in the URL.

> ➡ Note: Some free home page hosting sites ⬅
> will name your home page file for you and list your
> uploaded images in special directories.

Your home page should have links to any other pages in your directory. A home page is actually a "doorway" page to the rest of your site. It should act as an introduction and table of contents in one. Keep it somewhat simple and free of a lot of elaborate animation and images so viewers don't have to wait long for it to load. Any fancy stuff can appear on your other pages.

The best way to get ideas for your home page is to look at other Web sites. If you see one you like, adapt the general idea on your page.

Borrowing HTML Code

Borrowing is a nicer word than stealing. If you have Internet Explorer, you can borrow the HTML code from any page you can view. At the top of the browser in the menu bar is the word "View." If you click on this and select "Source" from the menu, the HTML code for the current page will open in the Notepad program. You can then save the HTML code to a file, alter any image paths or hypertext links, and adapt it for your own use. Many other Web browsers also allow the user to view the HTML source code.

Note: If the page is within a frame, you'll see the main frame setup page if you select "View Source" from the browser menu. Instead, right-click inside the frame and select "View page source" or the equivalent.

This is a great way to learn even more HTML. In addition, you can add some great stuff to your page.

What Makes a Good Home Page?

If you're like most Websurfers, you're going to love making pages. Since it won't be the only one in your directory, you should treat your home page as though it's the main page of a site. It should introduce the style and design of the rest of your site.

Note: I'll bet you a nickel that once you make one Web page, you'll make more.

A good Web site has certain characteristics:

• Contains new and unique content
• Allows visitors to have input, like with a guestbook
• Displays effective/innovative design
• Offers links to other pages or Web sites

In other words, a good home page will educate, engage, and entertain your visitors.

Things To Include

When you first attempt to make a personal home page, keep in mind what you want to include. Here are some ideas:

• Your personalized greeting to visitors
• A little about yourself
• Your hobbies and interests

- Photographs or images (small ones that load quickly)
- Links to your favorite sites
- Your guestbook

Later, you can tailor your site to whatever theme you choose by adding more pages with links from your home page.

Some people put their photograph on their home pages. This is a nice personal touch. Remember, though, that this is the *Internet*. Anyone with Internet access can look at your page and copy your photo to his or her hard drive where it can be used for all kinds of purposes. You have to decide if you want copies of your face in places you might not know about.

In this age of digital photography and sophisticated graphics programs, you might find your likeness where you don't want it if you anger the wrong person. On the other hand, it's nice to let your collecting friends know what you look like.

Here's an idea. Get a digitized picture of yourself and put it on your Web site. Be sure it's the only one you use anywhere on the Web. This way, if any variations turn up, others will know it's a copy of your home-page picture. You can even use a graphics program to turn the photo to monochrome so that others can see, but not easily replicate, your likeness.

As you surf around looking at home pages, you'll notice that most of them don't include a plethora of personal information about the author. Most revolve around the author's interests.

The best home pages include the author's first name, an e-mail address, a theme or attitude, and a list of links. These can include:

- Links to other pages in the author's site
- Links to other pages that the author enjoys
- Links to Web pages that pertain to the author's interests

The owner puts his or her stamp of identity on the page with its content alone.

What Not To Include

Never give out personal information about yourself on the Internet. When you're participating in bulletin board and chat room discussions, you leave yourself open for anyone to get an attitude about you.

Avoid offering information that can be used against you. Here's an example of what you should not include on your home page:

- Home address
- Home phone number
- Date of birth
- Social Security number
- Your mother's maiden name
- Political affiliations
- Marital history
- Employer

Carve out your Internet niche with what you know and what your page can offer in the way of information, not who you are and where you live. This is particularly important if you include photos of prized and valuable collectibles on your Web pages.

Also, avoid including anything that takes a long time to download. Nothing loses visitors faster than a slowly loading page.

☞Creating Your Page

The auction descriptions you coded in Chapter 7 were not a complete Web page — they were only part of an existing Web page. Each complete Web page starts and ends with a set of HTML tags that determine certain things about the entire page:

- Type of file (HTML)
- Title
- Background color or pattern
- Text color and style
- Hyperlink text color

Most sites that offer free space for home pages also include home-page builders. These are great for getting your home page up and running, but can be a pain to manage unless you're an HTML expert.

If you're going to make Web pages, it's best to learn the basics of HTML.

Home-Page Builders

Some home-page building programs let you make a Web page using a drag-and-drop interface, which automatically translates the page to an HTML file that you upload to a Web server. This is sometimes called WYSIWYG (What You See Is What You Get).

Some Web page designers feel that WYSIWYG Web page builders are a boon to the Web because you can make pages faster. I can't argue that they make great-looking Web pages and I like the idea of easily made pages, but I'd rather see folks learn how to code them in HTML. That way, you can create great-looking pages in Microsoft FrontPage or some other page building program, upload the page files to your Web directory, and then fine tune them with HTML.

If you know HTML, you don't need to go back to the page building program, make your updates, and then upload the file again. You can go right to the source file from the home-page editor for quicker updating; use the page building program for extensive page changes.

> ➡ Note: You'll have better control of how ⬅
> your auction descriptions look if you know how to code
> them yourself in HTML.

My advice is to make a very simple page with the site's home-page builder and then convert it into HTML. Most of them give you this option once your first page is completed. This gives you a start on your page and you can then use HTML tags to tweak it. It's much easier, and you're better off because you can effectively manage the page.

HTML for a Home Page

To code a Web page, you'll use HTML tags with attributes and values just like you did writing auction descriptions, but you'll include a few tags at the beginning and at the end of your HTML file. Each of the HTML tags that follow has a start tag and an end tag.

> ➡ Note: Use the next five HTML tags only ⬅
> when coding Web pages, not auction descriptions. They could
> adversely affect the way the auction page displays. Follow the
> examples in Chapter 7 for coding auction descriptions with HTML.

<HTML>

The main <HTML> tag lets the browser know that the file contains HTML-coded information. The other hint is the ".html" or ".htm" extension on the filename.

<HEAD>

The <HEAD> tag includes the prologue to the rest of the file. There are a few HTML tags contained between the <HEAD> tags, but no text is included except for the title, which is found within the <TITLE> tags.

<TITLE>

This contains a short title of your Web page. Whatever you code in here appears in the title bar of the browser when you view the page. This is also part of what Web-bots grab when they stop by to index your page for a search engine.

<BODY>

The entire body of your HTML document goes within the <BODY> tag, including your text, images, links, and everything else. Several attributes are used inside this tag:

- BGCOLOR – controls the background color of the page. The value is a color; the default is usually white.
- BACKGROUND – specifies a background image of the page. The value is the URL to a background image file. On some browsers, the BGCOLOR you specify shows through the background pattern on table borders and horizontal rules (lines).
- TEXT – indicates the color of the main text. The value is a color; the default is black.
- LINK – determines the color of hyperlink text. The value is a color; the default is blue.
- VLINK – controls the color of visited links. The value is a color; the default is purple.
- ALINK – specifies the color of links that the user is in the process of clicking on. The value is a color; the default is red.

➡ Note: Even if you specify a BACKGROUND ⬅ file, you should still specify a BGCOLOR. If your visitor has images turned off, he or she will see the BGCOLOR as the background of your page. Be sure the color complements your text and images.

<BASEFONT>

This indicates the basic size and typeface of the text on the page. The <BASEFONT> tag has two attributes, SIZE and FACE. The SIZE attribute can have a value from 1 to 7. The default size is 3. Internet Explorer, among other Web browsers, recognizes this tag.

Headings

HTML contains six heading-levels, with level 1 being the most prominent. Headings are enclosed in <H> and </H> tags, each one with a heading-level number, as in this example:

245

- \<H1>**This is a first-level heading**</H1>
- \<H2>**This is a second-level heading**</H2>
- \<H3>**This is a third-level heading**</H3>
- \<H4>**This is a fourth-level heading**</H4>
- \<H5>**This is a fifth-level heading**</H5>
- \<H6>**This is a sixth-level heading**</H6>

Similar to word-processing programs like Microsoft Word, the text for each heading gets smaller (or lighter) as the heading-levels decrease. Here's an example:

HTML Code
```
<H1>Here I Go Again, Demonstrating!</H1>
<H2>Why I Like to Give Examples</H2>
<H3>Example Types</H3>
```

Output

Here I Go Again, Demonstrating!
Why I Like to Give Examples
Example Types

You get the idea. Use the \<H> tags just as you would format any document with multiple heading levels. Just be sure to close the tag or the rest of your text will look exactly like the heading.

An extra space inserts automatically after each heading, so you don't need to include a \<P> tag. You might want to include the paragraph tag anyway, though, to make the code easier to edit.

Your Color Scheme

The Internet has more in common with television than it has with paper publications. You can get away with certain things in print because light shines toward it, not you. With a CRT, or cathode ray tube like your monitor has, the light comes from behind the screen right into your face. This is why long hours in front of a monitor strain your eyes more than reading a book.

Keep this in mind when you're designing anything that will appear on the Web, especially your home page. Too many different patterns and bright colors on one screen may cause people to lose interest, with good reason.

Avoid Complements

No, not the good kind. Compliments are nice! However, colors opposite each other on the spectrum, *complementary colors,* appear to bounce or vibrate when placed side-by-side.

When choosing the background and text color combinations for your Web pages, be sure your text color doesn't clash with the background. Avoid using these complementary colors next to each other on any Web page:

- Red and green
- Orange and purple
- Yellow and blue

This includes all variations or hues of these colors. When you view your Web page in your browser, stare at it for a few seconds to see if the colors seem to "wiggle." If they do, choose less psychedelic colors. You want to create an artistically pleasing Web page, not one that nauseates people.

If your background is a dark color, use beige, gray, or white text. Bold colors work fine on light or pastel backgrounds. Avoid combining bright shades.

A Very Simple Home Page

Not all home pages have to look like they belong to a heavy-metal rock band. The ones clogged with images and animated text usually take so long to load that you lose your visitor before he or she has a chance to read anything on your page.

Here's an example of a very basic home page coded in HTML:

HTML Code
```
<HTML>
<HEAD>
<TITLE>Jeff's Very Basic Home Page</TITLE>
</HEAD>
<BODY BGCOLOR=skyblue TEXT=black LINK=brown ALINK=sky-
   blue VLINK=maroon>
<BASEFONT SIZE=4
<FONT FACE=Verdana>
<CENTER>
<H1>Welcome to Jeff's Very Basic Home Page!</H1>
</CENTER>
```

```
<HR>
<P>
```
Here is my home page and here is a little bit about me:
```
<UL>
<LI>I like Harbour Lights lighthouses
<LI>I like Harmony Kingdom box figurines
<LI>My wife's OK
</UL>
<P>
```
Here are some of my very favorite links on the Web:
```
<UL>
<LI><A HREF="http://www.harbourlights.com">The Har-
   bour Lights Home Page</A>
<LI><A HREF="http://www.harmonykingdom.com">The
   Harmony Kingdom Home Page</A>
<LI><A
   HREF="http://www.angelfire.com/il/marble9">Nancy's
   Home Page</A>
</UL>
```
I made this page for anyone who wants to read it.
```
<HR>
<CENTER>
```
Send me e-mail!
```
<P>
<A HREF="mailto:jeff@email.com">jeff@email.com</A>
<HR>
</CENTER></FONT>
</BODY></HTML>
```

The example is on the following page.

Jeff can add images, tables, and background patterns the same way he did for his fancy auction descriptions. He should also include a guestbook so visitors can leave their comments and greetings. Once he learns the basics of HTML, Jeff can do a lot with his page.

A good Web page is easy to read and navigate. Here are some more tips:

- Use a background that contrasts well with the text so it's easy to read.
- Adjust the text font and make it bold if the default font is difficult to read.
- If you have other pages at your site, include a link back to your

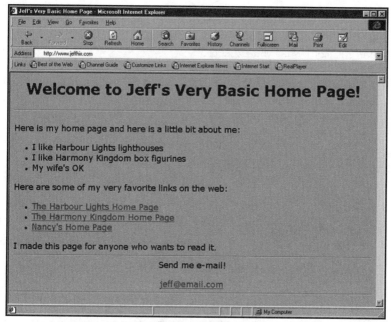

Figure 8-1. Jeff's Very Basic Home Page

home page on all of them.
- Don't use too much animation; it slows the loading time considerably.
- Be sure your images balance with the background.
- Include an e-mail link so your readers can communicate with you.
- View your home page in both Netscape and Internet Explorer, so you know how your visitors will see it. In addition, some of the HTML coding elements that work with Internet Explorer don't show up in Netscape, and vice versa.

Some Web developers advise against changing the color of link text. The default is blue, and people are accustomed to that. However, blue might not be a good match for your background.

A good choice for link text is to make the links one color, and the visited links a slightly darker shade of that hue. This way, the visited links will "fade" to let the user know that he or she has been there.

Test Your Page

Before you announce your URL to the world, test your page in at least one browser. You'll probably have to make changes to your

HTML code. That's part of learning how to design Web pages. If you forget one closing tag or even an end bracket, your page will look different from what you expected.

> Note: If you can, view your page from a few different computers. Monitor quality may also vary the results. You page might not look the same on your desktop computer as it does on your laptop screen, so you may need to vary your color scheme so it looks good on both.

Go through the whole page and check everything. Here are some things to look for:

- Is the formatting right?
- Is your text in familiar lower and upper case, so it's easy to read?
- Do all links work?
- Do your images line up correctly?
- Is the background correct?
- Is your e-mail address a MAILTO link so users can contact you?
- Is your text the right font and color?
- Is your link text the correct font and color?
- Does the page look the way you want it to?
- Have you used any colors that don't go well together?

> Note: If some of your link text is the color you designated for your visited links, it's because you've already been to those pages. Your browser stores this information.

Don't get discouraged if your page doesn't look right the first time. It takes time to get the hang of HTML and Web page design. Keep working on it!

Promote Your Page

Why not? You went through all the trouble of making it, so now be sure others see it. If you maintain the "build it and they will come" attitude, you probably won't get many visitors. Take advantage of registries to which most home page building sites have links.

Here are some promotion strategies for your page:

- Become part of a Web ring or link exchange.
- Make use of the <META> tags in your HTML code. <META> tags allow you to enter keywords about your site that Web-bots will pick up. Your HTML reference book will contain information about <META> tags.
- Trade links with other collectors who have home pages. Include links to their pages and let them do the same for you.

Some sites let you submit your page URL for indexing to many search engines at the same time. Some are free, and others charge a fee. Here are a few:

Uniform Resource Locator	Site Name
www.promoteyoursite.com	Website Promotion
www.announceit.com	Announce It!
www.powerpromote.com	Power Promote
www.qwiklaunch.com	QuikL@unch Web Site Announcer
www.register-it.com	!Register-It!
www.webdeveloper.com	WebDeveloper.com
www.urlsubmit.com	URLSubmit.com
tucson.com/market.html	Web Market Resources

For more information, check out the Search Engine Secrets site at www.searchsecrets.com.

A Few Hints from the Search Engine Pros

You can do some things to help Web-bots find and index your site:

- Don't put an image as the first item on your page. If you do, the search engine will index the image code, and your site won't come up in many searches.
- If you must have an image at the top of your page, enter some keywords above it that are the same color as your background. They won't show up on the page, but the Web-bot will see them. Don't overdo it, though, or "the Bots" may ignore your page.
- Avoid overloading your page with keywords. Search engines may ignore and disqualify sites that contain absurdly high instances of the same word.
- Web-bots index titles. Use a brief but descriptive title for your page, including keywords about your site.
- Read about <META> tags and use them correctly.

There are many ways to be sure that Web-bots index your page. In fact, some people make a living out of coding other people's Web pages to optimize indexing by search engines.

☞Web Sites That Offer Free Home Pages

It doesn't necessarily cost a lot to get a home page on the Web. In fact, you can get space for a home page (also called a *Web directory*) for free at many sites all over the Internet. All you need to do is find one you enjoy working with and you can have a home page on the Web in no time. A few of these sites are listed below.

My personal favorite is Angelfire, because it has many features that make maintaining a home page very easy and efficient. Users receive 5 megabytes (MBs) of space, which is substantial for a Web directory.

Uniform Resource Locator	Page Title
www.angelfire.com	Angelfire
www.tripod.com	Tripod
www.geocities.com	GeoCities
www.freenation.com	Free Nation
www.homepage.com	HomePage.com
www.homestead.com	Homestead
www2.fortunecity.com	FortuneCity
www.xoom.com	Xoom
www.conk.com	Conk World
www.oe-pages.com	Create uh Page
www.webspawner.com	WebSpawner
www.rotfl.com	ROTFL Online

Interior Decorating

Many free home-page sites also offer elements you can add to your page, such as:

- An image bank, so you don't have to fill up your Web directory with uploaded image files
- Page counters
- Guestbooks
- Editing capabilities
- Java and CGI scripts, with explanations and instructions
- Links to sites that will register your page with search engines
- HTML tutorials

☛Web Sites With Links To Free Stuff

Sites all over the Web provide free goodies for your home page. As with most free tools, the sites fund themselves with advertisements and welcome the exposure you give them by adding their items to your page. Most only request a link back to their main page in return for using the tools.

You can get scripts that welcome your visitors, greetings you write that scroll across the page, clocks, sound, and even movies. Some of them give you the HTML code to cut and paste right into your file.

What more could you ask?

Here's a list of Web sites offering home-page freebies:

Uniform Resource Locator	Page Title
www.forumcities.com	ForumCities – Free Message Boards
www.glacierweb.com/home	Glacier Web
www.freeindex.com	Free Index
www.thefreesite.com	The Free Site
www.freehomepage.com	FreeHomePage
www.alxbook.com	Alx' Guestbook Service
www.dboard.com	Dachshboard Software
desktoppublishing.com	desktopPublishing.com
www.fastcounter.com	Link Exchange FastCounter
www.dreambook.com	Dreambook Guestbooks
www.guestworld.com	The World Famous Guestbook Server
www.beseen.com	LookSmart's Beseen
guestbook.bloke.com	Bloke.com's Free GuestBook
counter.bloke.com	Free Java Hit Web Counter Applet
www.coolchat.com	Awesome-Chatrooms
www.counterart.com	The Museum of Counter Art
www.scrawlwall.com	Scrawl Wall
www.digits.com	WebCounter
jdante.hypermart.net	Free Stuff for your Web Pages

> ➤ Note: If you execute a Control-n (hold down ◀═
> your Control key and the letter "n" at the same time), this
> brings up another browser. You can access the Web sites
> with free tools in one browser, and work on your home page
> in the other.

☞Tying This In With Collecting

The last few chapters of this book provide information that's pertinent to all Web users, not just collectors. You may wonder why I covered so much of it.

Suffice to say that the more you use the Web for collecting, the better it is to know how to make Web pages. Having a page on the Web helps you effectively manage your collecting.

List Your Items for Sale

Posting items for sale on bulletin boards is great, but only when you have a few pieces. Otherwise, you'll have to keep track of what you sell and be sure that you post a follow-up when certain items are no longer available. With a home page, you can just change the code file, drop in the date the page was last updated, and post a link to your page on a bulletin board that everyone can access for the latest information.

Just remember to be careful about revealing your inventory. If you list pieces that you only want to sell, include a disclaimer that the sales are firm and you're not interested in trading.

If you have any items up for auction, you can list them and include a link right to the auction. By now, you should know how to get the URL for your auctions to include in your <A> tags, right?

It's great to be able to point people to your Web page for all of your information.

Build a Dedicated Web Page

With your HTML expertise, you can make a dedicated collectible Web site to which a company will want to include a link. Think about how proud you'll feel when others know you as both an authority in your hobby and a Webmaster.

The collectible company might notice you, too. I know of at least one individual who did such an outstanding job on his dedicated Web site that the company eventually hired him to do its main site.

Serve a Collecting Purpose

How about a Web page that tracks serial numbers of limited edition pieces? Other collectors will love having a place to go for this information. Here are some other ideas for your Web page that can be useful for your fellow collectors:

- Keep track of production numbers for retired pieces.
- Install a guestbook or chat room so your collector friends can

discuss their favorite items in the line.
- Describe variations.
- Write an information page about the history of the collectible line.
- Host a photo gallery of pieces and their descriptions.
- List collector clubs and their officers.
- Profile the company and its artists.
- Build a directory of collectors.
- Maintain a list of links to related Web sites.

Offer to host and maintain the home page for your local collector's club. You can include a list of members with links to their e-mail address and, of course, their home pages.

Become Part of a Collector's Web Ring

Refer to Chapter 2 for information on how to get your site added to a Web ring. The site sends you the HTML code to copy and paste into your page lets you know which parts you need to customize.

Additionally, you might be able to choose (from an image bank) the buttons used for the Web-ring links. Pick buttons that match your page.

Good thing you know HTML!

Get In on a Link Exchange

Why not? Register at www.LinkExchange.com or set up page-link exchanges with other collectors. You'll be surprised how many visits your site will get from visitors who surf in by clicking on a banner ad.

☞How Do You DO That?

The nicest thing about making your own page is that you'll attract other collectors to stop by and visit. They can sign your guestbook and add a link to your page from theirs. If you include a page counter, you can keep track of how many people visit your site.

Once you know HTML, plan on answering a lot of questions from your fellow collectors. When they see you add images in your bulletin board posts, enter fancy auction description coding, and sport a fancy new home page, they'll all want to know how you did it.

Of course, you can always do what I do and refer them to this book. :-)

Glossary

The Internet collecting community carries its own lexicon of terms. This glossary will help you identify them when you encounter them online. Also, as with any hobby or interest, followers adopt a special language as a form of "shorthand" when referring to the type, style, or condition of a collectible. Keep this list nearby as you manage your collecting on the Internet.

This glossary also provides basic Internet terms. If you can't find one you're seeking here, visit www.whatis.com for a huge index of terms.

Accessories – Anything originally included with the item.

Alias – Another name you're known by, such as a user ID.

Americana – Antiques or other items that reflect early American culture or history.

Antique – Traditionally, anything over 100 years old. This varies, however, within the collecting world. Cars over 20 years old are eligible for antique license plates in some states, yet fossils and gemstones aren't usually considered antiques. An antique is more broadly defined as "anything really old."

Applied decoration – A design added to an item after manufacture by soldering, painting, or gluing.

As is – Item has a flaw, variation, or aberration.

Art glass – Decorative glass made for display rather than function.

Art pottery – Pottery made for display rather than function.

ARPAnet – Advanced Research Projects Agency network, which was the precursor to today's Internet.

Attribute – Defines the way an HTML tag operates.

Auction – Presenting something for sale for a pre-determined period with the intent of selling it to the highest bidder.

Auction description – See Description.

Auto-ship – When a dealer agrees in advance to buy a certain number of each item that the collectible company produces.

Background file – A JPEG or GIF image which, when tiled, makes up the background of a Web page or a table cell.

Bid – An offer to buy an item listed for auction.

Bid increment – The amount by which the bid increases each time a new one is placed.

Bid retraction – Canceling a bid when the auction is active.

Bisque – Porcelain with no applied glaze.

Buyer – The winning bidder who actually buys the item at his or her high bid price.

Category – Main classes or sections for items on auction sites.

Cell – See "Table cell."

China – Fine porcelain and earthenware dishes.

Collectible – Any collected item for which there is a secondary market.

Collecting buddy – Someone you met in an Internet chat room or bulletin board with whom you share your collecting passion.

Collector membership – An offer available through dealers or directly from the company. It includes a kit with one or more pieces, and the option to purchase additional pieces only available to members. Members usually receive a newsletter or periodical dedicated to the collectible line.

Collector quality – An item in mint or excellent condition that would be acceptable for a collector.

Conservator – One who restores collectible items to the original condition or close to it.

Crazing – Minute cracks on the surface or in the glaze. Usually applies to ceramics or pottery.

Dated – A date mark added to an item to indicate its year of manufacture.

Deadbeat bidder – Winning bidder who never pays for the item. Auction sites revoke their user privileges.

Dealer – One who buys and sells antiques and/or collectibles for a profit.

Description – The text part of the auction page that is formatted and entered by the seller.

Double-click – Two rapid-succession clicks of a mouse button.

Disneyana – Any item produced by Walt Disney Productions or Disney Studios.

Disparate parts – Parts from one or more items applied to make another.

Dutch auction – An auction in which multiples of the same item are sold with one auction listing.

Dynamic auction format – An auction format in which the information is current up to the minute when you reload the page.

E-mail – Electronic mail. A message sent through cyber-space from one user to another.

E-mail mining – Collecting e-mail addresses from online auction sites for the sole intent of spamming. (See Spam)

Emoticon – A little face made out of keyboard symbols that illustrates the writer's intent or emotion.

Encryption – Scrambling data sent over the Internet so it can't be read if it's intercepted.

English auction – In online format, it's an auction that stays open as long as the seller wants.

Estate auction – An auction in which a collection of items owned by a recently-deceased person is sold, usually one by one.

Event piece – See Special-event Piece.

Excellent condition – Usually means near-mint condition; for example, if the item itself is in issue condition except for a flaw in the packaging that doesn't affect the piece.

Fake – In collectibles, a counterfeit or forgery. Selling a fake as an original constitutes fraud.

Feedback – Also called "Rating;" a comment left for one person by another after completing an online auction transaction with one another.

Featured auction – One for which an extra fee is usually paid to have the listing appear on the auction site home page, or first in the list of search results or category listings.

Fine art – Art produced for aesthetic purposes.

Folk art – Primitive art, usually that which was produced in the early 1900s.

First in series – Either item #1 in a series of items by the same collectible company, or items in a collectible line that were made before there was a market demand for the collectible. Usually the prime pieces in any collectible line.

Flame – A hostile remark toward another person made on a bulletin board or in a chat room.

Flame war – A barrage of hostile remarks by several users directed at each other.

Gently loved – A previously used item, such as an ornament hung on a Christmas tree for a few seasons, or a child's toy. Frankly, if all items in your collection are in mint condition, this one will be of noticeably poorer quality.

GIF – Graphic Interchange Format, a type of image file used for Web icons.

Giftware – An item purchased to give as a gift, with no intent for collecting any more of that type.

Glaze – A thin glossy coating usually applied to pottery or porcelain.

Guestbook – A program that allows Web page visitors to enter information into an on-screen form and type in a line or two of a message.

Hairline crack – A thin, almost invisible crack in porcelain, earthenware, or ceramic.

Handle – Your nickname in cyberspace.

Home page – The main page in a Web site, usually contained in a file called *index.html*.

Home page builder – A program at a home page site that helps you build your first page with the help of a menu-driven program. It then lets you convert your page to HTML so you can edit and update the file.

Hot item – An auction that draws a considerable amount of bids.

Hot spot – A string of text or an image that changes the mouse cursor into a little hand. This indicates a hyperlink, which takes the user to another page (or a different place on the current page) with a left mouse-click.

HTF – (Hard-to-Find) Signifies the item is in limited production and/or availability and cannot easily be found at retail.

HTML – (Hypertext Markup Language) The coding language used to create Web pages.

Hypertext links – Same as hyperlink text. Hypertext links connect Web documents. Hypertext links are underlined, color text that may change to a different color once you have visited the page that the hypertext links to. When you pass your mouse cursor over hyperlink text, the arrow changes into a little hand, indicating you're on a hot spot. If you click the left mouse button while on a hot spot, the linked page opens in your browser window.

Hypertext markup language – See HTML.

Icon – An image.

Image file – A JPEG or GIF file that contains an icon or a photograph. A JPEG file ends in .jpg and a GIF file ends in .gif. GIFs are usually graphic files, whereas JPEGs are usually photos.

Glossary

Impression – A design or monogram made by pressure on the surface of the item.

Inlay – A design made by cutting out a pattern and replacing it with a different material in the same shape as the cut pattern.

Internet – More simply the Net, a collection of networks, or a network of networks that allows computers all over the world to communicate with each other.

JPEG – Joint Photographic Experts Group, a type of image file used for photographs.

Left-click – Clicking on the left mouse button.

Limited edition – Collectible items produced in a specific quantity. They are marked with a serial number.

Link – See Hypertext Links.

Listing – Another term for auction, or the act of entering an online auction site.

Listing fee – Small assessment for starting an auction.

Lurk – To participate in a "read-only" mode on a bulletin board or in a chat room.

Maximum bid – The most you'll pay for an item that's up for auction. Once you enter a maximum bid you can raise the amount, but you can't lower it.

Membership – See Collector Membership.

Memorabilia – Nostalgia items collected to remind one of a time passed.

META tag – A code element used in an HTML document for use by search engines to categorize and index a Web site. They include keywords and short descriptions about the contents of the page.

MIB – (Mint-in-Box) Offers a way of being more specific about the term "mint." It means not only is the item itself in its original condition, but it remains in its original box.

Minimum bid – The amount at which bidding starts in an online auction.

Mint – An item in the same condition it was the day it left the manufacturer. There is no degree of mint — an item is either mint or it isn't mint, period. There is no such thing as "mint, except for..."

Some conditions that void the mint status of an item are:
• Placement of or damage caused by a price sticker
• Broken or dented packaging
• Missing or damaged product labels

- Chips or dents, even if repaired
- Incomplete set

MIP – (Mint in Package) An item that never came out of the original packaging. This usually means items sold in packaging that breaks when opened, like a piece mounted on a card. Since the item left the manufacturer in the package, it's mint only if it's still in the original package.

MOC – (Mint on Card) Same as MIP, only the item remains mounted on the packing card. The item, card, and any accessories are in perfect condition.

Motif – Design or style that earmarks an era.

Museum quality – An item in mint or issue condition suitable for setting a standard of perfection.

MWMT – (Mint With Mint Tags) Started with Beanie Baby traders to establish that not only was the item in issue condition, but it also had both the heart-shaped swing tag and the sewn-in product tag in their original places with no bends, dents, or price sticker residue.

MWT – (Mint With Tags) Another way of saying "mint," also of Beanie Baby origin

Near-mint – A term used by refreshingly honest sellers. Used to describe an item with a small chip, dented box, bend in the product tag, price sticker damage, or any other aberration from the issue condition of the item.

Net – See Internet.

NRFB – (Never Removed From Box) Another term for mint. Be wary of this term, because it could mean the seller never opened the box to inspect the piece for damage or to ascertain that all product documentation was included. Be sure to ask if the seller at least checked the item before putting it up for sale.

Numbered edition – Numbered collectible item not produced in a specific quantity.

Offline – Private communication via e-mail or telephone, away from the Web.

Open-ended auction – Any auction system that adds a specific amount of time, like five minutes, onto the end of an auction following any bid entered in the last hour.

Ordered list – A text list in which a sequential number or letter sets off each item.

Glossary

Outbid – When someone else bids more than your maximum bid and becomes the new high bidder for an auction.

Password – Private set of characters you must enter along with your user ID when you access certain Web sites.

Patina – Normal signs of age, usually used to describe wood or metal.

Physical tags – HTML tags that change text to boldface, italics, underline, or a few other options.

Plush – The soft fabric used to make stuffed animals, or soft toys made from a furry fabric.

Porcelain – A hard, fine-grained white ceramic ware.

Pottery – Earthenware made by low-temperature firing.

Post – To enter a comment on a bulletin board or in a Usenet newsgroup.

Primary market – Buying an item from a dealer for the suggested retail price.

Primitive art – See Folk Art.

Proxy bid – When your bid automatically raises to your maximum bid if someone tries to outbid you.

Rare – Difficult if not impossible to find; very few in existence.

Registered user – One who has an active user ID and password at an online auction site who can list and bid on auctions.

Repaired – When an item is fixed using the original parts or material.

Reserve auction – One at which the seller has determined a minimum bid required to purchase the item.

Reserve price – The lowest amount you'll accept for an item in an online auction.

Restored – When an item is fixed using material or parts that were not part of the original piece.

Re-strike – A new item made from an original mold or plate.

Retirement – When a collectible company ceases manufacture of a particular piece.

Right-click – Clicking on the right mouse button. Some actions require a fast double-click.

Search – An Internet feature used to locate information about specific items on the Web by certain criteria, such as the collectible line, the manufacturer, etc.

Search engine – A database of URLs linked to certain key-words. Excite, Alta Vista, and Lycos are some search engines. Yahoo is often called a search engine but technically is a directory because people, instead of Web-bots, index the entries.

Secondary market – Selling an item purchased at the suggested retail price for more or less than the retail price.

Secondary-market price – The resale value of an item. This can be either above or below the suggested retail price.

Secure Sockets Layer – (SSL) also called a Secure Server. A program that encrypts data so that it can't be understood if intercepted.

Seller – The person who enters an auction and receives payment from the winning bidder.

Shareware – Software programs you download from the Web that you try for a certain amount of time.

Shill – An illegal activity involving bidding on your own auction or encouraging someone to bid on your item with the intent of raising the price.

Site – See Web Site.

Sniping – Bidding at the very last second in order to secure the winning bid.

Spam – Sending the same e-mail message to a multitude of users in an effort to generate business. Also, posting to many Usenet news groups at once. Always considered obnoxious.

Special-event piece – A special piece you can only buy at special events, like in-store shows. Usually produced in a limited quantity.

Stoneware – A strong opaque ceramic ware that is high-fired, dense, and nonporous.

Super special-event piece – A special piece you can only buy at a major special event, like the International Collectible Exposition. Usually produced in a limited quantity.

Super-duper special-event piece – A special piece you can only buy at an exclusive event hosted by the collectible company. Always produced in a very limited quantity.

Surfing – What you do when you click on hypertext links to bounce from Web page to Web page.

Swap meet – A gathering of secondary vendors who sell or trade collectibles with admission-paying customers.

Glossary

Table cell – Component of a table in which text or an image appears. Table cells can also appear empty if you code only a <BR> tag (and nothing else) within the <TD> tag.

Tag – An element of HTML code contained within <brackets>.

Traffic – The volume of visitors to a particular page.

Uniform Resource Locator – (URL) An address that identifies the location of a page on the Web.

Unordered list – A text list in which a bullet sets off each item.

Usenet – A network that allows people to share messages. Another part of the Internet.

Value – Determines how an HTML tag attribute will function. Also, the price at which an item is expected to sell.

VHTF – (Very Hard To Find) Usually describes a nostalgia item, an early variation, or a super-duper special-event piece that was severely limited in quantity.

Visited link – A hypertext link that you've previously accessed.

Web – See World Wide Web.

Web-bots – Robot-like programs that scan the World Wide Web and build site indexes.

Web page – An HTML document containing text, images, and other online elements. It may be a stand-alone HTML document or one contained within a browser frame.

Web ring – A collection of linked URLs that are accessed in succession by visiting each page in order.

Web site – A collection of Web pages on a server that follow a common theme or belong to the same person or organization.

Webmaster – The person in charge of managing the Web site and often the writer of the HTML code for the individual Web pages.

Wimp feedback – Waiting for the other party to enter user feedback for you before you'll enter a comment in return.

Wimp trader – While conducting an item-for-item trade, someone who waits until he or she receives the item you sent before sending yours.

Winner's curse – The tendency for the high bidder at auction to pay too much for an item because last minute bidding drives the price up.

World Wide Web – Also called the Web. A system that uses the Internet to connect multimedia documents by way of hypertext links. A subset of the Internet.

About the Author

Nancy L. Hix collects online and frequents many Internet bulletin boards and collector chat rooms. She's a founding member of the Harmony Kingdom House of Peers, a collector's society that raises money for charity by auctioning artist prototypes on eBay.

The first edition of *Collector's Guide to Buying, Selling, and Trading on the Internet* drew great reviews from collectible and antique publications. She's also the author of *Collector's Guide to Online Auctions* and various articles appearing in *Mary Beth's Beanie World* and *The Queen's Courier.*

As a technical writer for a major telecommunications company, she is also an accomplished Web page designer and teaches the HTML code both in person and online.

Born in Chicago, she's a graduate of Illinois State University in Normal, where she specialized in Media Communications. She holds a master's degree in human resource management from National-Louis University in Evanston.

She and her husband Jeff live in Warrenville, Illinois, with their two sons, a cat named Mindy, and definitely too many collectibles.

Contact the author via her personal home page at http://www.angelfire.com/il/marble9. She accepts correspondence via electronic mail at Marble90@aol.com.

Index

Index

Index